A History of
child welfare

Edited by
Eve P. Smith &
Lisa A. Merkel-Holguin

A History of
child welfare

Transaction Publishers
New Brunswick (U.S.A.) and London (U.K.)

This book is printed on acid-free paper that meets the American National Standard for Permanence of Paper for Printed Library Materials.

Library of Congress Catalog Number: 95-677
ISBN: 1-56000-866-0
Printed in the United States of America

Library of Congress Cataloging-in-Publication Data

A history of child welfare / edited by Eve P. Smith and Lisa A. Merkel-
  Holguín.
     p. cm.
  "Original title: Lessons from the past. A history of child welfare (an issue of
the journal Child Welfare). Original publisher, The Child Welfare League of
America, Inc., January/February 1995"—Data sheet.
  Includes bibliographical references.
  ISBN 1-56000-866-0 (pbk. : alk. paper)
  1. Child welfare—United States—History. I. Smith, Eve P. II. Merkel-
Holguín, Lisa A.
HV741.H55 1995
362.7'0973—dc20   95-677
                                                                        CIP

CONTENTS

INTRODUCTION

A History of Child Welfare, a special volume commemorating the Child Welfare League of America's 75th anniversary, endeavors to (1) illustrate the importance of, and stimulate interest in, child welfare history; (2) demonstrate the linkages between historical and current child welfare practice and policy; and (3) encourage researchers to include child welfare history in their research perspectives. It is our hope that this historical issue will encourage readers to ask themselves a series of questions: What can the child welfare field learn from its past? How does and/or should child welfare history influence present-day practice and policy? How can I incorporate lessons from the past into my work?

Overarching Themes

The 15 chapters in this volume cover a range of social conditions, public policies, and approaches to solving problems. Though history does not repeat itself precisely, problems, controversies about solutions, and certain themes do. For example, our society is currently experiencing a recurrence of the kind of social and economic conditions that correlate with increasing rates of child abuse and neglect and an increasing number of children in out-of-home care. The public perception that we see being resurrected from the past is that many impoverished families are a bad influence on their children and that the children are better off removed from them, which is followed by controversy and polemics over ways to cope with the situation.

Some approaches have been useful, others have not. Success, however, has never meant that society would remember what worked. Some policy decisions, when viewed from a historical perspective, were clearly made in ignorance. It is evident that the child welfare system needs to make use of its own past,

1

evaluating the lessons learned, studying past mistakes, and building on successes.

The Chapters

Although it is impossible to cover all the arenas and aspects of
the child welfare field in one volume, we have attempted to provide a range of perspectives, and in doing so, we hope to demonstrate the uses of history.

Child Welfare's Challenge

The book begins with four chapters about conditions that led to
the need for child welfare services, and society's views of impoverished families and children:

- In "Child Welfare in Fiction and Fact," Robert Bremner
  describes the portrayal of child welfare conditions in
  novels and stories of nineteenth century English and
  American literature, and points out that these stories
  reflect then-prevailing views regarding the child welfare
  system. Prominent was the idea that keeping children
  with their own families, or placing them in new families that would love and care for them, was best for the
  children.
- The movement against child labor brought new difficulties
  for family service workers in the first few decades of the
  twentieth century. Beverly Stadum's chapter, "The Dilemma
  in Saving Children from Child Labor," concerns the actions
  of children, families, and social workers who were caught
  up in the conflict between the economic pressures of families who needed children's incomes and the implementation of new child labor policies.
- In "The Child Welfare Response to Youth Violence and
  Homelessness," Kristine Nelson compares the economic
  conditions and social crises of the growing number of homeless children and the rates of violence of the 1850s to those

of the 1980s. Nelson notes that both crises were consequences of laissez-faire economic policies.

- Despite research that almost always connects neglect with
problems of poverty, society continues for the most part to
blame mothers instead of working toward systemic change.
In "An Outrage to Common Decency," Karen Swift documents historical connections to present-day views of child
neglect.

Responding to the Need

Solutions to the problems discussed above were as varied as the
professionals who advocated for them. The eight chapters in the
next section include discussions of child day care, various forms
of out-of-home care, and adoption.

- William Tuttle, in "Rosie the Riveter and Her Latchkey Children," describes the U.S. government's swiftness in moving to create and fund a system of child day care during the
Second World War, as well as food programs for working
mothers and their children. This demonstration proved that
rapid program development and implementation for children and families is possible when the need of the nation is
great enough.
- In "Bring Back Orphanages? What Policymakers of Today
Can Learn from the Past," Eve Smith describes the orphanages of the nineteenth and early twentieth centuries, and
concludes that inherent difficulties would make it virtually
impossible—or at best, extremely expensive—to recreate
them. She also reminds us that even in the heyday of orphanages, many professionals criticized institutional living
as not being in children's best interests, and preferred family care.
- The social ethos that evolved during the nineteenth and
early twentieth centuries led to the development of institutions by the African American community. Struggling

against racism and segregation, African American women pursued the development of child welfare facilities for African American children. Wilma Peebles-Wilkins describes the nature of such developments with her chapter, "Janie Porter Barrett and the Virginia Industrial School for Colored Girls."

- Turning to the subject of family foster care, Tim Hacsi, in "From Indenture to Foster Care," affords an overview of the history of out-of-home care, stressing major societal changes that led to program changes. He shows how conflicting and difficult-to-reconcile goals and beliefs contribute to the current shape of government-funded care.

- Jeanne Cook, in "A History of Placing-Out: The Orphan Trains," describes the program of the Children's Aid Society, which sent approximately 150,000 children to homes in western states between 1853 and 1929. The Society deliberately removed children from the reach of parents—ostensibly for the good of the children.

- A new—and yet very old—form of family foster care receiving much attention of late is kinship care. In "From Family Duty to Family Policy," Rebecca Hegar and Maria Scannapieco describe the evolution of informal and formal kinship care—the full-time nurturing and protection of children separated from their parents and living with relatives. Kinship care, especially in child placement, is expanding.

- Over the history of child welfare practice, adoption has not escaped its share of controversy. Two chapters demonstrate the evolution of program and policies. In "Adoption and Disclosure of Family Information," E. Wayne Carp presents a picture of the cyclical nature—more openness, less openness—of adoption disclosure policies concerning children's medical and social backgrounds. He concludes that in response to lawsuits by adoptive parents accusing agencies of failing to provide information or fraudulently misrepresenting children's backgrounds, it is likely that the current trend toward fuller disclosure policies will continue.

- Patricia Collmeyer, in "From 'Operation Brown Baby' to 'Opportunity,'" traces the history of minority placements and transracial adoption from 1944 to 1977 at the Boys and Girls Aid Society of Oregon. As the need for adoptive families became apparent, the agency first recruited homes in minority communities and then began to accept Caucasian parents for children of color, a practice advocated by some today and looked on with disfavor by others.

Advocating for Change

Historically, advocacy groups have often been responsible for, or contributed to, major policy change. Marc Mannes, in "Factors and Events Leading to the Passage of the Indian Child Welfare Act," describes the long and tortuous path that led to the legislation's passage. On a similar note, Mary Jean McDonald, in her chapter, "The Citizens' Committee for Children of New York and the Evolution of Child Advocacy (1945–1972)," documents the waxing and then waning effectiveness over time of one kind of child advocacy organization, the Citizen's Committees for Children of New York, Inc. She describes the shifts in advocacy organizations, including agenda changes, strategy and goal modifications, and the importance of informal, unofficial contacts between advocates and officials.

Finally, to encourage further study of child welfare history, we conclude this volume with "Information Sources on Child Welfare Archives" by Murray Wortzel and Laura Delaney Brody. The authors offer sources and practical suggestions for those who would like to further pursue this fascinating area of study.

Special Acknowledgments

The editors are especially thankful to members of the Social Welfare History Group of the Council on Social Work Education. This group of scholars, practitioners, and supporters of historical research on social welfare issues helped bring to birth this interesting body of work through a special symposium in March 1992. Lastly, the editors wish to thank the contributors, external reviewers, *Child Welfare* editors, and all those who offered their help and support.

Eve P. Smith, D.S.W.
University of Windsor School of Social Work

Lisa A. Merkel-Holguín, M.S.W.
Child Welfare League of America

1

CHILD WELFARE
IN FICTION AND FACT

Robert H. Bremner

This article deals with the treatment of the welfare of children in fiction, particularly in nineteenth century English and American literature. Novels and stories depicting the social condition of children and exploring their psychological problems played an important role in arousing concern for children at a time when childhood was virtually without rights or protection. The works discussed are worth recalling because they reflected prevailing attitudes and practices in child care, inspired sympathy for and understanding of children, and contributed to a hostile stereotype of adult child welfare workers. The authors' favorite remedy for children's problems—keeping them with or getting them back to their own parents or, if that was impossible, placing them in a loving family—accords with current policy objectives that are easier to attain in fiction than in real life.

Robert H. Bremner, Ph.D., is Professor Emeritus of History, The Ohio State University, Columbus, OH.

Most of the children who are the principal characters in the novels under consideration are foundlings, orphans, or half-orphans. Except in rare instances, as in Charles Kingsley's *Alton Locke* [1850], the surviving parent is away or too weak to exert positive influence. Dandy Mick, a 16-year-old factory worker in Benjamin Disraeli's *Sybil* [1845] has a bedfast mother; her friends say she is dying; he says she is only drunk. The mother of one of Mick's friends went back to work two weeks after the boy was born. She put him out to nurse with an old woman who provided day care and a diet of treacle (molasses syrup) and laudanum (an opium-based sedative) for three pence a week. When the mother disappeared and the money stopped coming, the nurse thrust the two-year-old boy into the streets "to 'play' in order to be run over." He did not exactly thrive but of all his barefoot and half-naked playmates, he was the only one to survive. He slept on mouldering straw in a damp cellar, "a dung heap at his head, and a cesspool at his feet." Nameless in infancy, he was christened Devildust when at age five he went to work in a textile mill [Disraeli 1845].

In *Sybil*, subtitled *The Two Nations*—the rich and the poor—Disraeli presents imaginary characters against a factual depiction of English social and industrial conditions in the 1830s and 1840s. In a passage about girls and infants working in the mines, Disraeli incorporates materials from an official *Report of the Commissioner on the Employment of Young Persons and Children* issued in 1842 [quoted in Coveney 1967].

> Naked to the waist, an iron chain fastened to a belt of leather runs between their legs clad in canvas trousers, while on hands and feet an English girl, for twelve, sometimes for sixteen hours a day, hauls and hurries tubs of coals up subterranean roads, dark, precipitous, and plashy. [Disraeli]

"Trappers," boys and girls four and five years old, were the first workers to enter the mines and the last to leave. Their work—

opening gallery doors for coal wagons and keeping the doors closed after each wagon's passage—was not arduous but it was performed in darkness and solitude, and was a highly responsible task because the safety of the mine and all those working in it depended on the trappers' constancy in tending the doors.

We see the children through Disraeli's eyes and hear them through his ears. He tells us of their long hours, rough appearance, and foul language. We share Disraeli's alarm that the older girls are to be—and some of them already are—the mothers of England, and his wonderment at the interest mine owners take in the abolition of slavery and their obliviousness to the state of their own employees. We sympathize with the children but have to rely on the author's comments or our own imagination to know how the children feel about their treatment and condition.

The difference between *Sybil*, a social novel, and autobiographical ones such as *Jane Eyre* [1847] and *David Copperfield* [1849–50] is that the latter are primarily concerned with expressing how the heroine and hero feel about the hardships and misfortunes they encounter. The books are based on Charlotte Bronte's and Charles Dickens' childhood experiences so that the authors and protagonists speak as one and we see the children as they see themselves. What Jane Eyre and David Copperfield feel is self-pity. They resent the injustices, not of impersonal social forces, but of specific acts of meanness, neglect, and indifference of adults who should love and care for them.

Jane Eyre, a ten-year-old orphan, is made to feel unwelcome unwanted, and unappreciated in the home of her aunt. At Lowood School, which is very much like the Clergy Daughters' School that Charlotte Bronte attended when she was eight or nine, Jane is unfairly and undeservedly humiliated by the headmaster, Mr. Brockelhurst. Another girl tells Jane, "You and I and the rest of us are charity children"; the fees their guardians pay do not cover their expenses and have to be supplemented by charitable subscriptions. Mr. Brockelhurst, whose piety is as harsh as that of Charlotte Bronte's clergyman father, objects to the worldliness of girls wearing braids and curls in an evangelical charitable establishment. Either out of principle or economy or out of both, food is scanty, clothing ugly, and heating minimal. "My plan in bringing up these girls," Brockelhurst tells the matron, "is not to accustom them to habits of luxury and indulgence, but to render them hardy, patient, self-denying." He believes that missing occasional meals will do charity girls more good than harm. "Oh madam, when you put bread and cheese, instead of burnt porridge, into these children's mouths, you may indeed feed their vile bodies, but you little think how you starve their immortal souls" [Bronte].

"I become neglected" was the way Dickens' favorite child, David Copperfield, describes his situation when his mother died. His stepfather and stepfather's sister did not beat or starve him but "they disliked me; and they sullenly, sternly, steadily overlooked me . . . Day after day, week after week, month after month, I was coldly neglected." For some children, being sent to London to work and live on their own would have seemed a welcome escape from a stepfather's hostile indifference, but David didn't like it. His job was to paste labels on bottles in a wine-trader's warehouse. The warehouse was dark and dirty, the work dull, the hours long, and the pay poor, but what galled David Copperfield—as it had once galled Charles Dickens when sent to work at the same age as David—was the disregard of his worth and bright promise. In words similar to those Dickens used in an autobiographical sketch, Copperfield tells us that what had happened to him seemed incomprehensible:

> A child of excellent abilities, and with strong powers of observation, quick, eager, delicate, and soon hurt bodily or mentally, it seems wonderful to me that nobody should have made any sign in my behalf. But none was made; and I became, at ten years old, a little labouring hind in the service of Murdstone and Grinby. [Dickens 1849–50]

Although miserably unhappy, the boy suffers in silence and does his work. He really begins life on his own when he runs away, makes his way to Dover, and finds refuge with a kindly aunt.

Aunt Betsey Trottwood's willingness to take David into her household is an example of Dickens' customary way of solving his heroes' problems. After treachery and countless hardships, they meet a person with a good heart and modest fortune who adopts or befriends them and makes them a virtual part of his or her own family. Although Dickens was active in charitable enterprises and gave generously of his time and money to philanthropic institutions, his fiction celebrated individual rather than organized benevolence. Because he revered charity as the highest of virtues, he was quick to spot and condemn instances of self-interest, hypocrisy, harshness, and officiousness in its practice, whether by private individuals or public officials. With the single exception of the Hospital for Sick Children in London, whose work he praised in *Our Mutual Friend* [1864–65], he could not believe that a child could be as happy and well cared for in an institution as in a good family.

In *Oliver Twist* [1838], Dickens tells how churchwardens and overseers of the poor raise a boy unfortunate enough to be born in a parish workhouse. Oliver comes into the world in the late 1820s, his mother dying at his birth. Since no inmate of the house is available to nurse him, he is sent to a branch of the workhouse where a woman receives a few pence a week for each of the 20 or 30 babies farmed out to her. Her care consists of systematically starving and neglecting the children so that (Dickens estimates) in eight and a half cases out of ten, the infants sicken and die or succumb to injuries suffered in accidents that a little attention could have prevented. Oliver, like Devildust, is a survivor, and when he returns to the workhouse, it is operating under the rules of the New Poor Law of 1834. According to Dickens, one of the cardinal principles of that law, which he continued to denounce in later novels, was that "all poor people should have the alternative (for they would compel no one, not they!) of being starved by a gradual process in the house, or by a quick one, out of it" [Dickens 1838].

A parish child like Oliver is a burden to be gotten rid of by apprenticing him or her to an employer on the best terms available to the parish without consulting or considering the child's interest. Oliver, like David Copperfield, runs away from his master; he falls into bad company but is rescued from the clutches of the law and is eventually adopted by the kindly Mr. Brownlow.

Jo, a crossing-sweeper in *Bleak House* [1852–53], is less fortunate than Oliver. Although known to and harassed by the police, Jo is too dirty, scab-covered, vermin-infested—too much a native product—to be interesting to philanthropists, charitable societies, or even kind-hearted individuals until it is too late to help him. When he dies, Dickens reminds his readers that unfortunate, unlovable children like Jo are "dying thus around us everyday" [Dickens 1852–53].

Ginx's Baby, His Birth and Other Misfortunes [1870], a novel issued anonymously in the year of Dickens' death, records the history of another victim of social neglect. The author, Edward Jenkins, a missionary's son who was educated in Canada and the United States, was a lawyer in London and later a member of Parliament. The baby of the title, a boy, is the thirteenth child of a poor workingman who resolves to dispose of him at birth by throwing him in the Thames. The baby is rescued, or preserved for further misfortunes, by a nun who offers to raise him in the Sisters' Home. This solution to the boy's fate proves impracticable because his parents are Protestant and neither they nor church officials are willing to make the necessary concessions.

After satirizing sectarian rivalries more concerned with the baby's soul than his mortal welfare, Jenkins attacks, in turn philanthropic organizations who collect money in the baby's behalf and spend nearly all of it on administration (including legal expenses) and fund-raising, foster parents whose interest in the baby is confined to the money they receive for his care and can obtain by selling his clothes, Poor Law officials who are willing to devote large sums to litigation to establish that they are not responsible for the baby but who are chary of spending parish funds to feed or clothe him, and politicians who expound and rebut plans for social and educational reform while allowing the child to grow up ignorant and unskilled. In the last paragraph of the book, Jenkins exclaims:

> Philosophers, Philanthropists, Politicians, Papists and Protestants, Poor-Law Ministers and Parish Officers— while you have been theorizing and discussing, debating, wrangling, legislating and administering—Good God! gentlemen, between you all, where has Ginx's Baby gone to?

He has gone off Vauxhall Bridge and into the Thames where his father had intended to throw him "at a time when he was alike unconscious of life and death."

Neither Jenkins nor Ginx acknowledge Ginx's responsibility for bringing the baby into the world. Jenkins's language and logic seem to condone infanticide—a practice not unknown in Victorian England, especially as regards out-of-wedlock children [Pinchbeck & Hewitt 1973]. In fact, Jenkins advocated emigration for families burdened with more children than they could support. Ginx, his wife, and other children departed for Canada as soon as possible after getting rid of the baby.

By 1876, *Ginx's Baby* had gone through 36 editions. Its satire of sectarian rivalries influenced the religious compromise included in the Education Act of 1870, which made education a national rather than a parish duty. Operation of that act made clear the connection between undernourishment and poor learning ability and made feeding "the necessitous school child" a popular philanthropic cause.

Harriet Beecher Stowe's *Old Town Folks* [1869] takes place in rural New England between 1790 and 1820. The story involves two sets of orphans, and touches upon social class, foster care, informal adoption, child labor, and child abuse in the name of discipline. Horace, about 12 years old, and his slightly older brother, Bill, become half-orphans when their father dies. Bill, a normal, healthy boy, disappears from the story when an uncle takes him to live and work on his farm. Horace—bookish and not very strong—and his mother find a home with the boy's grand-parents.

The other orphans, Harry, age nine, and Tina, age seven, are left alone in the world when their mother dies while trying to get the children to Boston. Their father, an English army officer, had abandoned the family and returned to England at the end of the Revolutionary War. In the country parish of Needmore there is no difficulty in placing the children. A demanding, hard-fisted farmer takes the boy for what work he can get out of him; the farmer's sister, equally stern and hardworking, agrees to "fetch up" the girl. Stowe says of the sister that she was not the sort of woman a widower would choose to bring up his motherless children, but in Needmore she "would get all the votes as just the proper person to take charge of an orphan asylum" [Stowe 1869].

Stowe makes clear that Harry and Tina, although im-poverished, come from a higher social class than their would-be masters, and attributes the children's repugnance and refusal to accept their lot to social superiority. Harry defies the farmer's brutal demands; Tina fights back when her mistress tries to give her "a good spanking" to improve her character. They run away, are found and befriended by Horace, who takes them to his grandparents' house. A spinster, sensing Tina's gentle birth, adopts her; a clergyman and his aristocratic wife are attracted to Harry and arrange for him to board at the grandparents' home.

Little Men [1871], by Louisa May Alcott, is unusual in that the dozen children dealt with in it are happy and well cared for in an institutional setting. The institution is a progressive boarding school conducted by Mr. Bhaer and his wife Jo, one of the sisters in Alcott's earlier book *Little Women* [1868–69]. The boys range in age from eight to 14; most of them have been sent to the school by their parents, but one, who arrives as a "ragged urchin," has his expenses paid by a local philanthropist, and is not discriminated against. Billy, "a feeble idiot," and Dick, a hunchback, are treated considerately by Jo and Mr. Bhaer; the other boys, under threat of punishment by Mr. Bhaer, refrain from teasing them [Alcott 1871].

At the start of Jo's Boys [1886] Alcott presents glimpses of the boys ten years after the end of Little Men. They are scattered and have turned out well, or as well as can be expected. "Poor little Dick was dead and so was Billy," Alcott tells us, "and no one could mourn for them since life would never be happy, afflicted as they were in mind and body" [Alcott 1886].

In 1871, at the age of six, Rudyard Kipling, born in India, was brought to England to attend school, and for the next five years he was separated from his parents and lived with strangers. In at least two of his works, Kipling drew on his memories of these miserable years. In "Baa, Baa, Black Sheep" the woman who boards Kipling's alter ego, Punch, and his younger sister Judy, indulges the little girl but dislikes the boy. She calls him a liar, dubs him Black Sheep, destroys his self-respect, and fails to notice or take steps to correct his failing vision. Her own son, Harry, goes to school with Punch and acts as his mother's spy, inquisitor, and deputy executioner. Punch is beaten at home for having been beaten at school. To save himself from further punishment, Punch learns to practice deceptions, which the woman magnifies into deadly sins.

When The Light That Failed [1890] begins, Dick Heldar has been in the care of Mrs. Jennett for six years. "Where he had looked for love she gave him first aversion and then hate. Where he growing older sought a little sympathy, she gave him ridicule." Since she regards Dick as a hopeless liar, he, like Punch and, perhaps Kipling, "developed into a liar, but an economical and self-contained one, never throwing away the least unnecessary fib, and never hesitating at the blackest, were it only plausible, that might make his life a little easier" [Kipling 1890].

A story written from the viewpoint of Mrs. Jennett might present her as sympathetically as Jo and Mr. Bhaer in *Little Men*, and Dick Heldar as fatally flawed and unfit for happiness as the handicapped children briefly mentioned in *Jo's Boys*. Nevertheless, allegations that substitute families and parents, especially institutional ones, deny children the love they yearn for recur frequently in literature. *Tim All Alone* [1956], a children's story by Edward Ardizzone, uses words and pictures to show the sharp-beaked matron of a Home for Lost children and the gloomy Gothic institution she presides over in an unfavorable—and for young readers, frightening—light. In "Sweets from a Stranger" by J.I.M. Stewart [1980], an old woman who looks like a witch entices a frightened but fascinated schoolboy into a sinister-looking tenement house in Edinburgh. The boy expects the worst, but all the old woman wants is for him to visit her crippled, bedridden grandson. When the boy tells his family of his adventure, his father, a civic leader, is outraged that the authorities have allowed the unfortunate pair to live in such dangerous and unhealthy circumstances. He arranges to have the grandmother sent to a home for the aged and the boy to an orphanage. Stewart, recalling the incident many years later and thinking of the mutually sustaining love of the woman and child, concludes the story: "I don't suppose that either of them, thus sundered, survived long."

Late nineteenth and early twentieth century child welfare reforms such as compulsory school attendance, regulation and prohibition of child labor, and protection of children against neglect and abuse challenged family autonomy and limited parental authority. Advocates of the reform came from and represented the values of the middle and upper classes of society. For economic and cultural reasons, poor and working-class parents often resisted the reforms and became targets of their enforcers. Contemporary students of child welfare history with working-class backgrounds and sympathies feel obligated, even in cases in which "positive benefits accrued to children and youth" as a result of the reforms, to call attention to "the self-interest and righteousness of many of the reformers" [Rooke & Schnell 1983]. Self-interest and righteousness, however, are found in all classes and were as common among opponents as advocates of the reforms.

Animus against social workers in general and child welfare workers in particular continues, not so much for reasons of class as because their efforts to protect children sometimes bring them into adversarial relations with parents, and expose them to criticism by the press. We continue to believe that parents, even if immature and seemingly irresponsible, know what is best for their children. One week "Children's Services" is accused of being overzealous in discharging its duties, and the next week, of being lax. A recent mystery novel contains references to "phony" and "bogus" social workers suspected of sexually abusing children; when the children are rescued from their alleged molesters and placed in protective care, the author gratuitously observes, "Most people thought it was more likely the children needed to be protected from the social workers" [Robinson 1994].

Headlines and accounts of custody and foster care cases in newspapers read like episodes in fiction: "Escaping Abuse But Not Neglect: Languishing in Foster Care"; "Mom Would Pick Jail Over Giving Up Son"; "Mom Wins Long Fight for 2 Kids; Woman Regains Custody After Children's Services Gives Up 3–Year Battle"; "Mother, 24, Arrested After 6 Children Are Found Alone." Better funding and more vigorous implementation of the Adoption Assistance and Child Welfare Act of 1980 would probably help, but it is hard to believe that the stories will have happy endings as long as family poverty is compounded by lack of education, hopelessness, and drug and/or alcohol abuse, and the children's environment at home, school, and play is violent and unwholesome.

In the near future, the grown-up children of today will be counted as assets or liabilities to society. Some parents can offer their children advantages not available to others, but no parents are alone able to provide their children everything needed for intelligent and responsible citizenship. All adults bear part of the expense of bringing other people's children to maturity. It is in our own interest and very much in the national interest to give the welfare of children, especially those in need and at risk, our most serious consideration. Charles Dickens would be unhappy but feel at home in our age when the cost of keeping people in prison and detention homes leaves less money available for social services and education. Benjamin Disraeli would recognize the threat to social stability in the United States posed by the emergence of two nations, one highly skilled, highly educated, and well paid, the other an underclass of the unskilled, poorly educated, and low paid. ◆

References

Alcott, L. M. (1886). Chapter I. In *Jo's boys*. Boston: Roberts Brothers.

Alcott, L. M. (1871). Chapter II. In *Little men*. New York: E. P. Dutton (1967 reprint edition).

Ardizonne, E. (1956). *Tim all alone*. New York: Henry Z. Walsh, Inc.

Bronte, C. (1847). Chapter VII. In *Jane Eyre*. New York: Norton (1987 reprint edition).

Coveney, P. (1967). *The image of childhood* (p. 94). Baltimore: Penguin Books.

Dickens, C. (1853). Chapter XLVII. In *Bleak house*. Oxford: Oxford University Press (1987 reprint edition).

Dickens, C. (1849–50). Chapter II. In *David Copperfield*. Oxford: Oxford University Press (1981 reprint edition).

Dickens, C. (1838). Chapter II. In *Oliver Twist*. Oxford: Oxford University Press (1987 reprint edition).

Dickens, C. (1864–1865). Book II, Chapter IX. In *Our mutual friend*. Oxford: Oxford University Press (1987 reprint edition).

Disraeli, B. (1845). Book II, Chapters IX, X; Book III, Chapters I. In *Sybil or the two nations*. London: Oxford University Press (1969 reprint edition).

Jenkins, E. (1871). *Ginx's baby, his birth and other misfortune* (p. 224). London: Strahan & Co. Publishers.

Kingsley, C. (1850). *Alton Locke*. New York: Macmillan & Co. (1896 reprint edition).

Kipling, R. (1888). "Baa, baa, black sheep." In *Wee Willie Winkie and other stories*. New York: Standard Book Company (1930 reprint edition).

Kipling, R. (1890). Chapter I. In *The light that failed*. Garden City, NY: Doubleday (1988 reprint edition).

Pinchbeck, I. L., & Hewitt, M. (1973). Chapters XLX. In *Children in English society* (Vol. II). Toronto, ON: University of Toronto Press (1973 reprint edition).

Robinson, P. (1994). *Wednesday's child: An Inspector Banks mystery* (pp. 4, 20, 24). New York: Charles Scribner's Sons.

Roocke, P., & Schnell, R. L. (1983). *Discarding the asylum: From child rescue to the welfare state in Canada* (pp. iii, 5). Lanham, MD: University Press of America.

Stewart, J .I. M. (1980). "Sweets from a stranger." In *Parlour 4 and other stories* (pp. 175–184). London: Victor Gollanz.

Stowe, H. B. (1869). Chapter IX. In *Old town folks*. New York: Library of America (1982 reprint edition).

2

THE DILEMMA IN SAVING CHILDREN FROM CHILD LABOR: REFORM AND CASEWORK AT ODDS WITH FAMILIES' NEEDS (1900–1938)

Beverly Stadum

Early in this century, reformers lobbied for regulation of child labor and compulsory school attendance. This article draws on their publications, agency case records, professional literature, and historical studies to examine the role of social workers in implementing the new reforms and the reactions of parents and children in low-income households who were affected by the legislative changes. The precarious nature of family self-sufficiency and social workers' ambivalence toward child labor led to conflict between professionals and client families. Missing at the time was professional acknowledgment of economic security for families as a fundamental necessity for children's welfare.

Beverly Stadum, Ph.D., is Associate Professor, St. Cloud State University, Department of Social Work, St. Cloud, MN. The author expresses her appreciation to Clarke Chambers, who encouraged her work on this topic.

*C*hild saving was the broadly defined mission of many early twentieth century reformers.[1] Within their agendas, the prohibition of child labor became a prominent goal at a time when few protections existed against industry's enthusiasm for exploiting youngsters as cheap and pliable workers. The National Child Labor Committee (NCLC) organized in 1904 as the standard bearer for reform activity; social welfare leaders such as Jane Addams, Homer Folks, and Grace Abbott, as well as many lesser-known professionals, identified with its efforts [Abbott 1938a; Trattner 1970].

Hundreds of NCLC publications based on field investigations and the study of legal statutes raised the consciousness of women's organizations and religious and college groups, which lobbied for labor regulation.[2] In response, the federal and state governments documented working conditions for youngsters [U.S. Bureau of Labor 1913]. As the campaign against child labor developed, reformers' arguments remained constant: children were expected to help with tasks around the home or farm, but they had the right to a creative childhood and a productive adulthood. Work in "unhealthy or hazardous conditions" at "unsuitable ages" and "unreasonable hours," that "interfered with physical development and education," not only destroyed childhood, but jeopardized youthful workers' preparation for better-paying jobs as adults [Trattner 1970: 9–10]. The resulting failure of individuals to become economically self-sufficient could undermine the whole of American democracy [Abbott 1938a; Addams 1905; Adler 1908; Devine 1909].

Prominent reformers articulated these concerns, but it was anonymous caseworkers in private agencies who regularly saw firsthand the working child as part of a household. When child labor regulations were passed, some of these nascent professionals were in positions to oversee adherence to the new laws. Although children were assumed to be the beneficiaries of policy changes, many youthful laborers lived in families with grave economic needs. In these situations, the reform of child labor laws led to alarm and resentment rather than relief or celebration.

The successful introduction of child labor laws has been written about as a hard-won endeavor by committed social welfare leaders [Costin 1983; Trattner 1968; Trattner 1970]. This study, however, assumes that the full history of policy reform in child welfare also must include the activities of those who implement the policy and the reactions of families whose daily lives are to change because of it. The three parties in the story told here— NCLC reformers, agency social workers, and families in low-income households—did not share the same perspective.

NCLC literature advocated for children and the well-being of the nation, but gave slight acknowledgment to the needs and well-being of families as a whole. Pinched by economic need, many parents urged child employment, and youngsters undertook it to their physical detriment. Social workers and private agencies could be influential in creating or limiting job opportunities and were inconsistent in their assessment of the validity of work for youngsters. In responding to existing economic realities, both social workers and parents took practical actions that in the long term failed to support youngsters' well-being. This article explores how these conflicts were played out at the time and serves as a case study showing the need for broad systems change as the basis of progress in child welfare. It begins with an examination of the reformers' campaign actions and attitudes.

Reformers' Approach to the Problem of Child Labor

By 1909, after only five years of research, coalition building, and lobbying, efforts by NCLC had fostered new child labor legislation in 43 states. Most of these laws prohibited employment for youngsters under the age of 14 years, but state exemptions varied and enforcement was problematic [Loughran 1921]. In the next years, federal legislation to establish a *national* set of standards was twice passed and twice declared unconstitutional by the

U. S. Supreme Court. In response, forces organized by NCLC and the new federal Children's Bureau campaigned for a constitutional amendment prohibiting child labor [Abbott 1938a; Chambers 1963; Costin 1983; Ladd-Taylor 1994; Trattner 1970]. Amid changing strategies for reform, decennial census figures showed a continuing decline in the number of wage-earning children.

The number of employed youngsters ages ten to 13 years dropped from 121 in 1,000 in 1900, to 24 in 1,000 in 1930 [Abbott 1938a: 267]. Part of this change was illusory; the large numbers of migratory agricultural laborers were routinely excluded from both regulation and formal census counts, and employers learned useful deceits in documenting the presence of children.[3] Yet laws in some states did curtail certain employment; in addition, new technology in certain industries reduced the economic benefits of child labor. Then, in 1938, the Fair Labor Standards Act established general wage and hour rules for all workers. Grace Abbott, as chief of the Children's Bureau, lobbied successfully to extend this act, making 16 years the minimum age for employment in industries whose products were shipped interstate. The popular perception developed that child labor had been outlawed and the public's concern lessened. In truth, many kinds of work were still exempt from regulation, but the labor demands of World War II inhibited enforcement of even the existing child labor laws [NCLC 1938; Taylor 1944]. In the next years, NCLC's emphasis began shifting to support more adequate vocational training for youngsters leaving high school. This change in focus was completed in 1957 when NCLC was renamed the National Committee on the Employment of Youth [Trattner 1970].

In the earlier decades when NCLC activity centered on outlawing child labor, family poverty was acknowledged as basic to the problem, but conference speeches, annual reports, and circulated materials said relatively little about youngsters in the context of their families [Ladd-Taylor 1994; Zelizer 1985]. NCLC spokespersons quoted the Bible: "For the children ought not to lay up for the parents, but the parents for the children, 2 Corinthians 12:14" [Lord 1908]. Impoverished parents often were characterized as violators of that teaching and portrayed as lazy, greedy, or vicious people who sent children to the factory rather than seek employment themselves [Adler 1911; Draper 1909; Lindsay 1907; Taylor 1906; Trattner 1968]. Rarely did the public hear of households where adults labored hard and still needed children's incomes for survival [Ensign 1921; Folks 1907]. Owen Lovejoy, NCLC's director from 1907 to 1926, asserted that no one believed the argument that without the labor of children, families would starve [Kelley 1912; Taylor 1944: 10]. Ironically, organizations representing the businessmen—particularly southern mill owners—who took advantage of young workers were the ones who publicized scenarios of destitute widows saved only by the wages of a child lucky to find employment [Abbott 1938a; Trattner 1970].

In most states, the new labor regulations initially allowed children to be employed if officials determined that their families were in financial need. NCLC campaigned against such rules, however, saying that these rules maintained the child labor supply for business. After 1921, most states eliminated these exemptions because NCLC had convinced legislators that "the poverty plea was highly exaggerated" [Abbott & Breckinridge 1917; Ensign 1921; Trattner 1970: 112]. According to NCLC, the important issue was that children's low wages *contributed* to family poverty by driving down the pay for adults who should be the household supporters [Lovejoy 1908; Trattner 1970]. There is little evidence to suggest that working-class parents shared this understanding.

Implications of Child Labor for Impoverished Families

The need for multiple earners in working-class households was frequently acknowledged in government and academic wage and budget studies at the time. Given the growing number of

consumer items on the market, researchers debated what constituted "need," but they agreed that the cost of living was rising.
What many studies considered minimum subsistence exceeded
the wages routinely offered in low-skilled employment [Kyrk
1929; White House Conference 1933]. Some families could not
live on so little income; others refused to settle for scraping by.
The 1920 census data determined that children and adolescents
contributed to income in 88% of the households of unskilled
workers [Tentler 1981: 184].

Social historians have discovered that certain ethnic groups
were more likely than others to accept or assume that wage earning
was a role for children [Anthony 1914; Goldin 1981; Haines 1981;
Tentler 1981]. In general, however, unemployment, industrial accidents and ill health, husbands' desertion, and women's inability to
limit pregnancy introduced great unpredictability in the budgets of
many low-income families. The working child could well become
the means—if only temporarily—to the precarious economic survival of a household [Stadum 1992].

Reformers often described children's employment as a "sacri-
fice" made for the family, but youngsters also expressed their
own desire to contribute to the family as well as to have control
over funds of their own [Abbott & Breckinridge 1917]. Tentler
[1981] identifies obligation to family and affection for mothers as
a strong motivation for wage earning, particularly among daughters within certain immigrant communities. Some parents also
sought employment for children as a means of discipline, an
antidote to household conflict brought on by a young person's
willfulness and independence on the streets [Ladd-Taylor 1994;
Stadum 1992]. Regardless of children's roles as wage earners,
many low-income mothers relied on youngsters' work at home,
particularly on laundry day and with the tending of younger
siblings [Abbott & Breckinridge 1917; Holloran 1989; Stadum
1992]. When this meant absence from school, parents' priorities
again were in conflict with those of the reformers.

School Attendance as an Alternative to Child Labor

NCLC's opposition to any argument in behalf of child labor was accompanied by its advocacy *for* mandatory school attendance laws. These reformers believed that only formal education would increase youngsters' social and economic value to the nation and to the future employers they would encounter in adulthood [Lindsay 1907]. Thus, state governments were urged to pass compulsory school attendance laws in tandem with new regulations to discourage child labor. And as with labor laws, school regulations were ineffectual unless enforced; therefore, truant officers, monetary fines, and workhouse sentences were devised as repercussions for youngsters' failure to appear at school and for parents' failure to monitor their children's attendance [Abbott & Breckinridge 1917; Kelley 1912; Minnesota Bureau of Labor 1905].

Resistance to these laws existed among both parents and children. Many working-class adults were skeptical that formal education would deliver what reformers asserted. Education was promoted as the means to betterment, but in the distant future; employment now and wages at the end of the week seemed far more reliable and relevant to many parents [Abbott & Breckinridge 1917; Kett 1977; Stadum 1992; Tentler 1981]. But even for those youngsters without jobs, the classroom was often an undesirable environment.

Not all school personnel welcomed the presence of youngsters from low-income families. In a study of child labor and school laws at the time, Ensign [1921: 234] observed, "Teachers have not been anxious to receive in their well-ordered classes those who by taste or necessity placed foremost the breadwinning pursuits." Immigrant children were often above age and large in size for their assigned grade; foreign languages and mores complicated the traditional school curriculum. The children's poor clothing, scant opportunity for cleanliness, and chronic health problems could elicit sympathy or annoyance from those charged with teaching the youngsters [Kett 1977].

Contrary to what reformers expected as the benefits of education for future employment, the formal school experience offered many working-class children little opportunity for mastery or success. Class work was often unrelated to daily life or future job opportunities; the setting was controlled and lacked support for youngsters with special needs. Experiences that school provided often appeared less exciting than those offered in the workplace [Ensign 1921; Fuller 1927; Kett 1977; Woods & Kennedy 1913]. Whether or not youngsters felt welcome in the classroom, many chose not to be there as soon as their birthdays allowed them to leave.

The first compulsory attendance laws required youngsters to be in school to age 14; by 1927, 37 states had extended the requirement to age 16. But in practice, compulsory school attendance was a policy with multiple variations. Assessing children's ages was a problem because no uniform laws governed the registration of births in the United States or in some of the countries where immigrant children had been born [Costin 1983]. In many jurisdictions, exceptions existed whereby underage youngsters could get permits allowing them to leave school for employment—in many states, 14-year-olds could legally be absent simply by proving they had a job. Other states required a perfunctory health exam or a test indicating literacy or achievement of a certain grade level before granting the permit to leave. In some locations, proof of family poverty enabled a child to quit school for wage earning, just as many of the early child labor laws had included exceptions for underage youngsters coming from the neediest of families. In practice, employers often hired children who lacked permits or falsified the documents; parents frequently were unable to prove ages and lied to enable children's departure from school for wage earning [Abbott & Breckinridge 1917; Costin 1983; Ensign 1921; Taylor 1944]. And in most places, any youngster could put in a full week's work *after* school [Fuller 1927; NCLC 1937].

The new school laws often failed in their promise to protect children and enable a productive adulthood. While more working-class parents and youths were accepting the attendance mandates by the 1920s, even many who valued schooling saw formal education as a luxury dependent on "if we can afford it" [Lynd & Lynd 1929: 49, 186]. In urban areas, social workers were among those "officials" in the position of interpreting child labor and school attendance laws to the wary parents and children from low-income households.

Implications of Child Labor Reform for Social Work Activity

While reformers' discussion of child labor focused on the evils of wage work in factories, mills, and fields, personnel in various nineteenth and early twentieth century social programs accepted and even urged that children work for both economic and moral reasons. Agents employed by the Freedmen's Bureau to assist emancipated slaves after the Civil War negotiated work contracts that resembled indentured servitude between plantation owners and African American youngsters, in spite of opposition from parents [Scott 1985]. Federal boarding schools established for assimilation of Native American youths not only taught job skills, but relied on children's labor within the institution and on contracting it out to the community to support the schools' fiscal solvency [Szasz 1985].

"The importance of employment as a means of preventing deterioration and as a positive reformatory agency" was basic to the regimen in the first industrial schools for delinquent boys and to the strategies of private child welfare agencies [Folks 1904: 227; Holt 1992]. Well into the twentieth century, policies at many orphanages included options for indenture and apprenticeship [Clement 1979; Holloran 1989]. Rather than labor interfering with youngsters' development, it was consistent with traditional social values wherein the idle child compared unfavorably with the industrious child [Zelizer 1985].

Thus, while some professionals with social welfare concerns publicized the exploitation of young wage earners, other people in child-related programs designed work for youngsters with confidence that labor itself had merit. In urban family welfare agencies, social workers could engage in both surveillance and advocacy related to child labor and family economics when a referral was made for service or someone requested assistance from a program.

Mary Richmond, whose professional writing defined emerging casework practice, examined family economics in the records of 985 widows known to social workers at charities in 12 cities in 1910. She concluded that children's work was an important source of income in 44% of these families, but found that most case records were so incomplete that it was impossible "to ascertain if any [children] were working under the legal age, and also to compare the number of those who went to work immediately after the legal age with the number that remained in school a year or two longer." While most children known to charity agencies were joining the work force as quickly as legally possible, Richmond assumed that "it will not be long before most [charity] societies, taking a larger view of the problem, will be using their influence with the families in their care for the retention of children in school at least until they have completed the grammar school course [Richmond 1913: 31].[4] In various jurisdictions, the allocation of permits that exempted children from labor laws or compulsory school attendance provided social workers the direct means to influence youngsters' activity.

In states where a permit depended on the poverty of a child's family, the juvenile court often was charged with verifying household need. This task was frequently delegated to social workers in private agencies. In Minneapolis, Minnesota, staff members at the Charity Organization Society—renamed the Family Welfare Association—carried out the responsibility. Within a sample of 300 family case records generated there between 1900 and 1930, more than a sixth of the mothers requested that their children be granted permits to leave school for work. Social workers, however, usually decided against the request.

This action often led parents to voice anger and distrust of the agency; some parents appealed further to school superintendents, hoping to find them more amenable [Stadum 1992].

Having said no, agency workers often urged parents to pursue other means to enhance income, such as encouraging better efforts at budgeting, renting a cheaper apartment, getting older children no longer in school to find more lucrative employment, or asking relatives for financial aid. Social workers argued with parents that school attendance was important, not only as the path to adequate income, but because breaking the law meant fines and time in the workhouse [Breckinridge 1924; Stadum 1992].

Records from two cases opened at the Family Welfare Association in 1915 illustrate social workers interacting with families over these issues of school attendance and child labor.[5] One record began when the Attendance Department of the Minneapolis school system requested investigation of a family with an habitually absent daughter named Florence. Officials suspected her whereabouts because they knew that the immigrant mother had earlier sought a work permit for Florence. In arguing for this permit, the woman had explained that her "husband was sick and [the] older son [was] in the workhouse and the older daughter, Marie, employed in Sumner's Laundry, was [the] only support of [the] family." If Florence also could work, her wages would help fill the gap left by the absence of male income, but a social worker had recommended that the permit be denied. The girl had left school anyhow. On reaching the home to follow up, the agency social worker learned—via a neighbor who translated—that the "woman was angry because permit had not been granted. . . [Mother] refused to admit [social worker] to the home or discuss the necessity of assistance." When a meeting eventually took place, the social worker learned that the son had been released from the workhouse but had not returned home, and the mother had become more desperate. The woman also acknowledged that Florence's desire to work was related in part to wanting "good clothes like other girls and must earn them. [Social worker] tried to explain to her that she must comply and send Florence to school." With reluctance, the girl went, but only temporarily [FCS: C1048–113].

Case notes about a deserted woman with two young children and an adolescent son named Melvin described the mother's continuing inability to produce documents proving his age to enable employment. In the meantime, summer came and Melvin found work in a bakery. He had been "turning over every cent to his mother and she gives him back 10 or 15 cents a week ordinarily." However, "Melvin is getting anxious to have better things," and he spoke both of a heater for their home and a bicycle. He also said he would be employed only part-time once fall came in order to return to school, where classes were getting hard for him. Unknown to the social worker, but known to his mother, Melvin *did* purchase a bicycle from his employer, who took the money in time payments out of his wages. The annoyed social worker "explained to Melvin that the money [his wages] would have to go to his mother and that it was estimated in the monthly expenses [as budgeted by the agency], and that she could not possibly get along without it." The worker also said, "A boy of his age was not paying his own way and had no right to say how the money was to be used. [Melvin] said that as soon as payments finished on the bicycle [he] would turn over all his wages to his mother. Says he gets no time for recreation except in the evening and some on Sunday, but likes his job very much."

When read in full, the family's case record for the summer of 1915 shows the social worker disagreeing repeatedly with Melvin and his mother. Would Melvin return to school in the fall? Would he stay there? Should he stay there? Would he find work that paid better than the bakery? Could the bike be transportation to better employment or should he sell it? Should the agency assist a family with essentials when a luxury such as the bicycle had been purchased? One day's report reads, "'Woman comes. Is ragingly angry because [social worker] went to school for report on children and to employer's regarding Melvin. Said we must think her boy a thief. . . .Says her boy is not on probation and does not consider it any of our business how he gets along in school" [FCS: C685–111].

Although the casework encounter always held the possibility of such discord, exchanges with families over the issue of child labor were not always fractious. The Charity Organization Society in many cities encouraged certain children to stay in school by donating funds to their families as a "scholarship" that equaled a youngster's wages. In Oklahoma and Michigan, public money was allocated to certain families for this purpose [Abbott & Breckinridge 1917; Folks 1907; Leff 1973; Pumphrey & Pumphrey 1983]. These grants often placed social workers in the powerful position of designating a few youngsters as "promising" and deserving of continuing their education [Abbott & Breckinridge 1917; Breckinridge 1924; Folks 1907; Stadum 1992].

Edith Abbott and Sophonisba Breckinridge, founders of the University of Chicago School of Civics and Philanthropy, believed such scholarships were an important tool in encouraging youngsters' persistence in school. Studying wards of the Cook County Juvenile Court, they examined the correlation between school absenteeism and child labor in Illinois and concluded that most youngsters who failed to attend school did so because of problems at home rooted in miserable conditions brought on by poverty. They believed that intervention by school nurses and visiting teachers could lessen these obstacles to attendance, but they sought other remedies for the children who left school legally on their birthdays to go "unguarded and unguided" into the labor market [Abbott & Breckinridge 1917: 145, 455; Lynd & Lynd 1929; Stadum 1992].

Many urban adolescents, particularly those with foreign-born parents, knew little about the actual nature of available jobs [Abbott & Breckinridge 1917; Anthony 1914; Woods & Kennedy 1913]. To reduce ignorance about dangerous conditions in various industries, Abbott and Breckinridge established a small employment bureau at the School of Civics and Philanthropy. There, student social workers interviewed youngsters as well as their parents, and tried to find jobs for them that offered some semblance of safety, training, and permanency. Chicago women's organizations endorsed the idea and funded an agent who sought out the best available opportunities for working girls. Impressed by this utilitarian experiment, the Chicago school system began a similar employment bureau.

When children from client families at a social agency were *illegally* absent from school or earning wages, a social worker would lecture them and threaten legal action in adherence to the *letter* of the law. As a logical result, parents often were less than forthcoming with family information. But for a child whose age or situation made employment legal, a social worker could expect that the youth would quickly begin contributing to the household budget. Social workers were motivated in part by practical considerations. Many private agencies provided funds to impoverished families, but resources were limited and distrust was high. Therefore, personnel usually sought to oversee the budgets of client families and encourage development of additional income sources. The expectation that older youths were to find employment reflected the basic assumption that work and morality were interwoven, and that with effort, all families could achieve self-sufficiency [Pumphrey & Pumphrey 1983; Stadum 1992].

As an example of contradictory concerns that existed simultaneously at the Minneapolis agency in the summer of 1915, volunteers sent telegrams to federal legislators urging support of increased prohibitions against child labor while staff members sought information from the public schools on vocational training opportunities for youths.[6] Social workers there also initiated discussions with mothers and children about finding jobs and suggested which businesses in the city might be hiring. Staff members personally contacted employers and steered girls into domestic work in homes perceived as reputable [Stadum 1992].

Case records show how a social worker could debunk as unrealistic a child's dream for *extensive* education; conversely, a worker could support the vocational inclination of a bright and cooperative child. Help could be given in a variety of ways, for example, "A good linen dress is given to Rose with the understanding that she go out to look for some other work if she can secure a permit" [FCS: C390–108]. Case records suggest that youths often did not remain in the jobs that agency social workers arranged for them [Stadum 1992]. More importantly, access for one child to one position, or one scholarship in one household, fell short as a remedy for the family poverty that usually led to child labor.

Rather than needing admonishment, advice, or even contacts leading to youths' employment, most parents needed enough income to make reliance on children's wages unnecessary. Homer Folks, director of the New York State Charities Aid Association and lifelong NCLC member, was described by Trattner [1968] as more sensitive to poverty than were many "child savers." Early on, Folks urged reformers to carry commitment from their first agenda of seeking an end to child labor into a second agenda of finding ways to increase family income [Ensign 1921; Trattner 1968; White House Conference 1933]. Speaking at NCLC's 25th anniversary in 1929, Grace Abbott also voiced the sentiment that those who believed child labor was an unacceptable solution to family poverty had to find alternative ways to support family life [Costin 1983; NCLC 1930: 29; White House Conference 1933: 73].

Seeking economic reinforcement of the family ideal, many reformers with NCLC affiliation had lobbied successfully with others for "Mothers' Pensions" to be given to selected low-income women rearing children on their own. Enabling legislation was passed in 40 states between 1911 and 1921 [Abbott 1938b; Leff 1973; Pumphrey & Pumphrey 1983; White House Conference 1933). In many cities, the juvenile court administered this program, involving social workers at private agencies in the eligibility investigations. Rules related to citizenship, documentation of "legitimate" births, property ownership, and expectations for middle-class behavior interwoven with ethnic biases narrowed the pool of potential recipients [Ladd-Taylor 1994; Stadum 1992]. Most significant, the grants received by eligible mothers were minimal. In 1926, almost 15 years after the pension program had begun in Minnesota, the average grant was $39.75 a month, slightly greater than in neighboring states, but far less than the $60 for urban families advocated in a White House study [1933: 129].

In most states, these pensions provided support only for children under age 14 [Abbott 1938b; Abbott & Breckinridge 1917; Leff 1973; Pumphrey & Pumphrey 1983]. Thus, the program indirectly assumed that 14-year-olds could leave school for work and make up the loss of pension income [Breckinridge 1924; White House Conference 1933]. With its flaws, this program served as precursor to the contemporary Aid to Families with Dependent Children program established in 1935. Folks' "second agenda" of securing adequate family income for vulnerable households was not accomplished by the early twentieth century reformers, or by child welfare reforms that have followed to the present.

Conclusion

Opposition to child labor and the implementation of new policies included the activity of reformers seeking change, of social workers doing their jobs at private agencies, and of children and parents managing with scant income. This article draws attention to their separate perspectives and suggests the gulf that often existed between families and those intent on helping the children within them.

Contemporary historians have criticized the many early reformers and middle-class social workers who assumed they knew best what low-income families should do. Economic self-sufficiency was foremost in the hierarchy of values professed by many as they determined the worth of others [Lasch 1979; Pumphrey & Pumphrey 1983; Rothman 1981]. Yet, reformers often blamed members of impoverished families for needing and wanting more income if child labor was involved [Ladd-Taylor 1994]. Many reformers and social workers dismissed underlying economic realities in their confidence that legal sanctions would alter people's attitudes about employment and education [Finkelstein 1985].

Although many social agencies had historically encouraged the rigor of work as character development for youngsters, we see, in retrospect, ambiguities and contradictions in the professionals' definition of how employment fitted into child welfare and familial obligations. Passage of anti-child labor laws and school attendance laws gave certain social workers a role in interpreting, defending, and enforcing new policies. With this they gained arbitrary influence over children's opportunities. Many lacked sensitivity to the economic needs and wishes that sent children to the workplace; likewise, they underrated the negative school experiences that pushed youngsters away from formal education.

Changes in laws affecting children brought families new interactions with social workers and other officials intent on surveillance and intervention. More importantly, responsibilities *within* many low-income households shifted and budgets were squeezed in response to reforms [Hareven 1977]. Regardless of the promise of education or the attention of social workers, the economic struggle of many families with children continued unabated.

Abbott and Breckinridge wrote, "The ignorant and discouraged parent, weary of the desperate struggle with poverty, may be excused for wanting some help from the children he [sic] is trying to support." But they asserted as well, "The 'necessity' of the [children's] work must be estimated not by the poverty in the home, but in terms of its educative value from the point of view of their later industrial life and their fitness for citizenship. In the apparent conflict of interest between the community and the parent . . . the right of the community is slowly but surely being strengthened" [1917: 9, 330). Missing from their assertion is a demand that the community develop an economic environment in which family self-sufficiency is truly possible and financial need does not dictate children's roles.

In translating events here into a lesson for contemporary social work and child welfare reform, the importance of a systems perspective is apparent. As legislation ultimately is felt in daily lives, the viewpoint of affected clients must be prominent in the formative debate. In working through the difficult questions of competing rights and obligations among family members, and between family and community, action to eliminate families' economic insecurity is fundamental to other aims in child welfare. ♦

Notes

---

1. The term *child saving* arose in the nineteenth century; its twentieth century proponents supported family foster homes rather than institutions for children, state support for mother's pensions, and federal authorization of the Children's Bureau. Bureau publications related poverty, ignorance, and poor health to child labor [Kelley 1909; Costin 1983].

2. Taylor [1944] lists four decades of NCLC publications such as *Child Labor in the Southern Cotton Fields* (1906), *Accidents to Working Children of Ohio* (1927), and *Investigations of Homework in the Flower and Feather Industry* (1934).

3. Over time, the Census Bureau changed employment and age categories for grouping children; thus, comparisons of census figures have margin for error.

4. Mary Richmond's knowledge of low-income families grew from her work at the Baltimore, Philadelphia, and New York City Charity Organization Societies. She left direct practice for a position at the Russell Sage Foundation, which published her book *Social Diagnosis* [1917] outlining casework method.

5. COS/Family Welfare Association case records quoted here are from the Minneapolis Family and Children's Service [FCS] Collection at the Social Welfare History Archives, University of Minnesota; all persons' names have been altered. References in

the text relate to case numbers and microfilm reels as stored at the Archives. Findings from these records form the basis of *Poor Women and Their Families: Hard Working Charity Cases, 1900–1930* [Stadum 1992].

6. From Minutes of the Friendly Visiting Committee, Minutes March 3, 1915, Box 7, Minneapolis Family and Children's Service Collection.

References

Abbott, E., & Breckinridge, S. P. (1917). *Truancy and non-attendance in the Chicago schools.* Chicago: University of Chicago.

Abbott, G. (1938a). *The child and the state. Vol. 1: Legal status in the family, apprenticeship and child labor.* Chicago: University of Chicago Press.

Abbott, G. (1938b). *The child and the state. Vol. 2: The dependent and the delinquent child, the child of unmarried parents.* Chicago: University of Chicago Press.

Addams, J. (1905). Child labor legislation: A requisite for industrial efficiency. *Annals of the American Academy of Political and Social Science, 25,* 130–138.

Adler, F. (1908). *The basis of the anti-child labor movement in the idea of American civilization.* New York: National Child Labor Committee.

Adler, F. (1911). *Child labor: A menace to civilization.* New York: National Child Labor Committee.

Anthony, K. (1914). *Mothers who must earn.* New York: Russell Sage Foundation.

Breckinridge, S. P. (1924). *Family welfare work in a metropolitan community, selected case records.* Chicago: University of Chicago Press.

Chambers, C. A. (1963). *Seedtime of reform: American social service and social action, 1918–1933.* Minneapolis, MN : University of Minnesota.

Clement, P. F. (1979). Families and foster care: Philadelphia in the late nineteenth century. *Social Service Review, 53,* 406–420.

Costin, L. B. (1983). *Two sisters for social justice: A biography of Grace and Edith Abbott.* Chicago: University of Illinois Press.

Devine, E. T. (1909). *The new view of the child.* New York: National Child Labor Committee.

Draper, A. (1909). *Conserving childhood*. New York: National Child Labor Committee.

Ensign, F. C. (1921). *Compulsory school attendance and child labor* (Doctoral dissertation, Columbia University).

Finkelstein, B. (1985). Uncle Sam and the children: A history of government involvement in child rearing. In N. R. Hiner & J. Hawes (Eds.), *Growing up in America: Children in historical perspective* (pp. 257–266). Chicago: University of Illinois Press.

Folks, H. (1904). *Care of destitute, neglected and delinquent children*. New York: Macmillan.

Folks, H. (1907). Poverty and parental dependence as an obstacle to child labor or reform. *Annals of the American Academy of Political and Social Science, 29,* 1–8.

Fuller, R. G. (1927). *Fourteen is too early: Some psychological aspects of school leaving and child labor*. New York: National Child Labor Committee.

Goldin, C. (1981). Family strategies and the family economy in the late nineteenth century: The role of secondary workers. In T. Hershberg (Ed.), *Philadelphia, work, space, family, and group experience in the nineteenth century* (pp. 277–310). New York: Oxford University Press.

Haines, M. R. (1981). Poverty, economic stress, and the family in a late nineteenth century American city: Whites in Philadelphia, 1880. In T. Hershberg (Ed.), *Philadelphia, work, space, family, and group experience in the nineteenth century* (pp. 240–276). New York: Oxford University Press.

Hareven, T. K. (1977). Family time and industrial time: Family and work in a planned corporation town, 1900–1924. In T. K. Hareven (Ed.), *Family and kin in urban communities, 1700–1930* (pp. 187–208). New York: New Viewpoints.

Holloran, P. C. (1989). *Boston's wayward children: Social services for homeless children 1830–1930*. Toronto, ON: Associated University Press.

Holt, M. I. (1992). *The orphan trains: Placing out in America*. Lincoln, NE: University of Nebraska Press.

Kelley, F. (1909). *The federal Children's Bureau—a symposium*. New York: National Child Labor Committee.

Kelley, F. (1912). Efficiency in factory inspection. In School of Civics and Philanthropy (Ed.), *The child in the city*. Chicago: University of Chicago.

Kett, J. F. (1977). *Rites of passage: Adolescence in America, 1790 to the present*. New York: Basic Books.

Kyrk, H. (1929). *Economic problems of the family*. New York: Harper and Brothers.

Ladd-Taylor, M. (1994). *Mother-work: Women, child welfare and the state, 1890-1930*. Urbana, IL: University of Illinois Press.

Lasch, C. (1979). *Haven in a heartless world*. New York: Basic Books.

Leff, M. (1973). Consensus for reform: The mothers' pension movement in the progressive era. *Social Service Review, 41,* 397–415.

Lindsay, S. M. (1907). *Child labor and the public schools*. New York: National Child Labor Committee.

Lord, E. W. (1908). *Topics and suggestions for debates on child labor*. New York: National Child Labor Committee.

Loughran, M. (1921). The historical development of child labor legislation in the United States (Doctoral dissertation, Catholic University of America).

Lovejoy, O. (1908). *Selections from child labor day*. New York: National Child Labor Committee.

Lynd, R. S., & Lynd, H. M. (1929). *Middletown: A study in American culture*. New York: Harcourt.

Minnesota Bureau of Labor. (1905). *Special report of child labor in Minnesota*. St. Paul, MN: Author.

Minneapolis Family and Children's Service [FCS] Collection. Social Welfare History Archives, University of Minnesota, Minneapolis, MN.

National Child Labor Committee. (1930). *Proceedings of the 25th anniversary conference*. New York: Author.

National Child Labor Committee. (1937). *Child labor facts*. New York: Author.

National Child Labor Committee. (1938). *Child labor facts*. New York: Author.

Pumphrey, M. W., & Pumphrey, R. E. (1983). The widows' pension movement, 1900–1930: Preventive child-saving or social control. In W. I. Trattner (Ed.), *Social welfare or social control? Some historical reflections on regulating the poor* (pp. 51–66). Knoxville, TN: University of Tennessee.

Richmond, M. E. (1913). *A story of nine hundred and eighty-five widows known to certain charity organization societies in 1910.* New York: Russell Sage Foundation.

Richmond, M. E. (1917). *Social diagnosis.* New York: Russell Sage Foundation.

Rothman, D. (1981). The state as parent: Social policy in the progressive era. In W. Gaylin, I. Glasser, S. Marcus, & D. Rothman (Eds.), *In doing good: The limits of benevolence* (pp. 67–95). New York: Pantheon Books.

Scott, R. J. (1985). The battle over the child: Child apprenticeship and the Freedmen's Bureau in North Carolina. In N. R. Hiner & J. M. Hawes (Eds.), *Growing up in America: Children in historical perspective* (pp. 193–207). Chicago: University of Illinois Press.

Stadum, B. (1992). *Poor women and their families: Hard working charity cases, 1900–1930.* Albany, NY: State University of New York.

Szasz, M. C. (1985). Federal boarding schools and the Indian child, 1920–1960. In N. R. Hiner & J. M. Hawes (Eds.), *Growing up in America: Children in historical perspective* (pp. 209–218). Chicago: University of Illinois Press.

Taylor, F. (1944). *The long road: Fortieth anniversary report of the National Child Labor Committee.* New York: National Child Labor Committee.

Taylor, G. (1906). Parental responsibility for child labor. *Annals of the American Academy of Political and Social Science, 2*(2), 96–98.

Tentler, L. (1981). The world of work for working class daughters, 1900–1930. In M. Albin & D. Cavallo (Eds.), *Family life in America* (pp. 184–202). St. James, NY: Revisionary Press.

Trattner, W. I. (1968). *Homer Folks: Pioneer in social welfare.* New York: Columbia University Press.

Trattner, W. I. (1970). *Crusade for the children: A history of the National Child Labor Committee and child labor reform in America.* Chicago: Quadrangle Books.

United States Bureau of Labor. (1910–1913). *Report on the condition of woman and child wage earners in the United States.* Washington, DC: U. S. Government Printing Office.

White House Conference on Child Health and Protection 1930. (1933). *Dependent and neglected children: Report of the committee on socially handicapped, dependency and neglect.* New York: D. Appleton-Century Company.

Woods, R. A., & Kennedy, A. J. (1913). *Young working girls: A summary of evidence from two thousand social workers.* Boston: Houghton Mifflin.

Zelizer, V. A. (1985). *Pricing the priceless child: The changing social value of children.* New York: Basic Books.

3

THE CHILD WELFARE RESPONSE TO YOUTH VIOLENCE AND HOMELESSNESS IN THE NINETEENTH CENTURY

Kristine Nelson

The nineteenth century problem of street children, created by recurring economic crises, parallels contemporary problems of homelessness and youth violence. The programs developed to deal with these problems also have many similarities. Understanding the origins of both the social problems and the child welfare response is crucial to avoiding the mistakes of the past and developing effective programs.

Kristine Nelson, D.S.W., is Professor, Graduate School of Social Work, Portland State University, Portland, OR. An earlier version of this paper was presented at the Social Welfare History Group Symposium of the Annual Program Meeting of the Council on Social Work Education in 1993.

Once again the United States is facing the interrelated problems of homeless families and children, street gangs, and youth violence [Detweiler 1992; Gulati 1992]. In many cities, children are engaging in criminal behavior to support themselves and joining gangs that threaten the safety and stability of urban neighborhoods [Pryor & McGarrell 1993; Stark 1993]. Neither the problems nor society's response to them are new, however. Both closely parallel the conditions and responses prevalent in New York City and other developing urban areas in the nineteenth century. Confirming historical data are found in annual reports of the major organizations offering services to delinquent and dependent children, in newspaper articles, and in secondary sources describing social and economic conditions in mid-nineteenth century New York City. These sources provide descriptions of the origins, characteristics, and programs developed for street children.

The increase in street children in New York City nearly a century and a half ago resulted from economic changes that have parallels today. Thus, a knowledge of history is helpful in analyzing "innovative" programs and social policies to deal with "new" problems. Misconceptions about the origins and nature of both the social problems and the social welfare programs inhibit our ability to learn from the past and to respond effectively to social problems.

The Response of Charitable Organizations to Economic Crisis

Charitable organizations in the nineteenth century were, for the most part, responding to the social effects of economic change. The Panic of 1837, which lasted until the mid-1840s, for example, profoundly influenced New York City charities. With unemployment estimated at 33% [Schneider 1938: 262], cynicism and suspicion replaced the optimism and pious fervor of the previous decade's evangelical missions to the poor. Losing faith in the power of religion to reform, charity workers began to think of the poor and unemployed in terms previously associated only with the so-called "vicious poor"—criminals and alcoholics [Spann 1981: 71].

Increasing despair about the effectiveness of ministering to adults turned reformers' attention to the problem of street children, a problem publicized by Chief of Police George W. Matsell's 1849 report on juvenile crime. He documented the large number of vagrant children ages six to 16 in the lower wards of the city who survived by stealing, begging, and prostitution, or who simply made nuisances of themselves by hanging around street corners. He warned that this was a "deplorable and growing evil" that required an immediate remedy [Schneider 1938: 329].

Although a system of public schools had been established in New York City in 1842, in part to deal with problems of vagrancy and delinquency among the city's youth, only about half of the city's children attended school by mid-century. Since the schools emphasized moral education and character building rather than trade education, working-class students found them irrelevant and quit by age nine—if they went at all [Spann 1981: 260–261]. Matsell argued that street children should "be compelled to attend our schools regularly, or be apprenticed to some suitable occupation" [New York Juvenile Asylum 1860: 103].

Matsell's warning caught the attention of charitable organizations in the city. Both the New York Association for the Improvement of the Condition of the Poor (NYAICP) and the American Female Guardian Society (AFGS), previously oriented toward helping the adult poor, responded to Matsell's report with a change of direction [NYAICP 1849: 27; AFGS 1851: 26–27; AFGS 1853: 21]. Turning their energies toward "the thousands of children in our large towns and cities, without friends or home, who are growing up ignorant and vicious, thus becoming fit subjects for the prison or the gallows" [AFGS 1854: 8], the two groups established a shelter, an asylum, and a family placement program to remove children from the city.

In 1853, after five years of pressure, the New York State legislature responded to the increasing concern of city organizations about street children by passing the Truancy Act. Although AFGS had been petitioning since 1849 for legislation to ensure the "mental, moral, and physical education" of neglected and destitute children, NYAICP later took credit for the law [AFGS 1854: 10–11; NYAICP 1856: 44]. The legislature authorized local magistrates to compel parents of children five to 14 "found wandering in the streets or lanes . . . idle and truant, without any lawful occupation" to restrain the children or place them for employment and ensure that they be sent to school at least four months a year until the age of 14. If a parent, guardian, or appenticeship master could not be located or refused to comply, the child would be sent to a local institution for support, employment, and instruction. As a result of these efforts, the state and its agents had, for the first time, the power to arrest children who had committed no crime [NYAICP 1853: 23; NYAICP 1854: 61–63; NYAICP 1856: 41].

The most far-reaching response to Matsell's report, however, was that of the Children's Aid Society (CAS) founded by Charles Loring Brace in 1853. A Congregational minister and native New Englander, Brace had worked as a missionary with impoverished adults in the infamous Five Points district of New York City before finding his calling in service to the poor children of the city [Nelson 1980]. His letters [Brace 1894], newspaper articles, annual reports, and classic book, *The Dangerous Classes and Twenty Years Work Among Them* [1872], provide a view not only of the problem of street children in mid-nineteenth century New York City, but of the attitudes and ideas of reformers of the period.

The Social and Economic Context of the 1850s

In the years just preceding the founding of CAS, the United States experienced an economic boom following the prolonged depression that started with the Panic of 1837. The mechanization of many industries in the 1850s contributed to general prosperity, but the benefits of increased productivity went mainly to owners rather than to workers. Despite this prosperity, the burdens of immigration, urbanization, and industrialization weighed heavily on New York City. Statistics on crime and a growing number of immigrants added an aura of danger to the prevalent impression of disorder and disease. Many New Yorkers were afraid to walk the streets at night, in spite of a growing array of institutions and laws and a newly professionalized police force designed to restore order. Low wages, high unemployment, inflated prices, and housing shortages created a vortex that drew unskilled workers and their families into the depths of poverty, while propelling the middle and upper classes outward into suburban areas. The now familiar dilemma of suburban flight and central city decay had begun [Bremner 1956; Handlin 1973; Rosenberg 1964; Spann 1981].

With the influx of cheap immigrant labor in the 1850s, employers turned from hiring youths to employing more reliable adult male workers. For example, unemployment among Newark, New Jersey, youths ages 15 to 20 increased from 7% in 1850 to 22% by 1860. The unemployment of "large boys" in cities had always led to problems of delinquency and youthful gangs, but in the 1850s these problems were greatly magnified. Riots between rival gangs of boys as young as eight to 12 years old and between volunteer fire companies staffed largely by youths threatened peace and order in the city [Hirsch 1978]. As Matsell documented twice yearly after 1849, these youths constituted a threat to public safety and property [Mennel 1973]. In an effort to contain them, the number of houses of refuge and reform schools increased greatly between 1850 and 1860. Parents who were unable to effectively discipline their sons or keep them occupied turned to institutions for aid [Kett 1977].

At the time CAS was founded, 15 organizations and institutions served the needs of poor children in New York City. Three of them—the New York City Almshouse, the House of Refuge, and the Juvenile Asylum—could accommodate over 1,500 children. The remaining New York City institutions for children were of small scale or were quite specialized. The eight orphanages held only 50 to 300 children each. Two of the children's institutions were for the deaf and the mute or the blind. Although precise data are not available, it seems likely that in 1852, before CAS was established, at least twice as many poor children roamed the streets as were contained by the city's institutions and charity schools [Thurston 1930; Bremner 1970–74: 643; Schneider 1938; House of Refuge 1852: 8; Pickett 1969; Kaestle 1973].

The Founding of the Children's Aid Society

Charles Loring Brace announced a new organization to the public in a circular printed in the *New York Daily Times* on March 2, 1853. In it, he outlined the problem posed by street children, the inadequacy of existing efforts to aid them, and the proposed program of the Society, and called for public support. He described the squalid life of children who were "shrewd and old in vice when other children are in leading-strings" and reminded his readers that poor children "have the same capacities, the same need of kind and good influences, and the same Immortality [sic], as the little ones in our own homes" [Brace 1853]. Brace attributed the alarming increase in the number of street children to the influx of "poor foreigners" who left them "everywhere abandoned in our midst" [Brace 1853]. Brace blamed immigration, "a tide of population . . . to which there is no . . . parallel in history," for the rapid development in America of the "hideous and unnatural conditions of the European cities" [CAS 1856: 4; 1854: 3–4; 1855: 3].

The children, Brace felt, were "much superior to the parents." If caught in time, they could be saved from vice, beggary, and filth [CAS 1855: 35, 49]. Brace believed that many poor children, even if they were not orphans, had no semblance of the family life he advocated for all Americans. "Their memory of home is of a damp cellar, where they were kicked and cuffed. The gentle influences moulding childhood were curses and foul words, and bitter hunger and poverty." He emphasized their innocence, asserting that their suffering could not be connected directly to laziness, want of foresight, or vice but seemed to stem from distant social evils [Brace 1852; CAS 1860: 3].

Brace saw rescuing the children of the poor from the influences of their parents and neighborhoods as the only hope of avoiding "transmitted poverty," and a "fixed and hereditary" lower class. "The old heart of men," he wrote, "is a hard thing to change . . . the only hopeful reform through society must begin with *childhood*" (emphasis in original) [CAS 1855: 35; 1856: 3]. In Brace's view, however, the malleability of children had limits, which qualified them for the designation "the dangerous class." Although "they are comparatively easily influenced when young," Brace alluded to an undefined turning point after which they were "almost irreclaimable" [CAS 1854: 9, 22, 26, 31; 1855: 49].

The eventual program of CAS was fully outlined in its first circular [Brace 1853]. Religious meetings, industrial schools, lodging houses for homeless newsboys, reading rooms, and placement in the country proved to be CAS mainstays for the rest of the century. The first goal of CAS was work training or "honest" work in the city or country for street children. The overcrowded labor market in the city made it necessary for both adults and children to work to ensure the family's survival, and Brace accepted child labor as an integral part of family functioning. To keep the children from the "great temptations . . . arising from *want of work*" (emphasis in original), Brace established workshops for the boys and industrial schools for the girls. The workshops, however, could not obtain a steady supply of work for the boys, or support themselves as originally envisioned, and the business downturn of 1854 closed them temporarily [CAS 1854: 7–10; 1855: 6, 9, 38; 1861: 20].

Continuing Crisis and Resolution

The normal business of charitable organizations was severely disrupted, with lasting effects, by the Panic of 1854–1855 [Rosenberg 1971: 237]. NYAICP had already noted the impact of the business cycle on poverty and the oversupply of labor in the city [NYAICP 1850: 24–26]. After a particularly hard winter in 1852, the organization had observed that "the laboring population . . . appear not to obtain a proportionate share of the growing prosperity around them" [NYAICP 1852: 16–17]. Working people themselves had begun to protest high prices and low wages, especially egregious in the face of the increasingly conspicuous consumption of the rich [Spann 1981: 89, 307–308].

Haunted by the Communist Manifesto and the 1848 revolutions in Europe, a mere six years later the wealthy saw predictions of civil disorder in reaction to economic deprivation coming true before their eyes. Strikes and mass meetings of the unemployed to demand jobs and relief sparked rumors of socialist mobs advancing on the rich. The wealthy Peter Cooper, a founder of NYAICP and the Juvenile Asylum, called for a work relief program and was supported by the *Times* and the *Tribune*. In his inaugural address, the new Democratic mayor, Fernando Wood, spoke of redirecting taxes to relief for the unemployed and remonstrated with the rich not to "be ungrateful as well as inhuman. Do not let it be said that labor, which produces every thing [sic], gets nothing and dies of hunger in our midst, while capital, which produces nothing, gets every thing [sic], and pampers in luxury and plenty" [Spann 1981: 309–311, 367].

NYAICP had long railed against the demands of labor, and regarded it as an "absurdity" that the poor should believe "they have a *right* to subsistence, independent of their own earnings" (emphasis in original) or a right to a job [NYAICP 1853: 34]. However, to prevent the unemployed members of the stable working class from "sinking into the vagrant pauper class," NYAICP was eventually put in the embarrassing position of calling for more public outdoor relief due to the exhaustion of its own funds [NYAICP 1855: 20–21; Spann 1981: 308].

In 1857, a battle for control of the city between the Republican-dominated state government and the Democratic mayor and his immigrant supporters culminated in a Fourth of July riot that pitted the Irish Dead Rabbit gang, supporters of the mayor, against the newly organized and Republican-controlled metropolitan police. Newspaper headlines announced "AWFUL RIOTS AND BLOODSHED," "BARRICADES IN THE STREETS—CIVIL WAR IN THE BLOODY SIXTH—TEN KILLED AND EIGHTY WOUNDED—THE HOSPITALS OVER-FLOWING" (capitalized in original) [Spann 1981: 393, 378–389]. Brace attributed the riot to "the continued neglect of this class by the Christian public," and viewed it as "the explosion which those laboring to improve them have long ago expected and openly predicted" [CAS 1858: 8].

A mere two months later the stock market collapsed, initiating the Panic of 1857, even more severe in its immediate effects than its predecessors. As NYAICP related, "Bankruptcies now rapidly ensued, mills and manufactories stopped, thousands upon thousands were thrown out of employment, and a general panic, paralysis and distress, pervaded all classes." By the end of October, a quarter of a million persons were unemployed [NYAICP 1858: 15–17]. Running for re-election, the Democratic mayor called for expanded public works projects and warned, "If the present want of employment continues, many must rely upon either public or private charity, and I fear that not a few will resort to violence and force rather than submit to either of these precarious and humiliating dependencies" [Spann 1981: 395–96].

The charitable organizations felt the impact of the Panic as well. The House of Refuge reported overcrowding, reduced hours and wages for the boys' contract labor, and a reduction in the number of applications for apprentices [Society for the Reformation of Juvenile Delinquents 1858: 6–7]. CAS reported that "numbers of women, widows and others, who have been in respectable positions or in honest business . . . have brought to us their children to be placed in the West." The biggest increase, however, was in placements of children from two-parent families. Forced to turn away many "large boys" ages 15 to 20 in search of work, CAS established a special branch office to find homes and places in the West for the sewing girls who were especially hard hit. Even the newsboys in the CAS lodging house established a fund to feed the hungry [CAS 1858: 6, 13–14, 24]. Fortunately, increased gold and cotton shipments and a mild winter started to bring relief in December, but the lessons of two severe business downturns in succession were not lost on the child-caring organizations [NYAICP 1858: 27; Spann 1981: 416].

Looking back on CAS's first seven years, Brace concluded that they were dealing with "the most difficult problems in human nature and society." In treating the "young criminal and vagrant," they addressed questions of reform and prevention, childhood socialization, and parental neglect. The challenge, as Brace saw it, was to establish a system that could "manage numbers of persons . . . and yet . . . work in harmony with the great principles of political economy and the great impulses of human nature" [Brace 1859: 3]. Brace's programs were grounded in the ideology of laissez faire, relying on natural law, particularly the law of supply and demand, to produce the desired results in the economy and family.

Building on NYAICP's earlier diagnosis that incautious charity both corrupted human nature and distorted the labor market, Brace deduced two principles in his work with dependent children: (1) "the superiority of the *Christian family* [emphasis in original], to any and all other institutions for the education and improvement of a poor child" and (2) "the necessity, in treating the evils of the poor on a large scale, of following the natural laws of demand for labor." Brace emphasized that placing children with farm families in the West was the only feasible solution to "the great economic problem of poverty in our cities" [CAS 1855: 6]. Although he is remembered primarily as the founder of fam-

ily foster care, Brace saw himself, first and foremost, as responding to the needs of impoverished children generated by immigration and economic crisis.

It was not, however, a more liberal approach to aiding the
poor of the city or the expanding demand for child labor in the
western states, or even the sharp decline in immigration that
followed the Panic of 1857 that temporarily relieved the working
class of its desperate poverty and resolved the problem of street
children, but the classic solution to prolonged unemployment
and economic crisis: war. The Civil War provided military "employment" and discipline for husbands and fathers, city benefits
for wives and children of volunteers, and an "immense amount
of employment . . . in orders for clothes, harness, tents, arms & c."
[sic] [CAS 1863: 3]. The economic cycle, however, continued to
create unemployment and despair regularly throughout the next
three-quarters of a century, culminating in the Great Depression
of the 1930s and the formation of a modern welfare state to soften
its effects.

The Continuing Relevance of Economic Crisis

Since the 1980s, economic crisis and conservative ideology have
reproduced the related problems of homeless and disorderly
children and breathed new life into nineteenth century solutions:
reliance on the "natural forces" of family and the market, on
private voluntary efforts, or if those failed, on placement. Once
again, immigrants and the "underclass" are made to bear both
the burden of and the blame for the economy's reinvigorated
boom-and-bust business cycle [Gulati 1992]. Once again, we see
not only homeless families and children, but increasing rates of
violence both in the home and in the streets. Once again, a large
proportion of teenage males in inner cities cannot find a place for
themselves in the schools or in the labor market. As a result,
crime and welfare reform have moved to the top of the national
political agenda.

In many ways, the conditions of the 1980s paralleled those of the 1850s. In 1986, over 13,000 children in single-parent families passed through shelters for the homeless in New York City, and in 1988 *The New York Times* printed 71 stories about homeless children and families [Gulati 1992]. Unemployment, low wages, and inadequate welfare benefits produce the mobility and stress that lead to homelessness and family dissolution, particularly in families headed by single mothers [Mulroy & Lane 1992]. Shelters for the homeless and welfare hotels recreate the dehumanizing conditions of nineteenth century asylums and poorhouses [Gulati 1992; Keigher 1992], and a new "dangerous class" of children who are not expected to enter the economic mainstream is emerging in the inner cities [Wallis 1992].

In response to the sharp economic downturns of the 1970s and based on an ideology of individual responsibility and market solutions, the Reagan administration's social agenda was itself responsible for creating much of the problem by dismantling or downsizing the social programs of the New Deal and the War on Poverty [Rubin et al. 1992]. By reestablishing a "poor law" mentality that blames the victims of economic crisis for their problems [Gulati 1992], politicians of both parties reinforce the racism that keeps many in poverty by exaggerating the extent of crime, violence, and other social problems in African American communities [Belcher 1992; Stark 1993].

The proposed solutions should have a familiar ring. Like the juvenile reformatories of the mid-nineteenth century, boot camps for youthful offenders stress discipline and order. Mirroring NYAICP's philosophy, benefit cuts and mandatory work are advocated as welfare "reform." And the nineteenth century notion that children should be removed from their families to break the "debilitating cycle" of welfare, poverty, and crime has been revived by such prominent persons as the governor of Ohio [Stark 1993: 485]. Recognizing the heartlessness and ineffectiveness of removing poor children from their troubled families, others have responded with new approaches: family preservation and support·services and foster care programs for whole families [e.g., Whittaker et al. 1990; Nelson & Landsman 1992; Nelson 1992].

Despite the recent recognition of a growing gap between rich and poor and the perception that homelessness and youth violence are major social problems, solutions like these focus on individual victims and not on the economic system that creates them. Although social critics and reformers warn of the potential political and economic consequences of creating a disenfranchised and alienated "underclass," the civil unrest that so often stimulates reform has not yet been felt on a large scale. If history is allowed to repeat itself, however, it cannot be far behind. ♦

References

American Female Guardian Society and Home for the Friendless (AFGS). (1851). *Annual report*. New York: Angell, Engel & Hewitt.

American Female Guardian Society and Home for the Friendless (AFGS). (1853). *Annual report*. New York: Stephen Angell.

American Female Guardian Society and Home for the Friendless (AFGS). (1854). *Annual report*. New York: Author.

Belcher, J. R. (1992). Poverty, homelessness, and racial exclusion. *Journal of Sociology and Social Welfare, 19*(4), 41–54.

Brace, C. L. (1852, December 6). Public charity: Vagrant children. *New York Daily Times*, p. 3.

Brace, C. L. (1853, March 2). To the public—Children's Aid Society. *New York Daily Times*, p. 8.

Brace, C. L. (1859). *The best method of disposing of our pauper and vagrant children*. New York: Wynkoop, Hallenbeck and Thomas.

Brace, C. L. (1872). *The dangerous classes of New York and twenty years work among them*. Washington, DC: National Association of Social Workers (1973 reprint edition).

Brace, E. (Ed.). (1894). *The life of Charles Loring Brace chiefly told in his own letters*. New York: Charles Scribner's Sons.

Bremner, R. H. (1956). *From the depths: The discovery of poverty in the United States*. New York: New York University Press.

Bremner, R. H., et al. (Eds.). (1970–74). *Children and youth in America: A documentary history* (Vol. 1). Cambridge, MA: Harvard University Press.

Children's Aid Society of New York (CAS). (1854–1863). *Annual reports*. Reprinted by the National Association of Social Workers. New York: Arno Press, 1971.

Detweiler, B. (1992). Violence and our response: The violence and the underlying causes demand action. *Public Welfare, 50*(4), 4–5.

Gulati, P. (1992). Ideology, public policy and homeless families. *Journal of Sociology and Social Welfare, 19*(4), 113–128.

Handlin, O. (1973). *The uprooted* (2nd ed.). Boston: Little, Brown and Co.

Hirsch, S. (1978). *Roots of the American working class*. Philadelphia: University of Pennsylvania Press.

House of Refuge at Randall's Island, laying of the cornerstone: Addresses by Mayor Kingland and Robert Kelly, Esq. (1852, November 25). *New York Daily Times*, p. 8.

Kaestle, C. (1973). *The evolution of an urban school system*. Cambridge, MA: Harvard University Press.

Keigher, S. M. (1992). Rediscovering the asylum. *Journal of Sociology and Social Welfare, 19*(4), 177–197.

Kett, J. F. (1977). *Rites of passage*. New York: Basic Books.

Mennel, R. (1973). *Thorns and thistles*. Hanover, NH: University Press of New England.

Mulroy, E., & Lane, T. S. (1992). Housing affordability, stress and single mothers: Pathway to homelessness. *Journal of Sociology and Social Welfare, 19*(3), 51–64.

Nelson, K. E. (1980). *The best asylum: Charles Loring Brace and foster family care* (Doctoral dissertation, University of California at Berkeley).

Nelson, K. E., & Landsman, M. J. (1992). *Alternative models of family preservation: Family-based services in context*. Springfield, IL: Charles C Thomas.

Nelson, K. M. (1992). Fostering homeless children and their parents too: The emergence of whole-family foster care. *Child Welfare, 71*, 575–84.

New York Juvenile Asylum. (1860). *Annual report*. New York: W. S. Dorr.

New York Association for Improving the Condition of the Poor (NYAICP). (1849–50, 1852–56, 1858). *Annual reports*. New York: John F. Trow.

Pickett, R. (1969). *House of refuge*. Syracuse, NY: Syracuse University Press.

Pryor, D. W., & McGarrell, E. F. (1993). Public perceptions of youth gang crime: An exploratory analysis. *Youth and Society, 24*, 399–418.

Rosenberg, C. S. (1971). *Religion and the rise of the American city*. Ithaca, NY: Cornell University Press.

Rosenberg, C. S. (1964). Protestants and Five Pointers: The Five Points House of Industry, 1850–1870. *New York History Society Quarterly, 48*, 327–47.

Rubin, B. A., Wright, J. D., & Devine, J. A. (1992). The urban poor: The Reagan legacy. *Journal of Sociology and Social Welfare, 19*(1), 111–147.

Schneider, D. M. (1938). *The history of public welfare in New York State, 1609–1866*. Chicago: University of Chicago Press.

Society for the Reformation of Juvenile Delinquents. (1858). *Annual report*. New York: Wynkoop, Hallenbeck & Thomas.

Spann, E. K. (1981). *The new metropolis: New York City, 1840–1857*. New York: Columbia University Press.

Stark, E. (1993). The myth of black violence. *Social Work, 38*, 485–490.

Thurston, H. (1930). *The dependent child*. New York: Columbia University Press.

Wallis, J. (1992). Violence, poverty, and separation: No one really expects the children of the inner cities to enter the economic mainstream. *Public Welfare, 50*(4), 14–15.

Whittaker, J. K., Kinney, J., Tracy, E. M., & Booth, C. (1990). *Reaching high-risk families: Intensive family preservation in human services*. New York: Aldine.

4

AN OUTRAGE TO COMMON DECENCY: HISTORICAL PERSPECTIVES ON CHILD NEGLECT

Karen J. Swift

Drawing on historical documents and case files, this
article explores the roots of the perception that mothers
are the parents primarily responsible for child neglect.
It suggests that this focus on mothers has been at the
expense of an understanding of, and efforts to change,
the social and economic context in which child neglect
occurs.

*Karen J. Swift, Ph.D., is Assistant Professor, McGill University, Montreal, Quebec,
Canada.*

Today, child neglect is generally understood, defined, investigated, and acted upon in personal and in gender-specific terms. Most often, neglect is seen as the failure of individual mothers to carry out their mothering responsibilities [Swift 1991]. Gil [1970: 31], for instance, defined neglect as "a breakdown in the ability to mother." Polansky et al. [1972], the foremost scholars dealing with child neglect, have made the personal and home-centered focus of neglect explicit in their Childhood Level of Living Scale, a measure used to rate the adequacy of mothers' care [1972]. Polansky et al. [1972, 1981] and others [Jones & McNeely 1980] have emphasized the personal traits of mothers as primary causal factors in cases of neglect. This focus on mothers prevails, although research on neglect virtually always connects it to poverty [Wolock & Horowitz 1980], to other social conditions such as family violence [Gordon 1988; Swift 1990], and to community disorganization [Garbarino 1981]. This article examines the historical roots that contribute to this understanding of child neglect.

Sources

Besides secondary sources, this article derives from documents, intake records, and randomly selected case files of neglect from the agency now known as Metropolitan Toronto Children's Aid Society (MTCAS). Two time periods are examined: the late 1800s, when the concept of neglect and its legal and bureaucratic frameworks were developed; and the decade of the 1930s. The latter was chosen because it serves as a point about midway between the origins of child welfare work in Canada and the present time, and because it allows exploration of neglect in a period of severe economic distress.

The Historical Context

The concept of child neglect was originally conceived in relation to the significant problems of abandoned and neglected children

[Bala et al. 1990]. Canadian historians have attributed these problems to two main factors. First, the processes of industrialization and urbanization that occurred during and after the 1880s resulted in poor housing and sanitation, overcrowding, poverty, and sometimes early death for a large new underclass [Sutherland 1976]. Many children whose parents were unable to provide care for them were partly or completely abandoned; many others were orphaned. Second, a large number of destitute children in England were "rescued" and brought for placement into Canadian homes around the turn of the century. It is estimated that some 77,000 such children were brought into Canada between 1886 and 1923. Many of these children who found their new homes harsh and unsatisfactory eventually migrated to city centers as an alternative [Sutherland 1976]. By the 1880s, apparently unsupervised children were commonplace in Ontario cities. These children, seen sleeping in city streets, begging, loitering, and committing petty crimes, exemplified neglect to the original child welfare reformers, who were concerned both for the children themselves and for the stability of the social order [Jones & Rutman 1981].

Concern about neglected children culminated in protective legislation during the latter part of the nineteenth century, with the first child welfare agency in Canada (now MTCAS) being incorporated in 1891. Two years later, the province of Ontario passed the Children's Protection Act, which provided the administrative machinery to care for neglected children (defined as homeless, vagrant, and destitute) or those found in the company of "immoral" characters such as thieves and prostitutes [Falconer & Swift 1983: 9]. In these earliest years of child protection, two kinds of cases were handled by the new protection agency. As many as half the cases involved children referred or remanded by the courts [CAS Administrative History (n.d.): 1]. Although written records of these cases provide little evidence concerning the children's circumstances, many of these cases likely involved abandoned or runaway children—"street arabs," as they were known at the time—trying to support themselves by stealing or begging. Another group of cases handled by the volunteer protection "agents" concerned reports of neglect or other ill-treatment of children by parents [CAS Complaint Book 1899]. Many of these reports were made by husbands or wives against each other. One husband, for instance, complained that his wife "drinks and neglects the children"; another said his wife, a "bad character," was in the hospital with venereal disease. Wives complained that their husbands were drinking, beating them, or had abandoned them. Many reports recorded during this era involved the birth of out-of-wedlock babies; often the mothers themselves were seeking information concerning resources for boarding or "adopting out" these infants. Illness of the mother, notably "consumption," was another frequently reported problem. Remedies included the boarding of children in shelters; referral by the agent to private homes serving as "baby farms"; occasional foster care or adoption of children; "warnings" issued by the agent, especially to errant fathers; referral of abandoned mothers to the House of Industry (poorhouse); and, in extreme cases, the filing of criminal charges.

By 1906, 56 Children's Aid Societies existed in Ontario, with a total "volunteer force" of six or seven hundred [McBride 1983]. By this time, other Canadian provinces were using Ontario's model to guide the development of their own legislation and agencies. Although historians generally view child neglect of this period in its relation to broader social conditions, social reformers of the day perceived the neglect of children as the outcome of "improper parental training, indifference and drunkeness" [McBride 1983: 72]. In keeping with notions of individual responsibility embedded in Poor Law beliefs, these middle-class reformers directed their most vigorous efforts toward changing the morals and behavior of neglecting parents [McBride 1983; Farina 1982]. Further, the Children's Protection Act, which the reformers had helped develop, provided broad powers to remove children from homes considered unsatisfactory. Records from the first decade of this century show the beginnings of home investigations, attention to the various placements of children, and the placement outcomes. Although some parents continued to seek assistance from the agency, others objected to what they saw as interference in their affairs. One father, for instance, was reported to be in a "towering passion" concerning decisions made about his children in his absence, decisions quickly revoked in the aftermath of his response [CAS Complaint Book 1910].

In the new century, some reformers expanded the idea of child neglect to include problems of poverty faced by widowed and abandoned mothers. A 1911 review of Ontario children in the care of child welfare agencies revealed that as many as 50% had been removed from the homes of sole-support mothers on grounds of poverty [McBride 1983]. This shift in view of causation resulted in the support by many reformers of "Mothers' Pensions," a program adopted gradually by Canadian provinces during the second decade of the twentieth century. The program was controversial, however, and eligibility was extremely limited in all of the provinces that adopted it. Generally, the concept of an applicant's "worthiness" was included in eligibility criteria, and proponents of the newly developing profession of social work claimed expertise in differentiating those claimants whose need was "legitimate" from those whose own personal failings were the cause of child neglect [Guest 1980]. Charlotte Whitton, Director of the Canadian Council of Child and Family Welfare, proposed that this "unearned money" should not be given unless accompanied by "skilled social work investigation and supervision" [Guest 1980: 52]. Thus, even when poverty and single-parent status gained acceptance as causal factors in neglect, scrutiny of the personal characteristics of mothers continued as a primary focus for social workers concerned with the care of children.

In these beginnings, then, several themes continually reappear. The concept of child neglect arose from conditions of social and economic deprivation, and its resolution was pursued by

middle-class reformers who were both sympathetic to and frightened by the young victims and their families. While a powerful
emphasis on parental responsibility for children, especially by
mothers, was central to the approach these reformers took, the
obvious poverty of these mothers could not be overlooked. Thus,
the "dual" nature of neglect as an expression of both the character and the poverty of parents was born. It is important to note,
however, that it was parental responsibility for care and not
social responsibility for preventing poverty that was reflected in
the legislated child welfare mandate.

Children's Aid in the 1930s

Social and Economic Context

Social workers of the 1930s were faced with the effects of the
Great Depression. By 1933, nearly a third of Toronto's workforce
was unemployed. Many who continued to work saw their wages
drop dramatically and their standard of living suddenly reduced
[Lemon 1985: 59–60]. The relief effort in Ontario, although un-
evenly applied, was extensive and relatively generous. It was,
according to Cassidy [1932: 250], generally sufficient to prevent
serious malnutrition or health problems in the populace. However, families on relief or suffering from seriously reduced wages
often had to double up with other families, rent out rooms, or
engage in a series of moves in order to keep themselves housed
[Cassidy 1932; Lemon 1985].

In the ideal home of the 1930s, family responsibilities were
divided along gender lines. "It is the man's place to build and
subsidize the home," stated Dr. W. B. Atlee in 1932. "The
woman's place [is] to rear the young in it" [Maclaren 1990: 33].
This ideal, if it ever really existed, was certainly breaking down in
the face of economic stress and an employment market that had
some room at the lower end for women and children but much
less room for the higher-paid jobs that were traditionally held by
men. Milkman [1976] argues that the resulting shortage of

"male" jobs meant loss of status for unemployed men and increased psychological stress within families. Child welfare records provide evidence that unemployed men often resorted to drinking, violence, and abandonment of the family, while women often assumed breadwinning responsibilities even if the husband was living at home. At the same time, women maintained responsibility for the care of home and children, creating stressful conditions for themselves.

The families in the 1930s agency sample represent these conditions. Most were poor. Only a very few of the mothers were fully supported by their husbands through the life of the case; the majority of the mothers had jobs, were on relief, and/or found other sources of support such as renting out rooms. Where fathers were involved, most were working class and had periods of unemployment or underemployment. Poor and crowded housing conditions were the norm for these families, and there is ample evidence of alcohol and wife abuse as well as marital breakdown.

Professional Practices

The Canadian volunteers who originated child welfare work had their antecedents in the "friendly visitors," primarily women, who had worked in American volunteer charity organizations since the previous century [Treudley 1980]. The primary function of these visitors was to carry out personal investigations of supplicants to determine their "worthiness" for receipt of charitable assistance. Visitors also saw it as their duty to offer morally uplifting advice on self-improvement to the poor, often using themselves as examples of moral adequacy. Participation in the visitors' program declined during the early part of the twentieth century, and was supplanted by a more professionally oriented group of social workers who wished to emphasize expertise over morality. Both the investigative and moral uplift techniques, however, were preserved as part of the new profession [Lubove 1965].

By the 1930s, the investigative practices adopted by child welfare agencies were thoroughly geared to the investigation of home and family. Record-keeping procedures were organized around family units, and individual case planning was routine [Staff Minutes, Infant Homes of Toronto 1920–29; Gordon 1988]. As in modern times, Children's Aid Societies operated as part of a network of institutional services. Agencies traded information about families with each other through central registries of client families. As well, child welfare authorities were often asked to cooperate in identifying and investigating families for other agencies.

A central list of the neglect referrals made to the Toronto Children's Aid Society was maintained, and research shows that these "complaints" were restricted entirely to individual families [CAS Complaint Books 1937, 1939]. These records were all filed in the mother's name, on the supposition that the mother's identity was usually known whereas the father's sometimes was not [McDermott 1986]. The assigned worker investigated complaints first by visiting the family at home and later by interviewing other professionals, landladies, relatives, neighbors, employers, estranged husbands, or anyone else who might be able to give evidence. The worker then developed a "process recording" of case activity, in which observations about the family, and especially about the mother, were recorded in considerable detail, a practice in keeping with those of other North American social agencies of the day [Dixon 1938]. Although the Depression was producing serious economic problems for most of these families, such investigative practices quickly narrowed the focus of a neglect investigation to the personal characteristics and behaviors of family members.

Neglect: A Woman's Domain

The issue of child neglect highlights the dual role that single mothers have always faced as breadwinners and caregivers, a dilemma mediated but certainly not resolved by the introduction of Mothers' Pensions. Files demonstrate how mothers tried to cope, and how these efforts could be thwarted by child welfare authorities. Women who took jobs were unable to supervise their children, while those in overcrowded housing were subject to constant scrutiny by their neighbors. Those who stayed with unemployed husbands continued to bear more children and often endured abusive behavior from their mates, from which they had little or no protection, while those who sought relationships outside of marriage were considered immoral by child welfare authorities.

A variety of conditions could bring a family to agency attention on grounds of neglect, but these were confined almost exclusively to the female domain of home and child care. Even in cases of extreme poverty, the father's domain of "building and subsidizing" the home was rarely viewed as a cause for investigation. Complaints generally involved evidence indicting the physical care of the home or children and/or the behavior of family members. When a child was the focus of complaint, head lice; dirty, ragged, or inappropriate clothing; misbehavior such as truancy from school; or petty theft might be cited. Usually, as Houston [1982] notes, the "crimes" were small; one family came to the attention of Children's Aid, for instance, because one of the children had stolen four dollars. In other cases, the presenting complaint concerned a lack of supervision. For instance, one family was reported because a child was "allowed to run the streets." Often the major concern was the quality of housekeeping, with a dirty house or a "filthy room" cited as an indicator of neglect.

The most common complaints involved morality. Alcohol, loud parties, and the use of "bad language" in front of children were frequently cited in Complaint Books as reasons to investigate for neglect. Insinuations of sex outside of marriage on the part of the mother clearly caused the most concern. Mentioned in various complaints were that a mother had entertained a "foreign visitor," kept roomers, or went out at night; at times, it was simply that parents were separated.

Files show that the worker's subsequent investigation was also oriented to the mother's domain, that is, to the physical condition and upkeep of the mother and the house, and the cleanliness, discipline, and affect of children. Workers offered comments on these conditions at each visit, often in detail: the room was "most untidy, with cigarettes and orange peel and clothing on the dresser and no sheets on the bed," or "mother . . . untidy . . . hair unwashed and no stockings on." The physical appearance of children suspected of being neglected was especially mentioned on the first visit. If the worker was favorably impressed, she would record "cheerful, pleasant and well dressed" or "attractive, wearing clean clothes, and leaning close to her mother." In other instances, children were seen as "pitiful." If workers viewed the social context of the Depression as a causal factor in the deprivation and petty crimes they preserved in files, it was not expressed.

Expert Advice

Following the First World War, Canadians experienced a renewed interest in the requirements of proper parenting, an interest bolstered by knowledge development in the social sciences and by the advice of "experts" [Strong-Boag 1982]. In practice, as Strong-Boag makes clear, it was virtually always mothers who were held accountable for applying this knowledge, as well as for any failures or problems experienced by their children. File review demonstrates that by the 1930s child welfare workers were conversant with these expectations and regularly applied guidelines based on expert advice in their evaluations of mothers. One case file, for example, shows a mother of 11 judged inadequate by her worker because she could not recall the precise ages at which a particular child teethed, walked, and talked.

Child welfare workers, along with other professionals, were also interested in related social sciences [Simmons 1982]. The development of intelligence testing and taxonomies particularly captured their attention, as the following descriptions of mothers found in case files suggest: "is probably subnormal," "has the mentality of a child of nine," "is a low grade moron of the unstable type."

Workers' interest in intelligence levels reflected the tremendous appeal of the eugenics movement during the early part of this century, when public fear of the "feebleminded" population rose to considerable heights. A report examining the incidence of feeblemindedness among the citizenry of Ontario and recommending solutions to this public "threat" was published in 1919. One of the greatest concerns identified in it was "the feebleminded female of child bearing age" [Hodgins 1920: 126], who, it was feared, could add immeasurably to the size of this potentially dangerous and costly group. Thus, the morality of mothers, already a concern in terms of their "worthiness" for benefits, took on the greater meaning of constituting a potential threat to public security. The 1919 report consequently included recommendations for the segregation of women who posed such a threat, and suggested that child welfare agencies should cooperate in identifying feebleminded women of childbearing age.

Evidently this recommendation was followed, for the files of the 1930s commonly report the results of intelligence tests for both mothers and children. These results were generally treated as factual and often led to a recommendation for institutionalization of mother or child. One worker spent months trying to convince a mother that her daughter should be institutionalized because of a low intelligence-test result. The mother's vigorous resistance on grounds that she was managing perfectly well was challenged by the worker in her recording: "It is evident that the woman has not realized the difficulty she has been having with the child." This mother prevailed, however; her daughter remained at home.

Invidious Comparisons

A powerful belief in personal responsibility for the care of children, the ideal of gendered divisions of labor in the home, and reliance on expert knowledge about parenting were important contextual factors shaping perceptions of child neglect in the 1930s. The convergence of these factors led workers to pay far more attention to the characteristics and behavior of the mother than to the child, while fathers appear primarily as a point of contrast to mothers. When recorded, descriptions of men were likely to relate to the man's employment, actual or potential. Occasionally, glimpses of these men at home were seen. One young father sat reading a newspaper in the kitchen while the worker discussed the neglect complaint with *his* mother.

Prominent in a number of cases were contrasting images of the mother and the father. One mother was described as "not very bright mentally," for instance, while her husband's problems were ascribed to "limited opportunities." The mother, diagnosed as "a high grade moron of the unstable type," was married to a man with "highly influential friends." Associated with these contrasts was a marked trend to attribute family problems to deficiencies in women. In the case record of one couple with severe marital problems, each frequently accused the other of drinking and extramarital relationships. The woman was eventually found to be the "real problem," being "dull normal, alcoholic and immoral." In one case, the wife's repeated allegations of abuse by her husband were noted by the worker, who went on to say of the mother that she "is self-centered, does not think of the children, complains constantly, and takes no responsibility for the house." In instances where the couple gave different versions of their problems, workers tended to see the man as more credible. One woman was "charged with mental illness" and sent to an institution to recover. Evidence appearing in support of the charge was her husband's allegation that she had accused him "of acts of which he has no knowledge." The conclusion drawn by the worker was that "one cannot believe what this woman says." Her subsequent diagnosis was "conjugal psychopathy."

In some cases there is evidence that husbands could use child welfare authorities to control their wives. One wife stood accused by her husband of "dishonesty, failure to work with him, neglect of their children, encouraging disloyalty to him in the children, and instigating dishonesty in the children, which he attempts to check." In that case, the woman's mother, later interviewed, attempted to stand up for her daughter, blaming the husband for many difficulties. She herself was then described by the worker as "mentally unstable" and her testimonial was largely disregarded. Only rarely, in fact, were any family problems attributed to fathers. Although much evidence of wife abuse appears in these records, workers generally ignored this and instead targeted the deficiencies of mothers.

In spite of the attention paid to the character and capabilities of the mother, she was not necessarily expected to provide personal or full-time care for her children. Indeed, the presence of an unexplained man in a home was much more likely to bring attention from child welfare workers than the care of a child by someone other than the mother. "Boarding out" a child or getting help from the landlady and other female neighbors and relatives in caring for the child was perfectly acceptable, as long as the child was fed and clothed.

"An Outrage to Common Decency"

As is the case today, workers of the 1930s acted not only in an investigative role but frequently engaged in support and referral activities. In cases involving destitution, morality questions were deemphasized as workers organized needed supplies for families, including food, clothing, fuel, and even books and toys. In some cases, the task of obtaining resources continued over many years. The predominant tone of all the records, however, was one of moral disapproval and outrage, a tone that increased substantially when the case involved a single mother. On one unannounced visit, the worker encountered a man "in a nude condition" in the presence of a child and her mother. The embarrassed worker pointed out that "a man walking nude even before his wife and child was an outrage to common decency, let alone before another woman and a child." How the worker herself came to surprise the family in the bedroom remains unexplained.

Such incidents, by themselves, did not result in removal of children from their homes. Instead, they were used to justify continued "supervision" of the family by authorities. If a child appeared happy, was well-dressed and attending school regularly, it was unlikely that the mother's behavior would be zealously pursued. If any one of these matters became a concern, the worker would increase the number and intensity of her visits. Such supervision had contradictory purposes, as it does today [Swift 1990]. Citing in the record a need for supervision provided justification for ongoing assistance and resources to a family in need, and simultaneously justified ongoing advice, surveillance, and authority over the family. The files provided little evidence that "supervision" was necessarily related to substantiated cases of child neglect or that it led to any real or lasting change in the morals, economic circumstances, or lifestyles of families. The voluminous and ongoing documentation of poverty and problems in fact suggests the opposite. Nor did the records show evidence that legally defined neglect was required in order for ongoing supervision to occur. Only one legally substantiated case of child neglect was found, a significant fact given the vast amount of investigation and surveillance carried out in the name of neglect. In this instance, grounds cited for establishing neglect were that the child was "growing up without salutary parental control/or under circumstances tending to make him idle or dissolute," phrases taken directly from the legislation. The judge decided to make this child a permanent ward and "give him a chance."

Implications for the 1990s

Child welfare legislation and practice across North America have changed since the 1930s. Legal definitions of neglect are now geared less toward the child's guardian and more toward the actual or potential harm facing the child. Also, as various rights movements have developed, the protection process has come to be premised on the concept of due process [Bala et al. 1990]. Canadian law has incorporated the "least intrusive" principle, widely supported because of public weariness with the intrusive possibilities that child welfare work had previously included. Implementation of this principle means that social workers now have fewer opportunities to use the threat of neglect charges as a way of exerting authority over families; but also that fewer families can benefit from resource distribution through child welfare auspices. The professional literature on bonding and attachments [Bowlby 1969] has encouraged us to see ongoing personal care by mothers as essential to healthy child development. This view has not only changed perceptions of neglect to include a focus on the quality and quantity of time a mother devotes to caregiving, but has also helped to support the "family preservation" approach currently popular with child welfare authorities in both the United States and Canada.

These kinds of changes may encourage us to view our historical origins as relics of the past. Yet in a number of ways, modern perceptions of child neglect continue to reflect their personal and gender-biased beginnings. Historically, as we have seen, neglect has been located mainly in low-income, marginalized, and mother-led families. Within this domain, child welfare workers and scholars have continued to dwell on personal responsibilities of parents, and have sought explanations of poor quality child care primarily within the realm of mothering. Review of the literature concerned with child neglect [Swift 1988; 1995] reveals that this focus on the characteristics and behaviors of individual mothers has continued through the 1980s, while themes of poverty and deprivation have taken second place.

The gender bias seen in neglect has also remained a constant theme over the past century. Records show that the labeling of mothers charged with neglect is far from a thing of the past. Rather, it is regularly used in both professional discourse and in case files as justification for ongoing "supervision" of these mothers. Data from a recent study [Swift 1990] show that workers frequently assess mothers in neglect cases as "dull" or "intellectually limited." In addition, researchers often perceive these mothers as immature and needy, as "children themselves" [Young 1964], a focus that has developed in tandem with the popularization of theories such as Erikson's [1950] dealing with emotional and psychological development. This theme of immaturity also appears regularly in case files. Another and still developing theme is that of the "cycle" idea [Breines and Gordon 1983], which suggests that mothers pass on their "defects" to their children through their poor mothering, a view that has obvious parallels to the 1930s notion of neglectful mothers as dangerous to the social order. File review also shows that poverty, wife assault, drug abuse, poor housing, and social dislocation are important features of neglect cases that continue to be underemphasized both in professional discourse and in the programs funded to confront child neglect [Swift 1990].

Why has this personal focus remained so predominant in the face of the obvious and serious economic and social problems faced by these women? The original reformers were clear on this point. They believed that in "saving" neglected children, they also could save themselves and their positions of privilege [Sutherland 1976; McBride 1983]. They most certainly hoped to help neglected children, but they also wanted to reduce threats to the existing social order that they believed these children might come to pose. Their scheme was ingenious, providing themselves and their representatives with the authority of the state to intervene in and alter the private lives of those whom they saw as dangerous to their own interests. The arrangements were inexpensive and, at least in theory, easily carried out, since low-income mothers were lacking in political consciousness and power.

This basic approach, with continual refinements, remains in place today, and its attractions to middle- and upper-class Canadians are apparent. The alternative, after all, would be far-reaching changes in pursuit of a more equitable distribution of wealth and power. Indeed, the original child welfare purpose is almost perfectly preserved in the legal framework and work organization developed by the original reformers. Legislation continues to target the family as the locus of problems. Workers still have no real mandate to deal with social and economic conditions as causal factors of child neglect. Casework, which remains the primary mode of child welfare intervention, continually reinforces this approach, encouraging workers to attend to family relationships and dynamics. The more recent trend toward the legalization of child protection [Bala et al. 1990] exacerbates this approach by requiring social workers to continually collect evidence against mothers in anticipation of future court action. Social workers assigned to work on cases of child neglect, then, come to appear as competent professionals not by challenging and changing conditions of poverty, violence, and deprivation, but by the identification and containment of maternal deficiencies and error.

Given the serious social and economic problems faced by many mothers accused of neglect, we might wonder if the real "outrage to common decency" is the failure of child welfare services over the past century to confront the pressing need for change. It would not be correct to say that no change is possible as long as the traditional framework for coping with child neglect remains in place. New directions are being taken. The MTCAS of the 1990s, for instance, is placing new emphasis on housing as a factor in child neglect [Cohen-Schlanger et al. 1993]. The agency is also playing a central advocacy role in Campaign 2000, a community-based effort to eliminate child poverty in Canada [Rivers 1993]. There is increasing emphasis across Canada on the provision of in-home supports to low-income mothers. Some organizations now work specifically toward empowering clients, and a few now view mothers as partners in the child welfare endeavor rather than as perpetrators of offenses [Wharf 1994]. For some time, advocates of Native-controlled child welfare programs have been developing holistic program approaches that include the social and economic context of neglect [MacDonald 1985].

However, as Callahan [1993: 204] argues, the traditional mandate surrounding child neglect imposes serious constraints on social change. She has proposed a radical break from the past, advocating that the "so-called crime of neglect should simply disappear from the child welfare statutes." Her recommendation of an advocacy rather than an investigative model for child welfare holds great promise. What both actual and proposed directions suggest is that we can pay tribute to our history, and learn from it, but we need not and should not be slaves to it. ♦

References

Bala, N., Hornick, J., & Vogl, R. (1990). *Canadian child welfare law*. Toronto, ON: Thompson Educational Publishing, Inc.

Bowlby, J. (1969). *Attachment and loss*. New York: Basic Books, Inc.

Breines, W., & Gordon, L. (1983). The new scholarship on family violence. *Signs, 8*, 491–531.

Callahan, M. (1993). Feminist approaches: Women recreate child welfare. In B. Wharf (Ed.), *Rethinking child welfare* (pp. 172–209). Toronto, ON: McClelland and Stewart Inc.

Cassidy, H. (1932). *Unemployment and relief in Ontario, 1929–32*. Toronto, ON: J. M. Dent and Sons, Limited.

Children's Aid Society. *Complaint books*. City of Toronto Archives, 1899, 1910, 1937, and 1939.

Children's Aid Society. (n.d.). *Administrative history*. City of Toronto Archives.

Cohen-Schlanger, M., Fitzpatrick, A., Hulchanski, J. D., & Raphael, D. (1993). *Housing as a factor in child admission to temporary care*. Toronto, ON: Joint Research Report of the Faculty of Social Work, University of Toronto, and Children's Aid Society of Metropolitan Toronto.

Dixon, E. S., & Browning, G. A. (1938). *Social case records*. Chicago: University of Chicago Press.

Erikson, E. (1950). *Childhood and society*. New York: W. W. Norton and Company, Inc.

Falconer, N., & Swift, K. (1983). *Preparing for practice*. Toronto, ON: Children's Aid Society of Metropolitan Toronto.

Farina, M. (1982). *The relationship of the family to the state in Ontario: State intervention in the family on behalf of children* (Published doctoral dissertation, Ontario Institute for Studies in Education). *Dissertation Abstracts International*, A 44/03: 643, 1983.

Garbarino, J. (1981). An ecological approach to child maltreatment. In L. Pelton (Ed.), *The social context of child abuse and neglect*. New York: Human Sciences Press.

Gil, D. (1970). *Violence against children*. Cambridge, MA: Harvard University Press.

Gordon, L. (1988). *Heroes of their own lives*. New York: Viking.

Guest, D. (1980). *The emergence of social security in Canada*. Vancouver, BC: University of British Columbia Press.

Hodgins, F. E. (1920). Report on the care and control of the mentally defective and feeble-minded in Ontario. Public Archives of Ontario. File RG18 Series B49.

Houston, S. (1982). The "waifs and strays" of a late Victorian city: Juvenile delinquents in Toronto. In J. Parr (Ed.), *Childhood and family in Canadian history*. Toronto, ON: McClelland and Stewart.

Jones, A., & Rutman, L. (1981). *In the children's aid*. Toronto, ON: University of Toronto Press.

Jones, J. M., & McNeely, R. L. (1980). Mothers who neglect and those who do not: A comparative study. *Social Casework, 61*, 559–67.

Lemon, J. (1985). *Toronto since 1918: An illustrated history*. Toronto, ON: James Lorimer and Company, Publishers, and the National Museum of Man.

Lubove, R. (1965). *The professional altruist*. Cambridge, MA: Harvard University Press.

MacDonald, J. A. (1985). The child welfare programme of the Spallumcheen Indian Band in British Columbia. In B. Wharf, (Ed.), *The challenge of child welfare* (pp. 253–265). Vancouver, BC: University of British Columbia Press.

Maclaren, A. (1990). *Our own master race*. Toronto, ON: McClelland and Stewart.

McBride, M. (1983). *The development of child protection in Ontario, 1900–1954*. Unpublished paper, Faculty of Social Work, University of Toronto.

McDermott, S. (1986). Children's Aid Society of Metropolitan Toronto. Personal interview.

Metropolitan Toronto Children's Aid Society. (1920–1939). Client Records.

Milkman, R. (1976, Spring). *Review of radical political economics VIII*.

Polansky, N., Borgman, R. D., & De Saix, C. (1972). *Roots of futility*. San Francisco: Jossey-Bass, Inc.

Polansky, N., Chalmers, M. A., Buttenweiser, E., & Williams, D. P. (1981). *Damaged parents: An anatomy of child neglect*. Chicago: University of Chicago Press.

Rivers, B. (1993). Executive Director, Metropolitan Toronto Children's Aid Society. Personal interview.

Simmons, H. (1982). *From asylum to welfare*. Downsview, ON: National Institute on Mental Retardation.

Staff Minutes, *Infant Homes of Toronto*. City of Toronto Archives, 1920–1929.

Strong-Boag, V. (1982). Intruders in the nursery: Child care professionals reshape the years one to five, 1920–1940. In J. Parr (Ed.), *Childhood and family in Canadian history*. Toronto, ON: McClelland and Stewart.

Sutherland, N. (1976). *Children in English Canadian society*. Toronto, ON: University of Toronto Press.

Swift, K. (1991). Contradictions in child welfare: Neglect and responsibility. In C. Baines, P. Evans, & S. Neysmith (Eds.), *Women's caring: A feminist perspective on social welfare*. Toronto, ON: McClelland and Stewart.

Swift, K. (1995). *Manufacturing "bad mothers": A critical perspective in child neglect*. Toronto, ON: University of Toronto Press.

Swift, K. (1990). *Creating knowledge: A study of the production of knowledge about child neglect* (Unpublished doctoral dissertation, University of Toronto).

Swift, K. (1988). Knowledge about neglect: A critical review of the literature. *Working Papers in Social Welfare in Canada, #23*. Toronto, ON: University of Toronto, Faculty of Social Work.

Treudley, M. B. (1980). The "benevolent fair": A study of charitable organizations among American women in the first third of the nineteenth century. In F. R. Breul & S. J. Diner (Eds.), *Compassion and responsibility*. Chicago: University of Chicago Press.

Wharf, B. (1994). *Research on organizing and delivering child welfare services*. Paper presented at the National Research and Policy Symposium on Child Welfare, Kananaskis, Alberta.

Wolock, I., & Horowitz, B. (1984). Child maltreatment as a social problem: The neglect of neglect. *Journal of Orthopsychiatry, 54*, 595–602.

Young, L. (1964). *Wednesday's children*. New York: McGraw-Hill Book Co.

5

ROSIE THE RIVETER AND HER LATCHKEY CHILDREN: WHAT AMERICANS CAN LEARN ABOUT CHILD DAY CARE FROM THE SECOND WORLD WAR

William M. Tuttle, Jr.

During the Second World War, there was much public wailing about the plight of America's neglected "latchkey children." In truth, working parents—mothers especially—devised a variety of solutions to meet their child day care needs. It is past time to do full justice to America's mothers who helped to defend their country by working in the nation's shipyards and factories, and who did not neglect their children in the process, and to see what lessons we can learn. This article shows that the war was a time of successes in the provision of child day care and examines (1) the child day care arrangements made by families themselves during the war, (2) the Lanham Act child day care centers, (3) the child day care centers operated by private businesses, and (4) the hugely successful, but largely forgotten, Extended School Services.

William M. Tuttle, Jr., Ph.D., is Professor of History and American Studies, University of Kansas, Lawrence, KS. This article is dedicated to the memory of Lois Meek Stolz, late professor at the University, who was both a pioneer in child day care and a distinguished scholar and teacher of child psychology.

"**W**hat has happened to the nuclear family, which was once the backbone of American life?" asked the letter-writer in late 1985. "It taught love, generosity, caring and giving. It built character. Please answer, Ann. I am—Suffering from Culture Shock in Colorado."

"Dear Suffering," Ann Landers replied, assuming the mantle of the social historian: "The nuclear family began to fall apart when Rosie the Riveter went to work in the defense plant to replace the men who had gone to war. She liked the money and the independence"[Landers 1985].

Sadly, even today, many Americans agree with Ann's interpretation of recent American family history. It is time to revise this interpretation. America's working mothers had to confront many obstacles during the Second World War, not the least of which was people's hostility to the idea of mothers working outside of the home, even in defense plants. Feeding this sentiment were not only longstanding gender-role stereotypes, but also a slew of wartime magazine articles and speeches by Father Edward J. Flanagan of Boys Town, J. Edgar Hoover of the FBI, and other defenders of the father-led family in which the mother dutifully stayed at home. The hostility to working mothers was both intense and widespread [Schuyler 1943; Hoover 1943, 1945; Gilbert 1986; U.S. Senate 1943–1944; *The New York Times* 1942, 1943]. Indeed it is apparent that many of the wartime stories published about America's "latchkey children" were overwrought in their lamentations for the suffering boys and girls locked in cars, scared and lonely, or wandering the streets looking for trouble [Meyer 1944; Meyer 1943; U.S. Senate 1943]. Some children were neglected, but very few. It is past time to do full justice to America's mothers who worked in the nation's shipyards, aircraft factories, and other industries, and who did not neglect their children in the process.

Most of all, however, it is time to see what lessons can be learned from the experience of the Second World War, which was a time of notable successes in child day care, especially programs in industry and before-and-after school programs, which provided care for several hundred thousand children of working mothers. Perhaps in these successes from 50 years ago there are lessons for today.

Despite the many criticisms of mothers entering the labor force, Rosie the Riveter was clearly a reality—her muscles bulging, her hair tied in a kerchief, her hands holding a large pneumatic gun. Clearly, too, as one writer observed: "The hand that holds the pneumatic riveter cannot rock the cradle—at the same time." But many of the forlorn stories about neglected infants and toddlers were exaggerations, the ulterior purpose of which was to discredit the practice of mothers working. To be sure, not everyone accepted this viewpoint. Indeed, explained Anne L. Gould of the War Production Board, "The charge that because a mother goes to work she loses interest in her children is too absurd to comment" [Wetherill 1942; Gould 1943].

Many of the critics of working mothers failed to comprehend that millions of American women were their families' main breadwinners and had to work. Women headed between 17% and 18% of all families in the United States—almost one in five— during the war. Some mothers worked to supplement low family incomes, still others to boost the family's standard of living. Patriotism motivated many American women, just as it did many American men. "The motives for a mother's working are usually complex," wrote Hazel A. Fredericksen of the Children's Bureau. But then she asked a pertinent question, one that was not often heard during the war: "Who shall say at a time when labor is so necessary to a nation's winning the war that a mother's right to work should be questioned?" [U.S. Women's Bureau 1948; Chafe 1991; Milkman 1987; Frederickson 1943: 162].

The indictment of working mothers was especially cruel in the case of servicemen's wives, many of whom were the impoverished mothers of young children. With passage of the Servicemen's Dependents Allowance Act in 1942, the government had begun to pay monthly allowances to the families of service personnel, but the allowances were often insufficient to finance the running of a household [Employment in war work of women . . . 1942; Stevenson 1942; Cline 1943; Tarasov 1943; Bondy 1943]. In addition, mothers of young children under the age of two who had to work had no access to federal child day care until 1944 [U.S. Senate 1943; Aronson 1944; Gilbert 1944; *The New York Times* 1942 (October 16), 1943 (November 27)].

"Who's going to take care of me, Mother, if you take a war-plant job?" So asked the curly blond-haired boy of three or four pictured in the May 1943 issue of *Better Homes and Gardens*. The boy looked sad but resigned to his fate [Schultz 1943; Binford 1943; Carroll 1943]. Actually, the answer to the boy's question was a complicated one. In truth, working parents—mothers especially—devised diverse solutions to meet their particular needs.

In an effort to suggest "lessons for today from yesterday's experiences," this article examines (1) the child day care arrangements made by families during the war, (2) the Lanham Act child day care centers, (3) the child day care centers operated by private businesses, and (4) the hugely successful, but largely forgotten, Extended School Services.

Family Arrangements

First, it is important to recognize that most wartime mothers expressed satisfaction with the arrangements they had made. A 1943 survey in Milwaukee, for example, concluded that only 11% of mothers were dissatisfied with the child care they had arranged [Pifer 1983]. National surveys corroborated the Milwaukee findings. According to a Women's Bureau's investigation of ten major production areas, 30% to 45% of working mothers left the care of their children to relatives other than the husband or older children [U.S. Woman's Bureau 1946]. The author of another Women's Bureau study of 13 war plants concluded: "Care when the mother was away at work was given . . . most frequently by adult relatives living in the household." Husbands on different shifts from wives served as the second most frequent source. Only a few families paid for child day care services [U.S. Women's Bureau 1947; U.S. Senate 1943]. Perhaps most important, grandparents filled much of the void. One grandmother even suggested, "If anyone should ask for a name for this war, it's 'Grandmother's War.' I have had my house full of grandchildren for a month and so have all of my friends whose children are off for war work of one kind or another." [*The New York Times* 1942 (August 18, 24); 1943 (May 16); Strauss 1943; Gluck 1987].

Lanham Act Child Day Care Centers

In 1940 President Franklin D. Roosevelt signed into law the Lanham Act, which provided federal funds for the community needs of war-boom areas. Benefits under the Lanham Act included funds not only for child day care centers, but also for hospitals, water and sewer systems, police and firefighting facilities, and recreation centers. During the first two years of the war, intragovernmental disputes bedeviled the implementation of the Lanham Act provisions for child day care. On the one hand, the Federal Works Agency (FWA), which controlled the Lanham Act funds, urged the expansion of group child day care facilities. On the other hand, the Federal Security Agency (FSA), the Children's Bureau, and the U.S. Office of Education lobbied against group child day care outside of the home, criticizing it as a danger to parental authority, particularly the mother-child relationship, and advocated family foster care instead* [Hartmann 1982; Hartmann 1980; Michel 1987; Anderson 1981; Child Welfare League of America 1943; Dratch 1974; U.S. Senate 1943; Goldmintz 1987].

---

*The use of group or institutional care versus family foster care has been debated since the nineteenth century. Proponents of each position are still battling today, and arguments are again being made to "bring back the orphanage." This topic is covered in another article in this issue.

The dispute reached a showdown in 1943 when the FSA and its allies prevailed upon Senator Elbert Thomas (D-UT) to introduce a bill to end the FWA program. Known as the War-Area Child Care Bill of 1943, the Thomas bill would terminate Lanham Act funding of group child day care facilities in favor of individual family foster care. As with the Lanham Act, financing would be on a dollar-for-dollar matching basis; but under this proposal, the states rather than local governments would supply the matching funds [Greenblatt 1977]. And it would be the states, not the local communities, that would be responsible for initiating funding requests to the federal government, and, through their offices of education and child welfare, would be overseeing the programs. Ohio's conservative Senator Robert A. Taft, one of the bill's staunchest supporters, also conceded that it would be far easier, under the Thomas bill, to terminate federal involvement in child day care at the war's end, "if we avoid the situation of having one of the Federal Departments attempt to deal directly with the people of the various states." The program envisoned in the Thomas bill not only would be cheaper than the FWA program, but easier to dismantle. Although the bill won passage in the Senate, it died in the House, the victim of an incongruous lobby composed of the FWA and its allies, all urging a dramatic expansion in the number of FWA centers, joined by Catholic leaders who resolutely opposed federal child care of any kind [U.S. Senate 1943; Michel 1987; Dratch 1974; Anthony 1943; Whose Baby? 1943; Close 1945; The New York Times 1943 (June 9, 22, July 8, 10, November 22); 1944 (January 20)].

With the defeat of the Thomas bill, FWA's immediate future in assisting child day care seemed secure. In July 1943, Congress appropriated additional funds for FWA to implement the community facilities provisions of the Lanham Act. Child day care needs were spiraling, and experts predicted that by September more than one million children would require some sort of supervision while their parents worked. Shortages were so acute in one-third of the nation's war-production areas, the War Manpower Commission reported, "as to be a serious hindrance to the recruiting and retention of women in industry." Despite the acknowledgment of need, by the end of 1943 only 2,065 Lanham Act centers, enrolling just 58,682 children, were in operation. Although the number grew to 65,772 children in 2,243 centers by March 1944, the program's expansion was slowed due to shortages of physical facilities and trained staff. And, because of the near exhaustion of funds, applications from local communities for joint funding piled up on the federal bureaucrats' desks, unacted upon [U.S. Senate 1943–44; *The New York Times* 1943 (June 30, September 17, December 6); 1944 (May 18); Concerning Children 1944; *Congressional Record* 1944].

Gradually, however, the numbers grew. For one thing, the new women coming into the factories in 1944, especially on the West Coast, were young and had nursery or school-age children. "This gives the child-care program added momentum," explained the director of Los Angeles' child day care coordinating council, who added that "mothers are becoming interested who for a long time were skeptical. They are finding that leaving their children with the neighbors was not a satisfactory solution." Finally, the fees had dropped as public subsidies rose. In 1944 a mother could leave her child of two to five years for 50 cents a day, which also paid for lunch and morning and afternoon snacks [*The New York Times* 1944 (December 1)].

To keep the federal funding flowing, the proponents of group child care organized a potent lobbying effort. The women's auxiliaries of certain industrial unions, such as the United Electrical Workers and the United Auto Workers, joined with community leaders and FWA officials in the effort. Also influential were the six women members of the House of Representatives. In February 1944, Representative Mary T. Norton presented to the House "a joint appeal" for immediate funds to expand the wartime child day care program under the FWA. What was at stake, the statement said, was not only "the health and safety of our children," but also "the achievement of our war-production goals." "Therefore, we women members of Congress assume the responsibility of speaking for the millions of working mothers . . . and of impressing upon you the need for action." Responding to this importuning and to thousands of letters from union members, Congress increased funding for child day care [Dratch 1974; *Congressional Record* 1944; *The New York Times* 1944 (March 8, 10, 29, May 1)].

Beginning in the spring of 1944, child day care enrollments rose rapidly, one reason being FWA's decision to make funds available for the care of children under two. FWA explained that while it "frowned upon" the employment of women with children under two, "we know that, realistically, many women with young children have been forced to take war jobs." By mid-May, a total of 87,406 children were enrolled in 2,512 war nurseries and child day care centers. Enrollments, which reached their peak in July 1944, with 3,102 centers serving 129,357 children, had doubled in just five months. Although the FWA centers never served the predicted clientele of 160,000 children, they did help to meet families' wartime needs. Lanham Act child day care centers ultimately received federal funds totalling $52 million, with matching sums from states and local communities. By the war's end, a large number of children, estimated at between 550,000 and 600,000 for the Lanham Act programs, had received care at one time [U.S. Women's Bureau 1947; Greenblatt 1977; Anderson 1981; *The New York Times* 1944 (May 1, 18); Close 1945].

Finally, the federal government had made an important declaration, even if belatedly: In this national emergency, the public should provide subsidized care for the children of working women. One scholar, Bernard Greenblatt, has written that the Lanham Act programs "represented a major shift of national policy on preschool progams. The federal government had essentially declared that . . . if the national interest is served, public funds should help wage-earning mothers carry the burden of the cost of day care" [Greenblatt 1977; Kerr 1973; Auerbach 1988].

Child Day Care in Private Industry

By mid-1944, happy stories of child day care successes had begun to supplant the sad tales of latchkey children highlighted in many magazines just the year before. Both local efforts, including cooperative nursery schools begun by mothers themselves, and federally funded programs were beginning to prosper [*The New York Times* 1942 (March 14); Schooler 1944; Carson 1943; Ross 1943; Anderson 1981; Bragdon 1943; Evans 1946]. So, too, were a handful of initiatives by private industry. In the fall of 1942, for example, the Douglas Aircraft plant in Santa Monica announced plans to open a nursery within four miles of the plant, but "out of range as a target for the enemy." In efforts to recruit female workers to its airplane factory in Buffalo, the Curtiss-Wright Corporation announced that it would double the size of the plant's nursery school [*The New York Times* 1942 (August 24); Marvelous for Terry? 1943].

Probably the most innovative child day care program was the product of an industrialist's fertile mind. Edgar F. Kaiser was general manager of the two massive Kaiser shipyards in Portland, Oregon. To house workers and their families, the government erected its largest wartime civilian housing project, a town called Vanport City, Oregon. Recognizing that with 25,000 female workers, child day care would be an immediate problem, Kaiser constructed two large child-care centers. Lois Meek Stolz, formerly the head of the Institute of Child Development at Columbia University, became the centers' director [Slobodin 1975; Skold 1980.] In addition to stabilizing women's employment in the shipyards, the Kaiser centers promised to be innovative in their own right. Buildings were located "not out in the community but right at the entrance to the shipyards, convenient to mothers on their way to and from work." The centers were to be large, accommodating 1,125 young children apiece, or 375 each during the three daily working shifts. Finally, the centers were to be run not by the federal government, nor by the local schools, but by Edgar Kaiser's staff [Kaiser Child Service Centers 1978; Takanishi 1977; Stolz 1942; *Congressional Record* 1943; Hymes 1944].

The federal government actually funded these centers, but not directly. Kaiser wrote these costs—minus the nominal fees paid by the mothers—into the company's cost-plus-fixed fee contracts with the government. Furthermore, the U.S. Maritime Commission bore the construction costs. The centers' innovative wheel-spoke design included large grassy play areas, four wading pools, and 15 spacious classrooms. Large classroom windows enabled the children to see the ships on which their mothers worked. Each center also had an infirmary with a trained nurse, a social worker, and a fully staffed kitchen. In addition to the children's meals, take-home meals for the families of mothers coming off their shifts were prepared here. Called "Home Service Food," this program had been suggested by Eleanor Roosevelt. Nutritionally balanced and neatly packaged, the meals contained directions for reheating and for "supplementary salads and vegetables to make a full dinner." Available at 50 cents a portion, each meal was sufficient for an adult and a child [Wolff & Phillips 1944; Kaiser Child Service Centers 1978; Dratch 1974; Auerbach 1988].

Peak attendance at the Kaiser Child Service Centers was substantial (1,005 children in September 1944), but never reached its stated goal. Despite low enrollments, however, the Kaiser centers stand as examples of what private industry might accomplish. As one student of the Kaiser program has written, "Their existence serves to prove that quality, center-based child care services can be made available, given the necessary ingredients of priority, leadership, and professionalism" [Kaiser Company 1945; Kaiser Child Service Centers 1978; Slobodin 1944; *The New York Times* 1944 (November 12, 17)].

It is evident that with the approach of victory in 1945, child day care was gaining acceptance, and enrollment in the centers continued to climb. Another factor was the large percentage of America's working women wanting to stay on the job after the emergency, thus presaging a postwar demand for child day care. In the spring of 1945, working women, government officials, and child development experts began to agitate for a national peacetime child day care policy. Letters and petitions descended upon Congress from scores of organizations—among them, the San Francisco Board of Supervisors, the East Hollywood Club of the Communist Party, and various chapters of the Veterans of Foreign Wars, the American Legion, and the American War Mothers—in support of continuing the Lanham Act centers. Local governments, labor councils, and educational associations also sent telegrams. In all, FWA received 5,914 letters, wires, cards, and petitions in favor of the centers. Although originally scheduled to expire on October 31, 1945, Lanham Act child day care funding received a reprieve from Congress—an additional $7 million to keep the centers alive until March 1, 1946 [*The New York Times* 1945 (March 15, May 22, August 21, 28, September 20, October 18); Baruch 1945; *Congressional Record* 91; Pfister 1944; Close 1945; Owen 1946; Concerning Children 1946; Child Care Programs 1947; Dratch 1974; Greenblatt 1977].

Extended School Services

Another option for wartime child care was an unheralded but unique program called Extended School Services (ESS), which was one of the biggest success stories of the war. In August 1942, in a little-noticed move that proved fateful beyond mere dollars, President Franklin D. Roosevelt allocated $400,000 to the U.S. Office of Education (part of the Federal Security Agency) and the Children's Bureau (part of the Labor Department) "for the promotion of and coordination of [Extended School Services] programs for the care of children of working mothers" [Policy of the War Manpower Commission 1942; Extended School Services for Children of Working Mothers 1942].

Relatively few women with young children took jobs during the war (the wartime labor force participation rate for mothers of children under the age of six only increased from 9% to 12% [Campbell 1984]). The much larger group of children needing care—the real latchkey children—were those between the ages of six and 12 or 13. Charles P. Taft of the FSA estimated that 80% of the children needing care attended school. The need of America's latchkey children was thus for a place to go before and after school, a supervised environment in which to wait until their mothers ended work and picked them up [U.S. House of Representatives 1943; Employment in war work of women . . . 1942].

In the fall of 1942, the U.S. Office of Education announced its ESS program for the school-age children of working mothers, and by early 1943 the agency had granted funds to seven states to promote the program. Actual federal financial assistance was minimal. Funds were available only for organizational and administrative purposes; nothing was to be spent for child care personnel or operational costs, or for the maintenance of children enrolled in the centers and nursery schools. But the $400,000 grant funded 222 positions nationwide and stimulated the creation of 450 more. New Jersey, for example, used its initial funds to hire two staff members for the Department of Public Instruction, one serving as a field worker, the other as the state coordinator for extended school services. Other states followed this pattern. Funding was the key issue, and in New Jersey as elsewhere, it originated at the local level, with the public schools assuming major responsibility for school-age children [Education for Victory 1942 (October 15, November 16), 1943 (January 15); U.S. Senate 1944; Kandel 1974].

ESS programs were usually initiated by individual communities. After the local school system, welfare department, or office of civil defense first perceived a critical need, the community attempted to meet it. The federal government's function was limited to start-up funding and advice giving. By February 1943, the Office of Education had granted funds to one territorial (Hawaii) and 17 state departments of education to hire field workers to help local communities organize extended school services, and for administrators to coordinate statewide committees. Throughout the spring, the number of state programs grew. The Office of Education distributed leaflets in its "School Children and the War" series. Leaflets 1 and 2—*School Services for Children of Working Mothers* and *All-Day School Programs for Children of Working Mothers*—answered such questions as, "What is the all-day school program?" "How can a community interested in such a program get one started?" "What general principles underlie the program before and after regular school hours?" "What equipment is necessary for the expanded program?" "What are the possible sources of financial support?" [Extended school services . . . 1943l; Education for Victory 1943 (February 15, April 15, June 1, 15, July 15)].

By mid-1943, local communities in 33 states had benefited from federal guidance in establishing ESS programs. The Office of Education proudly announced that ESS "at present, takes care of some 320,000 children," including 60,000 preschoolers and 260,000 of school age; this figure is far higher than historians have appreciated. Summer vacation, of course, posed especially vexing problems: "Schools are closing," explained Bess Goodykoontz, assistant commissioner of the office of education. "Children for whom after-school care was needed now need all-day and all-week care. The same school facilities can be used" [Pidgeon 1953; 17; *The New York Times* 1943 (June 30); U.S. Senate 1943].

To notify parents of the availability of extended school services, announcements were included in pay envelopes or sent home from school with the children. There were also informational visits by civil defense block leaders, signs on streetcars and busses, "announcement flashes" in movie theaters, and posters in employment offices, union halls, and in classrooms offering vocational training classes for women. Local radio stations and newspapers also publicized these services [Education for Victory 1943 (August 16, December 15)].

The publicity paid off, and cities and towns across the country boasted of their ESS programs. Enrollment rose rapidly in
communities that provided transportation to program sites. For
example, to the ESS programs located at Detroit's Hutchins Inter-
mediate School, children from the neighboring schools were
"convoyed" daily by "student assistants" from Wayne University and the Merrill-Palmer School. With guidance from their
professors, the college students had charge of games, dancing
and singing, dramatics, handicrafts and hobbies, gardening, mar-
keting for food, setting up for meals, and cleaning up afterwards.
In Youngstown, Ohio, the public library supplied books and
instructed teachers' aides in storytelling, rhymes, and finger
painting. The aides themselves—senior high school girls taking
courses in home nursing and child care—were also benefiting. As
the mothers of tomorrow, explained the director, "they will be
able to work more wisely with their own children" [Education
for Victory 1944 (April 3, May 20), 1945 (March 3)].

In the ESS programs in Vallejo, California, enrollment
reached 1,000: 350 children were preschoolers cared for in nurseries located in the public schools, and 650 were school-age children. As in Youngstown, the child-care services were integrated
with the regular school program. Centers were placed in public
school buildings, and high school home economics students were
utilized as child-care aides. The first children arrived at 6:00 A.M.
If the mothers' working hours required it, the children were
given supper and departed for home as late as 6:30 P.M. [Educa-
tion for Victory 1945 (February 3); U.S. Senate 1943; Baruch 1944].

On June 30, 1943, federal funding for ESS expired. Some
programs were discontinued, but the programs in many communities were by that time self-sustaining. Cleveland's program,
which provided in-school care after school, all day on Saturday,
and during vacations, received funds from a variety of sources.
Financing originally came from parents' fees and contributions
from civic foundations, but eventually, with the aid of Lanham

Act money from FWA, the Cleveland Board of Education assumed the primary responsibility [Groves & Groves 1947].

Likewise, in Kansas City, Missouri, enrollment in ESS programs was booming in 1943. Funding came from the school board as well as parents' fees and contributions from the Community Chest. Kansas City's schools, which opened at 7:00 A.M. and closed at 6:00 P.M., provided children arriving early in the morning with "warm cereal with a generous serving of milk." Mothers as well as children ate meals in the schools. In 1945, Will S. Denham, the area director of the War Manpower Commission, expressed the opinion of employers and worker mothers alike when he applauded the school system for rendering "a magnificent service in caring for thousands of these children of workers taking war jobs" [Board of Education 1943a, 1943b, 1943c, 1944, 1945a, 1945b; Hunt 1943; Denham 1945].

Not just in Kansas City, but in communities throughout the nation, Extended School Services provided working parents with an invaluable option for day care. Many seized the opportunity, even after the expiration of federal funding for the program. It is impossible to tabulate the total numbers of children served by ESS, since we do not know to what extent state and local governments assumed fiscal responsibility for the programs or initiated their own programs. It is clear, though, that the number was in the hundreds of thousands: ESS constituted a homefront victory [Pidgeon 1953].

Lessons for Today

Today, the United States faces overwhelming child day care problems. Shortages of affordable, quality facilities and of caregivers are severe. This was true in some areas at some points during the Second World War, but today's crisis is more dire and widespread than the wartime emergency. Currently, 60% of all mothers with children under the age of six work outside of the home. As for mothers with infants under the age of one, 53% were in the labor force in 1991, up from 39% in 1980 and more than double the rate in 1970 [Children's Defense Fund 1992].

In some towns, working parents are responding to today's exigencies by establishing programs that closely resemble the extended school services of 50 years ago. Parents in Ithaca, New York, have obtained the cooperation of the principal of their local grade school. Opening its doors at 7:00 A.M., the school serves breakfast to the early arrivals. The official school day runs from 9:00 A.M. to 3:00 P.M., but the building is open until 5:30 P.M. The after-school program, which is operated by two certified teachers and two aides, consists of educational activities, including those in which fifth- and sixth-graders tutor first-graders, and lots of fun: games in the gymnasium or on the playground, ice skating at a local rink, and field trips to museums. Increasingly around the country, similar programs are being initiated by working parents, particularly those in white-collar jobs.

Before-and-after school care can help to ameliorate the child-care needs of the nation. It is at the heart of a proposal made by Edward F. Zigler of Yale University and former Chief of the Children's Bureau. "We can solve the child-care crisis," Zigler has promised, "by implementing a second system within already exisiting elementary school buildings, where formal education takes place, and create the school of the 21st century" [Hamburg 1987; Zigler & Lang 1991].

It is clear that the Second World War experience produced a new appreciation of the demands of child day care. Children's expert Catherine Mackenzie wrote in *The New York Times* that "if day care of children in wartime has done nothing else, it has brought better understanding of the exacting nature of round-the-clock supervision of small fry, and its fraying effect on adult nervous systems" [*The New York Times* 1944 (October 15)]. The tragedy of the Second World War experience is how little carry-over value it has had in the decades since 1945, even in the face of the country's mounting need for child day care.

In the past half-dozen years, the federal government has made progress in providing child day care, not only boosting aid for Head Start, but also establishing Child Care and Development Block Grants and "At-Risk" Child Care Programs for low-income families. In recent years too, federal block grants have provided start-up and operational funds for child day care programs, and the dependent care tax credit has helped working parents to make ends meet [Children's Defense Fund 1992].

Still, the United States was probably closer to having a national child day care policy in 1945 than it is today. Today, though the child-care crisis is more urgent than ever, there is no thoroughgoing national commitment to eradicating it. In the mid-1990s, many American families are suffering from overwhelming problems of poverty, not to mention lack of either health insurance or child care.

Families are falling apart, but the culprit is not Rosie the Riveter, who has much to teach us. Indeed, if I were to respond to Ann Landers' letter to "Suffering from Culture Shock in Colorado," I would have to write: "Dear Ann—Sorry, you blew it." ♦

References

Allowances for Servicemen's Dependents. (1942, August). *Monthly Labor Review, 55,* 226–28, 1–8; 9–21.

Anderson, K. (1981). *Wartime women: Sex roles, family relations, and the status of women during World War II.* Westport: Greenwood Press.

Anthony, S. B. II. (1943). *Out of the kitchen—into the war: Women's winning role in the nation's drama.* New York: Stephen Daye.

Aronson, P. (1944). The adequacy of the family allowance system as it affects the wives and children of men drafted into the armed forces (M.S.W. thesis, Wayne University).

Auerbach, J. D. (1988). *In the business of child care: Employer initiatives and working women.* New York: Prager.

Baruch, D. W. (1944). Extending extended school services to parents. *Journal of Consulting Psychology, 8,* 241–52.

Baruch, D. W. (1945). When the need for war-time services for children is past—what of the future? *Journal of Consulting Psychology, 9,* 45–57.

Binford, J. (1943, February). The war must be won, but—don't forget the children. *The Rotarian,* 38–40, 62.

Board of Education of the School District of Kansas City, Missouri. (1943a). Board minutes for July 13, August 19, and September 16. Kansas City, MO: Board of Education Files.

Board of Education of the School District of Kansas City, Missouri. (1943b). Resolution of July 23. Kansas City, MO: Board of Education Files.

Board of Education of the School District of Kansas City, Missouri. (1943c). Children's War Service Program—Report to the advisory committee (August 2). Kansas City, MO: Board of Education Files.

Board of Education of the School District of Kansas City, Missouri. (1944). Superintendent's reports for January 20 and March 16. Kansas City, MO: Board of Education Files.

Board of Education of the School District of Kansas City, Missouri. (1945a). Board minutes for February 15. Kansas City, MO: Board of Education Files.

Board of Education of the School District of Kansas City, Missouri. (1945b). Superintendent's reports for March 15, April 19, June 21, August 2, and September 20. Kansas City, MO: Board of Education Files.

Bondy, R. E. (1943). Special welfare services to families of men in service. *Proceedings of the National Conference of Social Work, 70,* 76–79.

Bragdon, E. (1943). A day care project. In *The impact of war on children's services.* New York: Child Welfare League of America, 10–12.

Campbell, D. A. (1984). *Women at war with America: Private lives in a patriotic era.* Cambridge, MA: Harvard University Press.

Carroll, J. L. (1943, October). Raising a baby on shifts. *Parents' Magazine,* 18, 20, 77–78, 80.

Carson, R. (1943, January 30). Minding the children. *Collier's,* 46, 48.

Chafe, W. H. (1991). *The paradox of change: American women in the twentieth century.* New York: Oxford University Press.

Child Care Programs. (1947, February). *School Life, 29,* 26.

Child Welfare League of America. (1943). *The impact of the war on children's services.* New York: Author.

Children's Defense Fund. (1992). *The state of America's children, 1992.* Washington, DC: Author.

Cline, D. C. (1943, May). Allowances to dependents of servicemen in the United States. *Annals of the American Academy of Political and Social Science, 227.*

Close, K. (1945, May). After Lanham funds—what? *Survey Midmonthly, 81,* 131–35.

Close, K. (1943, July). Day care up to now. *Survey Midmonthly, 79,* 194–97.

Concerning Children. (1944, February) *Survey Midmonthly, 80,* 58.

Concerning Children. (1946, November). *Survey Midmonthly, 82,* 300–1.

Congressional Record, *89.* (1943) A4729–30.

Congressional Record, 90. (1944, February 25, March 9). A983; A983, 2449–57.

Congressional Record, 91. (1945). 8657, 9337, A700, A943, A3868–69, A3928–29, A3998–4002, A4010, A4015, A4025–26, A4076–77, A4155–57, A4194–95, A4290–91.

Denham, W. S. (1945, February 23) Letter to Herold C. Hunt. Board of Education files.

Dratch, H. (1974, Summer). The politics of child care in the 1940s. *Science and Society, 38,* 177–80.

Education for Victory. (1942; October 15, November 16). 1–2; 13–14, 22.

Education for Victory. (1943, January 15, February 15, April 15, June 1, 15, July 15, August 16, December 15). 1, 14; 28–29, 30; 27, 32; 27–28; 15; 23–24; 22; 3–4.

Education for Victory. (1944, April 3, May 20). 14; 5–6.

Education for Victory. (1945, February 3, March 3). 9; 12–13.

Employment in war work of women with young children. (1942, December). *Monthly Labor Review, 55*, 1184–85.

Evans, M. E. (1946, May). Nursery school lessons learned in wartime. *Journal of Home Economics, 38*, 257–60.

Extended School Services for Children of Working Mothers. (1942, November 16). *Education for Victory, 1*, 13, 14, 22.

Extended School Services for Young Children. (1943, April). *Elementary School Journal, 43* 439–41.

Fredericksen, H. A. (1943, June). The program for day care of children of employed mothers. *Social Service Review, 17*, 162.

Gilbert, H. N. (1944, January). Green checks for the folks back home. *American Magazine, 137*, 94.

Gilbert, J. (1986). *A cycle of outrage: America's reaction to the juvenile delinquent in the 1950s.* New York: Oxford University Press.

Gluck, S. B. (1987). *Rosie the riveter revisited: Women, the war, and social change.* Boston: Twayne.

Goldmintz, L. R. (1987). The growth of day care: 1890–1946 (Doctoral dissertation, Yeshiva University).

Gould, A. L. (1943, October 30). The child care program and its relation to war production. United Auto Workers Papers, War Policy Division, Women's Bureau. (Reuther Library, Wayne State University, Box # 1).

Greenblatt, B. (1977). *Responsibility for child care.* San Francisco: Jossey-Bass.

Groves, E. R., and Groves, G. H. (1947). *The contemporary American family.* Chicago: Lippincott.

Hamburg, D. A. (1987). *Fundamental building blocks of early life.* New York: Carnegie Corporation of New York.

Hartmann, S. (1980). Women's organizations during World War II: The interaction of class, race, and feminism. In M. Kelley (Ed.), *Woman's being, woman's place: Female identity and vocation in American history* (p. 321). Boston: G. K. Hall.

Hartmann, S. (1982). *American women in the 1940s: The home front and beyond.* Boston: Twayne.

Hoover, J. E. (1943, July). Wild children. *American Magazine, 136–40,* 105.

Hoover, J. E. (1945, April). There will be a postwar crime wave unless——. *The Rotarian, 66,* 12–14.

Hunt, H. C. (1943, July 15). Letter to the Board of Education of the School District of Kansas City, Missouri. Kansas City, MO: Board of Education files.

Hymes, J. L. Jr. (1944, July–August). Child care problems of the night shift worker. *Journal of Consulting Psychology, 8,* 225–28.

Kaiser Child Service Centers. (1978). An interview with Lois Meek Stolz. In J. L. Hymes, Jr. (Ed.), *Early childhood education: Living history interviews, Book 2* (pp. 27–32). Carmel, CA: Hacienda Press.

Kaiser Company, Inc. Portland Yard and the Oregon Shipbuilding Corporation. (1945). Child Service Center, 1943–1945: Final report. Portland, OR: Mimeo.

Kandel, I. L. (1974). *The impact of the war upon American education.* Westport: Greenwood (reprint edition).

Kerr, V. (1973). One step forward—two steps back: Child care's long American history. In P. Roby (Ed.), *Child care—Who cares? Foreign and domestic infant and early childhood development policies.* (pp. 162–65). New York: Basic Books.

Landers, A. (1985, December 2). Where are family support systems?" *Lawrence Daily Journal-World.*

Marvelous for Terry? (1943, March 22). *Time,* 40.

Meyer, A. (1943, August). War orphans, U.S.A. *Reader's Digest, 43,* 98–102.

Meyer, A. (1944). *Journey through chaos.* New York: Harcourt, Brace and Company.

Michel, S. (1987). American women and the discourse of the democratic family in World War II. In M. R. Higonnet et al., (Eds.), *Behind the lines: Gender and the two world wars* (pp. 165–64). New Haven, CT: Yale University Press.

Milkman, R. (1987). *Gender at work: The dynamics of job segregation by sex during World War II.* Urbana, IL: University of Illinois Press.

Owen, M. B. (1946, March). Save our child care centers. *Parents' Magazine, 21,* 20.

Pfister, E. S. (1944, July–August). The case for child care centers. *Journal of Consulting Psychology, 8,* 199–205.

Pidgeon, M. E. (1953). Employed mothers and child care. *U.S. Women's Bureau Bulletin,* 246. Washington, DC: U.S. Government Printing Office, 17.

Pifer, R. L. (1983). A social history of the home front: Milwaukee labor during World War II. (Doctoral dissertation, University of Wisconsin).

Policy of the War Manpower Commission on Employment in Industry of Women with Young Children. (1942, October). *The Child, 7,* 49–50.

Ross, A. (1943, May). What seven mothers did. *Parents' Magazine, 18,* 32, 97.

Schooler, R. (1944). Child care program in a city of steel mills. *Journal of Home Economics, 36,* 331.

Schuyler, J. B. (1943, April). Women at work. *Catholic World, 157,* 26–30.

Shultz, G. D. (1943, May). Who's going to take care of me, mother[,] if you take a war-plant job? *Better Homes & Gardens, 21,* 9.

Skold, K. B. (1980). The job he left behind: American women in the shipyards during World War II. In C. R. Berkin, & C. M. Lovett (Eds.), *Women, war, and revolution.* (pp. 55–72). New York: Holmes & Meier.

Slobodin, C. (1944, November 12, 17). When the U.S. paid for day care. *The New York Times,* 23.

Slobodin, C. (1975, September–October). When the U.S. paid for day care. *Day Care and Early Education, 23.*

Stevenson, M. (1942, December). New governmental services for people in wartime. *Social Service Review, 16,* 595–602.

Stolz, L. M. (1942, May). War invades the children's world. *National Parent-Teacher, 36,* 4–6.

Strauss, C. A. (1943). Grandma made Johnny delinquent. *American Journal of Orthopsychiatry, 13,* 343–46.

Takanishi, R. (1977). *An American child development pioneer, Lois Meek Stolz.* Oral history. On deposit in University Archives, Stanford University Libraries, 185–225, 241–58.

Tarasov, H. (1943, May). Family allowances: An Anglo-American contrast. *Annals of the American Academy of Political and Social Science, 227.*

The New York Times. (1942, March 14, June 25, August 18, August 24, October 16).

The New York Times. (1943, March 18, May 16, June 9, 14, 22, 30, July 2, 8, 10, September 17, November 27, December 6).

The New York Times. (1944, January 20, March 8, 10, 29; May 1, 18, October 15, December 1).

The New York Times. (1945, March 15, May 22, August 21, 28, September 20, October 18).

U.S. House of Representatives. 78th Cong., 1st Sess., Committee on Appropriations. (1943). *Hearings on the first deficiency appropriation bill for 1943* Washington, DC: U.S. Government Printing Office.

U.S. House of Representatives, 78th Cong., 2nd Sess., Subcommittee of the Committee on Appropriations. (1944). *Department of Labor-Federal Security Agency appropriation bill for 1945.* Washington, DC: U.S. Government Printing Office, 301–2.

U.S. Senate, 78th Cong., 1st Sess., Committee on Education and Labor (Thomas Committee). (1943). *Wartime care and protection of children of employed mothers.* Washington, DC: U.S. Government Printing Office, 71.

U.S. Senate, 78th Cong., 1st Sess., Subcommittee of the Committee on Education and Labor (Pepper Committee). (1943–44). *Wartime Health and Education.* Washington, DC: U.S. Government Printing Office. 68, 100–20, 262–63.

U.S. Women's Bureau. (1947). Women's wartime hours of work: The effect on their factory performance and home life. *Bulletin No. 208.* Washington, DC: U.S. Government Printing Office.

U.S. Woman's Bureau. (1946). Women workers in ten war production areas and their postwar employment plans. *Bulletin No. 209.* Washington, DC: U.S. Government Printing Office.

U.S. Women's Bureau. (1948). Handbook of Facts on Women Workers. *Bulletin No. 225.* Washington, DC: U.S. Government Printing Office.

Vanport City extends its school service. *Recreation, 37,* 510–12.

Wetherill, G. G. (1943, September). Health problems in child care. *Hygeia, 21,* 634.

Whose Baby? (1943, March 20). *Business Week,* 32, 34, 37.

Wolff & Phillips (architects). (1944, March). Designed for 24–hour child care. *Architectural Record, 95,* 84–88.

Zigler, E., and Lang, M. E. (1991). *Child care choices: Balancing the needs of children, families, and society.* New York: Free Press.

6

BRING BACK THE ORPHANAGES? WHAT POLICYMAKERS OF TODAY CAN LEARN FROM THE PAST

Eve P. Smith

Contemporary proposals to revive the use of
orphanages raise two questions: Is a return to
orphanage care for children without special needs
feasible? If so, would such institutions benefit
children? Examination of the historical record of
orphanages of the nineteenth and early decades of the
twentieth century reveals characteristics that would
make the creation of a new system of orphanages
expensive and highly unfeasible. Proponents of new
orphanages would also have the burden of disproving
past criticism by professionals, based on the perceived
harm done to children by institutional care.

*Eve P. Smith, D.S.W., is Assistant Professor, University of Windsor School of Social
Work, Windsor, Ontario, Canada.*

In many jurisdictions in the United States, proposals to "bring back the orphanages" are gathering momentum. Charles Murray of the American Enterprise Institute, a proponent of institutional care, espouses an end to AFDC payments to single mothers, with resultant savings to be spent on orphanages [1993]. Milwaukee Mayor John Norquist advocates the removal of children (and the termination of parental rights) of welfare recipients who refuse to accept jobs, and the placement of the children in institutions [Walsh 1994]. Both men have called for public action. Similar suggestions have also come from human service professionals who are looking for better ways to care for children of drug-addicted or HIV-positive parents. Joyce Ladner, a professor at Howard University, has concluded that finding families for "so-called high risk youngsters" is so difficult that "small-scale, caring institutions" should be created that can "offer children . . . a place they can count on to nurture them" [1989]. Even Sally Provence [1989], whose 1962 research documented the inferior development of institutionally reared infants, now suggests the use of institutions for some young children. The move toward the re-creation of orphanages for children without special needs has gone beyond mere discussion to serious consideration. The Illinois legislature, for example, has established a task force to study the need for a system of "child residential facilities" in Illinois.

What leads proponents to conclude that children's institutions are desirable or necessary? Some cite the growing rate of births to adolescent mothers, especially to teens 15 to 17 years old, and tell us that ending AFDC support to unwed mothers and placing the children in orphanages will reverse the current trend. Others believe that the current policy priority of maintenance of children in, or early return of children to, their own families or relatives is contrary to the children's best interests, and that they will be better off if they are reared in institutions. Still others point out that while the number of children living in out-of-home care is increasing (from 323,765 children in 1987 to 424,379, or

31.1% more in 1991), the number of licensed foster family homes has declined from approximately 147,000 in 1984 to 100,000 in 1990 [Merkel-Holguín 1993].

While the above issues deserve discussion, this article will focus solely on the efficacy of the solution. The policy changes now being discussed are antithetical to current child welfare policies and should be considered only after a careful review and analysis of all available data. Before making major changes, policymakers should be able to predict how long-term institutions for children might function in the current environment, and what children's experiences might be as residents of new orphanages.

This article reviews the historical picture, describing the orphanages of the past, their uses, population, funding, staffing, and contemporary views of the care they provided. Using this information, this article will attempt to answer two questions: Is a return to orphanage care feasible? If so, would the re-creation of orphanages benefit the children who would be placed in them?

The Emergence of Orphanages

The orphanage in North America appeared in the context of the development of specialized institutions for free persons who were perceived as needing special structure and training because they were dangerous to the welfare of society. Before 1850, outdoor relief was provided for destitute families in some localities, but other cities and towns built almshouses where paupers, including children with or without parents, could live and work.

Before 1800 there were only five orphanages in the United States, and by 1851, only 77 [Folks 1902]. The number quickly multiplied: Trotzkey [1930] noted that the 13 years from 1890 to 1903 saw an expansion of institutions, with 400 being established (see table 1). Consistent with a growth in the general population, the number of institutionalized children increased through the 1920s, though the growing use of free or boarding homes in the 1920s and 1930s resulted in a slight decrease by 1933.

TABLE 1

Growth in number of orphanages and children in orphanages in the United States, 1800–1933[1]

Year	Number of Orphanages	Number of Children in Orphanages
1800	5	—
1851	77	—
1880	613	50,579
1890	—	74,000
1900	—	85,000–90,000
1910	1,151	110,000[2]
1923	1,558[3]	142,971
1933	1,613	140,352

[1]Statistics taken from U.S. Bureau of the Census, (1910, 1927, 1935); Hart, H. (1892). The economic aspects of the child problem from *Proceedings of the National Conference of Charities and Correction* as quoted in Bremner, R. H., *Children and Youth in America, Vol 2*, p. 283 (Cambridge, MA: Harvard University Press).
[2]Includes a small number of children adjudicated delinquent.
[3]Includes 1,341 institutions for children only and 217 institutions accepting both children and dependent adults.

The number of residents per so-called *orphan asylum* varied. Although very large institutions existed, such as the New York Catholic Protectory, which in 1891 housed 2,000 children at one time, many institutions housed relatively few. In 1880, the median size institution held 42 children, and of the 960 agencies reporting to the U.S. Census Bureau in 1923, about one-fourth (27.5%) held fewer than 30 children. Almost two-thirds of the so-called *homes* (64.7%) housed fewer than 80. Despite the small number of large orphanages, however, many children lived in large institutions: in 1923 approximately 18% (25,350) of all orphan children lived in institutions holding from 250 to over 1,500 children [U.S. Bureau of the Census 1927].

Although there were a few state and county government institutions, particularly in the Midwest, the majority of North American orphanages were begun by religious groups, independent philanthropists, or "well-placed citizens with an eye to the protection of society as well as the welfare of their inmates" [Sutherland 1976]. In New York, in reaction to Charles Loring Brace's program of sending children west to live and work with Protestant farm families, Jews started their own sectarian institutions, and Roman Catholics increased the number of theirs as well. In creating institutions, religious groups could ensure that children of their coreligionists would be brought up in their parents' tradition. In addition, Henry Dwight Chapin [1929] noted the popularity of the building and endowment of a great many institutions by some rich philanthropists to perpetuate their names. In addition to this measure of personal immortality, philanthropists could enjoy the visible evidence of their largess, which they could not do if children lived with their own or other families.

Life in the Orphanages

The institutions varied in number of residents, physical conditions, and atmosphere. It is generally agreed, however, that life in pre-1920 orphanages, and in many post-1920 orphanages, was likely to be regimented and sparse. Trotzkey, a proponent of what he termed "modern" institutional care, described conditions prevailing in most child-caring institutions until 1915 and continuing until the time he wrote in 1930. He used the term, "institutionalism," which meant "closed walls, children segregated from the community . . . commanded by the sound of the cowbell not by word of mouth, every minute of the day from rising to retiring regulated with mathematical precision, the child seldom seen apart from a line but moved in serried ranks, always marching." Corporal punishment was not uncommon, nor was "lack of understanding of the need of educational opportunities, lack of sympathy for the higher and finer interests of life . . . under which conditions alone is possible the relentless application of the iron heel and mailed fist which is all the more hideous when applied to defenseless childhood" [Trotzkey 1930: 64–65].

Statements and letters from former orphanage dwellers document the variety of institutional atmospheres: some depicted an
environment that approximated Trotzkey's description; a few
described a positive and loving atmosphere. Three examples
illustrate the differences. First, the following statement, from a
"national figure who wished to remain anonymous," described
an impoverished environment:

> Life for a typical boy in an institution . . . meant essen-
> tially shelter, the actual necessities in the way of clothes,
> and food which primarily served the purpose of prevent-
> ing starvation, rather than scientific or, may I say, com-
> mon sense nourishment. The attitude of those responsible
> for the institution was that the boys and girls were un-
> fortunate objects of charity. [Thurston 1930: 70–71]

Second, a statement by E. J. Henry, "an orphan asylum boy
who became a superintendent," depicts not only impoverish-
ment but also regimentation. Henry, whose widowed mother
placed him in the orphanage and paid $1 per week for his care,
described his experience. He noted that before he entered, he had
had "the threat held over my head that if I were not a good boy,
I would be put in an institution." He described the day room to
which he was brought upon entrance:

> I found about twenty-five boys, averaging from six to
> fourteen years. . . . There were no furnishings in the room,
> except for a small table and chair, in which the governess,
> as we called her, sat. The floors were of rather rough
> boards, but very clean. It was the boys' job to do the
> scrubbing.
>   When night came, we all had to be in our places in the
> playroom. We took off our shoes and stockings and
> placed them in front of the bench where we sat, before
> which we knelt for our devotional exercises. Then we

formed in line and marched upstairs to the dormitories. There were ten iron beds . . . two boys slept in each bed . . . This dormitory was a very plain room—no pictures on the walls, and no furniture except the beds.

In the morning when the rising bell rang, we all jumped up, dressed and marched downstairs where we washed and combed our hair. The dining room and kitchen were in the basement. We marched down single file, to long, roughly made tables . . . there was mush and milk for breakfast. At noon we would have soup and bread and water, or once in a while, chopped meat made into a gravy to put on our bread. At night we would have bread and milk—and only one helping. We growing boys were never satisfied when the bell tapped to get up from the table—there was no danger of stomach trouble from overeating. Very strict discipline was maintained . . . The girls' playroom was across the hall from the boys' and the playgrounds were separated by a high board fence. There would be weeks at a time when brothers and sisters in the same building would have no chance to talk with each other. [Thurston 1930: 77–79]

Third, the following letter from a former inmate of the Home for the Children of Seamen in New York implies a kinder, loving, and more benevolent atmosphere. In 1927, Mrs. McCabe of New York City wrote: "My name was Lizzie Walker brought up in that dear home for Seamen's children on Staten Island some 50 years ago. The only real home I have known and every one was so good and kind . . . That dear home is always in my memory."

By the 1920s, some institutions had modernized their programs. Uniform dress was discarded, food was improved, and children of many but not all homes were sent to public schools [Hacsi 1993]. Attempts were made to normalize the children's lives. Some philanthropists and wealthy institutions provided summer camp, books, magazine subscriptions, trips, and birthday presents. Now the best of homes were seen by some parents, professionals, and philanthropists as private schools for the poor, where children could receive more "advantages" than their parents could supply [Reeder 1929]. A number of model programs were developed during the second and third decades of the twentieth century. Institutions such as Edenwald, in Westchester County, New York, and Carson College for Orphan Girls at Flourtown, Pennsylvania, were lauded by professionals of the day and seen as serving specific populations well [Deardorff 1924].

Despite these improvements, some of the negative aspects of institutional life continued. Physical punishment, sometimes severe and abusive, was commonly used in institutions to control children's behavior, and extreme incidents were sometimes reported in the media. One late nineteenth century example described abuse that led to the death of an eight-year-old boy, Harry, who died following a severe beating by L.T. Prime, "caretaker of the boys' wing of the asylum." When the mother, a widow with nine children, five of them placed in the institution, visited the orphanage after being informed of her son's death, "some of his companions said that he had been taken from his bed and carried to the bathroom, where Mr. Prime had whipped him with a heavy cane . . . [Mr. Prime] admitted . . . that in severe cases he had stripped boys and beaten them in the bathroom . . . He has 140 children to look after." It is important to note, however, that the rules of the asylum forbade severe punishment [Affairs in Brooklyn. . . 1894].

Despite the asylum's policy, however, the use of corporal punishment was difficult to control and continued. The issue was frequently discussed in board meetings, and two staff members who used this method of discipline were dismissed in 1923 and 1924 [Smith 1993].

It is likely that sexual abuse was prevalent in group facilities, and was also difficult to control because so much of institutional life was hidden from the general public. Children may also have been afraid of the consequences of reporting their powerful care-givers. Many occurrences, therefore, went unreported. A 1989 Royal Commission inquiry in Newfoundland, Canada, for example, documents widespread physical and sexual abuse involving pedophile Christian brothers in a Roman Catholic orphanage over a lengthy period of time. Although incidents of abuse had been reported to the police, over time, the abuse was glossed over and hidden from public knowledge by authorities who were unwilling to confront a powerful Roman Catholic hierarchy, and the perpetrators went unpunished for many years [Harris 1990]. Allegations and/or descriptions of sexual abuse may also be found in the literature and in case records. Bogen [1992], for example, noted the persistence of such activity through several generations of the Hebrew Orphan Asylum of New York. The case records of another institution reveal such statements as: "[Child] has told his mother of various sexual happenings at the Home . . . particularly about the relations of a man, the boys' caretaker, with one of the young girls" [Agency "Y" (Case Record D.M.) 1928].

The Orphanage Residents

Before the availability of AFDC or other financial support, residents of orphanages were likely to be children of the "worthy poor," young and generally well-behaved. Institutions could be selective about the children they accepted, generally preferring to serve those whose parents they considered "deserving"—that is, in need through no fault of their own. Institutions frequently discriminated against children whose parents were considered immoral. Children from "genteel" families, children born in wedlock rather than out of wedlock, and children whose poverty was a result of the death of one parent were preferred. Table 2 reveals the statistical disparity between all children in care and those placed in institutions. Of all the dependent children in out-of-home care in 1933, 57.8% were in institutions. Of all of the

TABLE 2
All Dependent Children and Dependent Children with One Viable Parent[1] in
Out-of-Home Care, by Type of Care, 1933[2] (Percentages)

Type of Care	All Children	All Children with One Viable Parent	Children Born in Wedlock (Parent Not Viable)			Children Born Out of Wedlock (Parent Viable)
			Dead	In Inst.	Whereabouts Unknown	
	(N=242,929)	(N=115,476)	(N=63,517)	(N=11,760)	(N=23,204)	(N=16,995)
Institution	57.8	62.9	72.8[3]	58.9	62.9	29.0[4]
Boarding Home	27.3	26.1	19.2[4]	33.5	27.6	44.6[3]
Free Home	13.0	9.5	6.1[4]	6.3[4]	8.2	25.8[3]
Work Home	1.9	1.5	1.9	1.3	1.3	0.6
Total Percent	100.1	100.0	100.0	100.0	100.0	100.0

[1]For the purpose of this paper, *viable parent* is one who, given proper support, might be able to care for the child. Parents listed in the 1933 Census as being "at home" or "elsewhere" are counted as "viable"; parents "in institution," or "whereabouts unknown," are considered "not viable."

[2]Data taken from: U.S. Department of Commerce, Bureau of the Census. Table 24: "Children under each type of care, according to whereabouts of father and mother (39–40)." In *Children under institutional care and in foster homes, 1933*. (Washington, DC: U.S. Government Printing Office, 1935).

[3]Greater likelihood of receiving this type of care than all children, or children with one viable parent.

[4]Less likelihood of receiving this type of care than all children or all children with one viable parent.

children of widows or widowers, however, 72.8% were in institutions. Children born out of wedlock were more likely to be placed in boarding or free homes: only 29.0% were in institutions.

Agencies' own literature often described the type of child that would be admitted. The Leake and Watts institution, for example, stated that it accepted only "well-behaved . . . orphans of respectable parentage . . . physically and mentally sound. Disorderly and ungovernable children are not admitted" [U.S. Bureau of Education 1875: 118–120].

The term *orphanage* was a misnomer. A minority (approximately 10%) of all orphanage residents in 1933 were true orphans; the majority were children with one or two living parents. Even as early as the 1830s, available institutional beds were filled by children of single parents who had to work. The Orphan Asylum Society of the City of Brooklyn, for example, was founded in 1832 by a group of well-meaning citizens who mistakenly believed that a recent cholera epidemic would result in an abundance of friendless orphans. During the first year, however, only eight such orphans appeared. The remaining 18 children admitted were half-orphans, children of destitute widows, who [were] enabled by their daily labor, to pay the small sum of 50 cents a week for their support" [Orphan Asylum Society in the City of Brooklyn 1835: 4]. Most cholera epidemic orphans were taken in by relatives or friends, but many children were admitted who, by death, desertion, or institutionalization had lost only one parent, and whose remaining parent, while not able to perform the roles of breadwinner and homemaker at the same time, was able to work and pay a small sum for child care. Living in institutions also were children of two-parent families in which the caregiver was ill.

Other institutions followed similar patterns, some devoting themselves exclusively to the care of children with single parents. In 1875, for example, the Rev. Thomas W. Peters, D.D., a founder of the Sheltering Arms institution in New York, said his agency's services were needed because there were "many families abandoned by fathers . . . such mothers had little recourse but to "break up the household and go out herself to service" [U.S. Bureau of Education 1875: 271]. Similarly, many of the children of the Chicago Protestant Orphan Asylum in 1875 were described as having "one parent, who for various reasons cannot care for children in a home of their own, yet can contribute to their support in the asylum by paying a small amount for board" [U.S. Bureau of Education 1875: 60–61].

Statistics for 1933 demonstrate the continuation of these patterns into the first third of the twentieth century. More than half of all *dependent* children (51.8%) in institutions had one viable parent* [U.S. Bureau of the Census 1935].

That few teens were in institutions before the 1920s meant that the residents were relatively easy to control. Depending on the year and place, most impoverished children were employed by the time they were 12 or 14. Institutions followed the pattern of the larger society. By their teen years when they were likely to become troublesome, orphanage children were generally working—either indentured, placed in a *work home* (where work was to be exchanged for room and board), or returned to their own families and presumably contributing financially. When institutions began to keep children beyond the age of 12 or 14, they were faced with the problem of sometimes defiant, troublesome teenagers who were difficult to manage.

Children were expected to be compliant, respectful, and well-behaved, and were not to "talk back" to their adult caregivers. Although some disobedience was tolerated, for the most part, children whose behavior proved disruptive were either sent home or to other institutions. Letters to parents demanding that they "take your child home: we can't tolerate his behavior" were common. The widower father of one five-year-old boy, for example, was told to remove his child because Dr. LeGrand Kerr "made it very plain that it was impossible for [the institution] to keep him in a group with other children." The "home" was therefore leaving him with [the father] "as we know of no place to advise you to put him . . . . Hoping you will be able to find the right place for your little boy." This child was described as "abnormally troublesome at all times," hurting the smaller children, going into violent tempers, and kicking and biting anyone who tried to control him. He was "destructive, breaking his own and

---

*Parents are described as "viable" when whereabouts are described as either "at home" or "elsewhere"; not "dead," "in penal institution", "in other institution," or "unknown."

other children's toys." He had "bad sexual habits," and needed constant watchfulness to keep him from teaching the other children "bad tricks." He was also "bright, a leader in kindergarten work, and loved music" [Orphan Asylum Society of Brooklyn (OAS) (Case Record 3370) 1927].

Another letter gave a mother one week's notice to remove her son, the superintendent noting that "I feel sure you will agree with me that he is a boy that needs individual attention which you as a mother will give him."[OAS (Case Record 3509) 1928]. In 1933, a child who could not be sent home was sent to another institution because he was considered "not suitable for the Seamen's Home." The board and staff were afraid that his behavior would "cause the Seamen's Home to get a bad name" [Society for the Children of Destitute Seamen (SCDS) 1933]. In 1939, a staff person, dissatisfied with the behavior of one teenager, reported to the Board of Managers of the Society for the Children of Destitute Seamen that this girl had been told that "the society was not going to continue to keep any older children who were not self-respecting and anxious to do for themselves; that we were not going to raise a generation of chiselers; and that unless her attitude was very different and unless she was willing to work and help herself we would have to transfer her to another Society" [SCDS (Case Record S.R.) 1935]. In May 1924, a letter was sent to the single-parent father of a 16-year-old girl described as a "troublemaker." It read, "The Committee feels that, as Gilda will be 17 this summer, she should leave the Home at the close of the school term. We will be glad to know what arrangements you make in reference to this matter"[OAS (Case Record 2870) 1924].

Although some children stayed for 10 years or more, others went home when widowed parents remarried, when deserting fathers returned, or when single parents could either take them or place them with extended family or friends. Other parents moved children from one institution to another, either because they were dissatisfied, or because financial arrangements were more favorable at another home. Temporary placements were common: an analysis of the records of 109 children who were in the Orphan Asylum Society (OAS) during the 1920s revealed that 32% spent one year or less in the institution.* This is consistent with the 1933 national census statistics indicating that 36.8% of all institutionalized children had spent one year or less in the institution, and almost half (49.3%) two years or less [U.S. Bureau of the Census 1935]. Of all children released from OAS from 1913 to 1915, and 110 children released in the 1920s, 66% were returned to parents. When other relatives (such as grandparents, older siblings, aunts, or uncles) are added, 80% returned to families.** Returns were precipitated by parents who either took the children home or placed them with relatives, friends, or in another institution; or by the orphan homes, because the children or parents were not living up to institutional standards; or because the children had aged out.

Parental Involvement and Influence

The early assumption that virtually all dependent children were better off separated from their parents, and the widespread practice of discouraging parents from visiting with or having other involvement with their children, practically disappeared by the end of the nineteenth century. When parents were considered "worthy," when they were polite and respectable, and particularly when they paid for the care of their children, they were permitted to retain custody, to visit—at least monthly—and to send and receive letters. Most children not receiving public funding were supported at least in part by a parent. Parents who paid could apply to the institution of their choice and had the right to

---

*Fifteen percent of all residents of the Orphan Asylum Society of Brooklyn spent one year or less in the institution.
**Fairly consistent with the 1913-1915 survey and the 1920s sample were the findings of a survey of all children released from the Orphan Asylum Society of Brooklyn from 1873 to 1875 and from 1883 to 1885: 62% of all children released during those years were returned to parents. An additional 13% were returned to relatives other than parents.

maintain a relationship with their children and to visit, move, or remove them.

Institutional records contain notes and correspondence illustrating that parents were sometimes consulted and often maintained an active role in their children's lives. Many parents developed relationships with their children's caregivers and, when necessary, advocated for them. The records of the Orphan Asylum Society of the 1920s contain letters to and from parents that reveal a pattern of consultation and involvement. Parents were viewed as being ultimately responsible for their children and as having the power to make their children behave. A series of letters from the superintendent to the mother of a teenage girl, Phyllis, illustrates the expectation that parents could influence the behavior of their children. "The time has come when you and I will have to work together," stated the superintendent in her first letter. "There seems to have been quite a change in her . . . she has an indifferent air about almost everything and quite a 'high hat' attitude, which . . . must be curbed." The superintendent then described her unsuccessful efforts to make Phyllis behave: she had talked to her and had threatened to curtail her music lessons. She therefore asked the mother, whom she perceived to have greater power than she had over Phyllis' behavior, to "give Phyllis a real, motherly severe talking to; and, if necessary, do not take her out and give her as much as you have been doing." The superintendent's perception that she and parents shared responsibility is evident in a subsequent letter. She wrote: "Mrs. W., my responsibility is so great for your daughter and every woman's daughter and every boy in this place, that I do not feel that I want to carry it alone" [OAS (Case Record 3430) 1933].

One mother advocated for her son, explaining his behavior to institution personnel, and asking that he be treated with greater understanding. In a letter to the superintendent, she said that he "liked the institution but kept thinking of home and missed his freedom . . . He feels inferior to his school chums . . . due to the fact that he has to be in an Institution." She hoped that the superintendent would "understand how he feels." She said that her son was "influenced by older boys in the home . . . he has promised me to try and do better." This mother moved her son to another institution several years later. In announcing the child's removal, she wrote that she felt "sorry for the boys and girls there who have no one to defend them" [OAS (Case Record 4000) 1930].

Staffing and Funding

Low personnel costs and minimal expenditures for food, housing, clothing, and recreation were common to most institutions. Institutionalization, therefore, was a fairly inexpensive way of caring for dependent children. In addition, congregate care was more likely to attract voluntary funds than boarding or placing-out. Parents' board payments also contributed to institutional budgets.

Personnel costs were minimized by the use of low-paid staff, members of religious orders, and volunteers. With the exception of a very few unusual homes operating after 1920, workers and teachers were selected in part for their willingness to accept low salaries or, in the case of the religious, maintenance only. Some institutions hired mothers of their own residents: in 1924, for example, Mooseheart in Illinois employed more than 80. Mature unmarried women who had few jobs open to them could also be hired for low wages and were therefore frequently employed in institutions [Deardorff 1924].

The best of these workers, dedicated individuals, contributed their all despite low recompense. The worst were exploiters of children, or at least, persons who were unable to obtain any other type of work. Some unmarried women dedicated themselves to the rearing of other people's children. One woman of this type was Miss Anna M. Drew, matron of the Home for the Children of Seamen, who died in 1906. Her obituary depicted a devoted woman whose charges, all under age 14, received more than routine care. She was described as a "quiet, gentle but firm disciplinarian, with a loving motherly disposition, she won the friendship and respect of everybody near her . . . generations of boys and girls have grown up under her intelligent guidance." As a single parent, Miss Drew also adopted one of her charges [Miss Drew at Rest. . . 1906]. A description of another matron, however, as reproduced by Henry Thurston and told to him anonymously, reveals a very different attitude: "Well do I remember the . . . ridicule [matron] heaped upon me when I ventured to urge a plan of giving me an opportunity of entering high school. Her question as to "who had ever heard of an orphan boy having a high school education" reflected the attitude of the institution towards me . . . as well as the other boys" [Thurston 1930: 70–71].

By the 1920s and 1930s, the board and administration of the Child Welfare League of America (CWLA) were expressing concern regarding the qualifications of children's attendants, the difficulties of their jobs, and the low rates of pay. CWLA Board of Directors' minutes of 1926 described the conditions of work of some 5,000 cottage mothers:

> Most of them work for less than $50 per month with maintenance. Few of them get away from their strenuous duties for one full day each week . . . Often they have too little assistance . . . they find themselves loaded with responsibilities from 6:30 in the morning until 8 or 9 at night. Sometimes they must occupy living quarters which permit but little privacy. It is not strange, therefore, that women break down or are dissatisfied because of these burdens. [Special report . . . 1926]

In 1933, C.C. Carstens, the executive director of CWLA, discussed the seriousness of the situation. He pointed out that "[The cottage mothers] are usually untrained . . . and yet occupy the most important posts in the daily lives of the children." He also noted that the Great Depression "has led to serious reductions in salaries that in the first place have never been adequate to ensure good service . . . A higher grade of cottage mother is needed in many institutions than is now generally found."

From the onset of the orphanage system and continuing into the 1920s and 1930s, board members and "lady manager" volunteers assumed many tasks currently assigned to professionals. Middle-class and upper-class women, with servants at home, assumed supervisory tasks as an extension into the community of normal tasks with their own families. Volunteer boards not only oversaw budget and made policy, but also made decisions regarding admissions and discharges and approval or disapproval of families to whom the children were to return or be placed out or adopted, and governed many other phases of the children's lives, deciding what they would eat, wear, and how much and how they would work and play. Board members and "lady managers" were regularly present at the institutions and oversaw their functioning [Letchworth 1886; Thurston 1930].

Few institutions were fully funded by government, and many received no public funds at all. Support came from memberships; small and large contributions; endowment; wise investments, including return from mortgages; membership dues; and direct board payments from parents. The 1933 U.S. Census report noted that a *minimum* of 76,252 (54.3%) of all institutionalized children and almost one-quarter (24.7%) of African American children received no public support at all [U.S. Bureau of the Census 1935].

Policy Changes and the Decline in the Use of Institutions

The decline in the use of institutions was preceded by at least 60 years of debate, and the conclusion, after the first 40, that family care was preferable to institutionalization. The debates began during the last third of the nineteenth century, and by 1886 were well under way. While most opponents of orphanages accepted that short periods in receiving homes might be useful for some children, they were highly critical of long-term placement. Letchworth [1886] described the objections of these critics of institutions. They contended that: "the simple routine of the asylum does not give sufficient variety of mental or manual employment for proper development; and that the children thus become institutionalized, and graduate inefficient, lacking confidence in themselves to cope with the world in a struggle for a livelihood." Richardson argued that it is "hurtful, to retain in institution life, longer than . . . absolutely necessary as a preparation for outside life, those committed to it . . . it [is]not a natural condition" [Wolins & Piliavin 1964: 12, 22]. In 1896, Folks stated several reasons for preferring family homes over institutions: the institutions' "unbroken monotony. . . a measure of restraint and repression which tends to obliterate individual distinctions, to discourage originality and inquiry . . . practically no opportunity to learn the value of money," a lack of opportunity to develop "local relations and attachments which are a safeguard and an assistance in starting out in life," and little opportunity to develop continuing affections and relationship with adults. He asserted that children "need fathers and mothers" [Folks 1896].

The White House Conferences on the Care of Dependent Children in 1909 and 1919 were supposed to have settled the issue in favor of families, with preference given for helping children in their own homes through mother's aid. In 1909, Booker T. Washington, speaking out at the conference about "destitute colored children of the south," said that his "observation and experience" was that "in many cases the child would be better off if left to chance to get into some home than he is in the average orphan asylum." From his experience with former orphanage children who were enrolled at Tuskeegee, he had "become very suspicious of the average orphan asylum, organized and built up for the support of the members of my race" [Washington 1909: 114–117]. The 1919 conference emphatically endorsed the statement, "The carefully selected foster home is for the normal child the best substitute for the natural home."

Articles by advocates for family care and against institutions for children began appearing in professional journals and the popular press during the second and third decades of the twentieth century. Henry Dwight Chapin, M.D., the founder of a family care agency, wrote in 1926 that the United States was an "institution ridden" country, and cited experts who substantiated his position that family care was superior. Professor Boas of the Jewish Bureau of Social Research found that "children in boarding homes showed a much better physical development than children in institutions." Prison warden Mott Osborne said that "an undue proportion of his prison wards had their early training in institutions" [Family vs. Institution 488]. The Literary Digest [1921] described a highly successful "experiment" by the board of trustees of Hancock County, Ohio, in which children were boarded out rather than placed in institutions. Sophie Irene Loeb, a reporter, not only produced many anti-institution articles but also organized the Child Welfare Committee of America, Inc., an organization of prominent Americans, and held two conferences (1925 and 1928) at which professionals and politicians voiced their opposition to institutions. Ethel Verry [1939] listed problems facing children who graduated to the community after long periods of institutional care, describing difficulties in economic adjustment (too little realism in use of money, too few opportunities for making choices), family adjustment (difficulty in accepting family and personal imperfections, setting schedules, meeting appointments), and personal adjustment (making adequate personal social lives, making adequate marriages and relationships with partners, making lasting, not superficial relationships).

During the 1940s and 1950s, institution personnel also spoke of the limitations of institutional care. At a meeting of the Association of Children's Institutions in Syracuse, New York, on April 16, 1948, Miss Lillian Johnson, Executive Director of the Ryther

Center in Seattle, Washington, said that the pretense that an institution is a home must be given up, that most children come to institutions because there is no other place for them and that they must be prepared for going elsewhere. She noted that an institution is not life and cannot be made to be. She compared the institutional plan to a life jacket that holds the child above water but without putting solid ground beneath the child's feet. At a 1952 institute for institutional personnel given at Case Western Reserve University, Morris Mayer, the executive director of Bellefaire, in Cleveland, an orphanage that became a treatment center, characterized the best-rated institutions as third choice, after the children's own homes and family foster homes. He believed that institutions should be used only for those children with personality difficulties who could not adjust to families [Thomas Orphan Asylum (Box 2 Folder 6)].

The impact of preference for family over institution, in conjunction with the development of the ADC program as part of the 1935 Social Security Act and the continuing development of foster boarding care, was felt over the years. While the number of children in out-of-home care increased from 1951 through the 1960s, the percentage of children in institutions dropped significantly, from approximately 43% in 1951 to 31% in 1962 [Wolins & Piliavin] and from 21.5% in 1982 to 17.1% in 1989 [Merkel-Holguín]. Most institutions either closed or were transformed into residential treatment centers for the emotionally disturbed.

Lessons for Today

Is it feasible to re-create the orphanages? The preceding pages describe the orphanages and the conditions that enabled them to develop and continue well into the twentieth century. In the last several decades, however many structural and demographic changes have taken place in society, and the re-creation of orphanages would therefore be extremely expensive and so difficult as to be virtually impossible. Three changes stand out.

First, the old orphanages depended on having a population that was generally well behaved and easy to control. Today's children differ in behavior. Before the 1920s, most children in institutions were young. Children generally graduated to the work world by the time they were 14, either sent home to their own families or placed out. When institutions began to keep children through the high school years, the population became more difficult to control. Today's children enter the adult world at about 18, so institutions would have to deal with adolescents.

In the past, children living in institutions were the most, not the least, desirable of all children cared for by child welfare agencies. The old institutions preferred to care for children whose families were respectable and worthy by the standards of the day. In addition to selective admissions, institutions could, and frequently did, get rid of troublesome children by sending them home or to another institution, or by placing or boarding them out. In this manner, they could maintain a population relatively free of children who were difficult to control or who would exert negative influence on others. Given the present preference for family care over institutional care, institutional residents are likely to be those with the most, rather than the least, behavior problems.

Second, unlike parents of the past who had some influence and power to determine the course of their children's lives, most of the parents of children currently being considered for institutional care will be unable to retain control and custody, advocate, and move their children if the children are subjected to poor conditions or to abuse. Because many parents in the past paid for their children's board, they could and often did move or remove them from the care of a particular institution, either taking them home, moving them to another institution, or placing them privately. They could oversee their children's care, explaining their behavior and acting as advocates with institutional personnel. Though some children lived in orphanages on a long-term basis, many children were only temporary boarders. Most children returned to parents or to other relatives.

Unlike the many children of the past, today's children will be more likely to spend most of their growing-up years in institutions. The proposed curtailment of welfare payments to unmarried mothers, and time limits on welfare benefits, will mean that, even if parents are employed at minimum wage jobs, few will have the resources that will enable them to assume the care of their own children. Given the lack of financial support for families and the increasing incidence of parents whose drug habits make them unsuitable custodians, it is likely that the length of time children spend in care will increase, and that children will be less likely to experience family life at any time during their childhood years.

Third, in comparison to the orphanages of the past, contemporary costs to the public for institutional care would be extremely high, and would be borne almost entirely by government. Not only did many parents make board payments, but the old institutions also attracted endowments and contributions from philanthropists, religious organizations, and well-meaning individuals. Philanthropy now follows different channels, and government has largely assumed the cost of contemporary child welfare. It is unlikely that private money can be diverted back to support orphanages. If it cannot, the public purse will have to bear the whole cost. This includes a large up-front expenditure for capital costs for renovations and/or new buildings.

In addition, it appears unlikely that orphanages can be reconstituted to operate at reasonable cost. In the past, expenditures were minimized by the utilization of low-paid, untrained personnel, members of religious orders, and middle-class and upper-class women who contributed time to overseeing the facilities and decision-making. Such low-cost personnel are no longer available, and health, safety and other regulations now mandate higher staffing ratios and consequently higher staff costs. With the current emphasis on social welfare retrenchment, adequate funding is unlikely.

In practical terms, the re-creation of orphanages without such adequate funding would be highly unrealizable. However, if, for discussion sake, it was assumed that the public would be willing to pay the bills, another question would remain: Would the re-creation of orphanages benefit the children who would be placed in them? Opinions and experiences of past professionals, quoted above, lead one to believe that the children would be harmed more than they would be helped. Advocates for modern-day orphanages might argue that they would not intend to re-create the harmful aspects of orphanage life, but would create new forms of institutionalization that would benefit the children. Based on the historical record, however, they face a very high burden of proof that this can be done. If history is any guide, the experiential evidence is to the contrary.

Aside from history, there is contemporary evidence that institutions can be harmful to children. For example, although abuse may also a be problem in children's own families and in some foster homes, it appears to be more prevalent in institutions.* The problems described by Folks and other family advocates, and the reasons they gave for preferring families, seem still valid.

Goldstein et al. [1973] have corroborated the experiences of earlier professionals and advocates, describing the reality that constant changes in caregivers and a lack of what they describe as "psychological parents" create children who tend to be behind other children in skills, achievement, and social adaptation. The consequences of this deprivation become even more apparent in adulthood, when the lack of self-love and self-regard leads to a diminished capacity to love and care for others, including the individual's own children. ◆

*Current statistics imply a rate of founded or substantiated abuse or neglect in institutions to be more than twice that of abuse or neglect incidence in foster homes. According to Merkel-Holguín [1993], 13 states responsible for approximately 30% of all children in out-of-home care provide statistics for number of children in out-of-home care, and number of founded abuse and neglect cases for institutions and foster homes. Applying the latest estimate (1989) that 17.1% of all children in out-of-home care live in group homes, residential institutions, and emergency shelters, it appears that in those 13 states, approximately 5.1% of institutional children and approximately 2.2% of children living in foster homes are victims of reported and founded abuse and neglect. Based on the rationale stated in the text, even these figures are likely to be underestimated.

References

Affairs in Brooklyn: A caretaker charged with cruelty. Mrs. Huckans asks the coroner to investigate the death of her son at the Brooklyn Orphan Asylum. (1894, May 9). *Brooklyn Eagle*, p. 9.

Agency "Y". (1928). Case record D.M. Reference available from the author.

Bogen, H. (1992). *The luckiest orphans: A history of the Hebrew Orphan Asylum of New York*. Urbana and Chicago: University of Illinois Press.

Carstens, C. C. (1933, June 15) Report: Child Welfare today and tomorrow. Address delivered at annual meeting held at the Detroit-Leland Hotel, Detroit, Michigan. Full report included in minutes of Board of Directors, same date. Available at the Social Welfare History Archives, University of Minnesota.

Chapin, H. D. (1926). Family vs. institution. *The Survey, LV*, 485–488.

Chapin, H. D. (1929). Homes or institutions? *Review of Reviews*. New York: Child Welfare Committee of America (reprint).

Deardorff, N. R. (1924). The new pied pipers. *The Survey, LII*, 31–47, 56–59, 61.

Department of Commerce, U.S. Bureau of the Census. (1927). *Children under institutional care 1923*. Washington, DC: Government Printing Office.

Folks, H. (1896). Why should dependent children be reared in families rather than in institutions? *Charities Review, V*, 140, 141, 143. Quoted in Wolins, M., & Piliavin, I. (1964). *Institution or foster family: a century of debate* (pp. 15–16). New York: Child Welfare League of America.

Folks, H. (1902). *The care of destitute, neglected, and delinquent children*. New York: The Macmillan Company.

Goldstein, J., Freud, A., & Solnit, A.J. (1973). *Beyond the best interests of the child*. New York: The Free Press.

Hacsi, T. A. (1993). *A plain and solemn duty: A history of orphan asylums in America* (Dissertation, University of Pennsylvania).

Harris, M. (1990). *Unholy orders: Tragedy at Mount Cashel*. Markham, ON: Viking, Penguin Books Canada Ltd.

Homes better than orphan asylums. (1921, December 17). *Public Opinion in Literary Digest,* pp. 29–30.

Johnson, L. (1948, April 16). Notes on "Modern day trends dealing with children in institutions." Meeting of representatives of Association of Children's Institutions, Elmcrest Center, Syracuse, NY. Box 2, Folder 6, Thomas Indian School series B0640–85. Available at the State University of New York, State Education Department, State Archives and Records Administration, Albany, NY.

Ladner, J. (1989, October 29). Bring back the orphanages. *The Washington Post,* pp. B1–B2.

Letchworth, W.P. (1886). Children of the state. *Proceedings of the National Conference of Charities and Corrections.* Reprinted in Bremner, R.H. (Ed.) (1971), *Children and youth in America: A documentary history. Vol. II: 1866–1932* (pp. 296–298). Cambridge, MA: Harvard University Press.

Mayer, M. (1952). Remarks at institute on children's institutions held at Case Western Reserve University. Notes. Box 2, Folder 6, Thomas Indian School series B0640–85. Available at the State University of New York, State Education Department, State Archives and Records Administration, Albany NY.

McCabe, M. (1927). Letter to Annie E. McCord, executive secretary, Home for the Children of Seamen, October 10, New York City. Correspondence File. New York: Society for Seamen's Children.

Merkel-Holguín, L.A., with Sobel, A. (1993). *The child welfare stat book 1993.* Washington, DC: Child Welfare League of America.

Miss Drew at Rest: Beautiful life of matron of children's home. Impressive services at institution—Her life reviewed. (1906, January 13). *The Staten Islander,* p. 5.

Murray, C. (1993, October 29). The coming white underclass. *The Wall Street Journal,* p. 413.

Orphan Asylum Society in the City of Brooklyn (1835). The constitution and bylaws of the Orphan Asylum Society in the City of Brooklyn, with the annual report for the year 1834.

Orphan Asylum Society in the City of Brooklyn (1924–1933) Case records 2870, 3370, 3430, 3509, 4000. Available from the Social Welfare History Archives, University of Minnesota.

Provence, S. (1989). Infants in institutions revisited. *Zero to Three, IX(3),* 1–4.

Reeder, R. R. (1929, January 15). The place of children's institutions. *The Survey Mid-monthly*, 482–484.

Richardson, A.B. (1880). The Massachusetts system of placing and visiting children. *Proceedings of the 7th Annual Conference of Charities* (pp. 186–200). Boston: A. Williams & Co. In Wolins (1964), pp. 12, 22.

Smith, E. P. (1993). Characteristics of social welfare stasis and change: A comparison of the characteristics of two child welfare agencies in the 1920s. *Journal of Sociology and Social Welfare*, XX(2), 105–122.

Society for the Children of Destitute Seamen. (1939). Case record S.R.

Special report on description of job of cottage mother in 1926. (1926, March 8). Minutes of the Board of Directors, Child Welfare League of America. Unpublished microfilm. Available from Social Welfare History Archives, University of Minnesota.

Sutherland, N. (1976) *Children in English-Canadian society: Framing the twentieth-century consensus.* Toronto ON: University of Toronto Press.

Thurston, H. W. (1930). *The dependent child.* New York: Columbia University Press. Reprinted in Bremner, R.H. (Ed.) (1971) *Children and youth in America: A documentary history. Vol. II: 1866–1932.* Cambridge, MA: Harvard University Press.

Trotzkey, E.L. (1930). *Institutional care and placing-out: The place of each in the care of dependent children.* Chicago: The Marks Nathan Jewish Orphan Home.

U.S. Bureau of Education. (1875). Circular of Information No. 6. Statements relating to reformatory, charitable and industrial schools for the young. Washington, DC. Reprinted in Bremner, R.H. (Ed.). (1971). *Children and youth in America: A documentary history. Vol. II: 1866–1932* (pp. 269–271). Cambridge, MA: Harvard University Press.

United States Children's Bureau. (1919). *Standards of child welfare: A report of the children's bureau conference, 1919.* Pub. No. 60. Washington, DC: U.S. Government Printing Office.

U.S. Department of Commerce, Bureau of the Census. (1927). *Children under institutional care, 1923.* Washington, DC: U. S. Government Printing Office.

U.S. Department of Commerce, Bureau of the Census. (1935). *Children under institutional care and in foster homes, 1933.* Washington, DC: U. S. Government Printing Office.

Verry, E. (1939, February). Problems facing children who have had a relatively long period in institutional care. *CWLA Bulletin, XVIII*, 2–3.

Walsh, E. (1994, March 1). As at-risk children overwhelm foster care, Illinois considers orphanages. *The Washington Post.*

Washington, Booker T. (1909). Destitute colored children of the south. Proceedings of the Conference on the Care of Dependent Children, held at Washington, D.C., January 25, 26, 1909. Reprinted in Bremner, R.H. (Ed.) (1971), *Children and youth in America: A documentary history. Vol. II: 1866–1932* (pp. 300–303). Cambridge, MA: Harvard University Press.

Wolins, M., & Piliavin, I. (1964). *Institution or foster family: A century of debate.* New York: Child Welfare League of America.

7

Janie Porter Barrett and the Virginia Industrial School for Colored Girls: Community Response to the Needs of African American Children

Wilma Peebles-Wilkins

During the late nineteenth and early twentieth centuries, a social ethos evolved among African American women that led to internal child welfare reform in legally segregated African American communities. This article describes the nature of these child welfare developments and provides a historical example using the Virginia Industrial School for Colored Girls. Prevailing themes derived from the historical account are discussed in a contemporary context.

Wilma Peebles-Wilkins, Ph.D., is Acting Dean, Boston University School of Social Work, Boston, MA.

135

Virginia will not forget that she is indebted to the colored women of the Commonwealth for the Industrial Home School. [Davis 1920: 362]

Historically, African American child welfare services have evolved as a response to exclusion, differential treatment, segregation, and other forms of racial oppression [Billingsley & Giovannoni 1972; Smith 1991; Stehno 1988]. Internal social reform and selective services for African American children have resulted from mutual aid-oriented responses on the part of African American churches and voluntary associations, and benevolence originating from interracial cooperation, the work of Caucasian philanthropists, and governmental sponsorship. The Virginia Industrial School for Colored Girls, founded in 1915, was initially maintained by the Virginia Federation of Colored Women's Clubs through organized interracial cooperation. Existing today as the Barrett Learning Center, this institution responded to dependent and delinquent African American girls and exemplifies the fulfillment of one of the national directives of the National Association of Colored Women. Using guiding principles from educational theory and from the Child Welfare Department of the Russell Sage Foundation (forerunner of the Child Welfare League of America), the Virginia Industrial School, under the leadership of Janie Porter Barrett, provided "convincing reform efforts" by means of a humanistic living and learning environment and preparation for transition to the community [Davis 1920: 358].

Child Welfare Work and the African American Community

Between 1877 and 1900, the status of African Americans was being socially redefined [Ogbu 1978]. In general, conditions for impoverished African American children in the South were deplorable. Emancipation resulted in the problem of who would care for dependent African American children. African American children were excluded from any meaningful and structured governmental care aside from the in-home services offered to former slave families by a few pre-Civil War private orphanages [Billingsley & Giovannoni 1972: 27–33], the orphanages established by the short-lived Freedman's Bureau, and almshouses. Mutual aid organizations and voluntary associations or self-help efforts became the dominant mode of care for dependent African American children immediately after emancipation and beyond [Billingsley & Giovannoni 1972]. African American status was based on separation laws and customs between 1900 and 1930 [Ogbu 1978], and the existing governmental child welfare system was not adequately responding to the needs of African American children.

The child-saving activities of the mid-nineteenth through the early twentieth centuries led to the establishment of industrial schools and other institutions primarily for the care of poor Caucasian immigrant children who were dependent, abused, neglected, or delinquent. For the most part, African American children were not the focus of this early crusade for children. Although the juvenile court system was established as early as 1899, the practice of putting African American children in jail persisted in many communities well into the twentieth century. In 1976 in Virginia, for example, 75 years after the practice was prohibited by state law, a large number of children under age 15 were still being jailed, generating community concern [Child Jailings Decline . . . 1976]. As segregation customs and laws persisted, young dependent African American children were either jailed or sent to reform schools even when not delinquent because communities were slow to respond to the need for homefinding and family foster care services for African American children.

During the early decades of the twentieth century, voluntary associations founded by African American women began to confront the unmet needs of African American children and youths.

Kindergartens, day nurseries, and schools for dependent and delinquent African American children were developed in response to the racial uplift mandates emanating from the philosophy of the National Association of Colored Women. Founded in 1896, this association represented African American clubwomen from coast to coast in about 40 states. Its organizational philosophy was promulgated by the first president, Mary Church Terrell, whose words [1899: 346] are typical of the clubwomen's collective moral authority in the African American community:

> As an Association, let us devote ourselves enthusiastically, conscientiously, to the children . . . Through the children of today, we must build the foundation of the next generation upon such a rock of integrity, morality, and strength, both of body and mind, that the floods of proscription, prejudice, and persecution may descend upon it in torrents, and yet it will not be moved. We hear a great deal about the race problem, and how to solve it . . . but the real solution of the race problem, both so far as we, who are oppressed and those who oppress us are concerned, lies in the children.

The perceived internal social reform duties of African American clubwomen to the race are best chronicled and understood through their autobiographical and other personal and biographical accounts. Community perceptions, as expressed in anecdotal accounts in the African American news media, are also useful. For the most part, child welfare services that developed through the clubwomen's movement were residual in nature and were replaced by institutionalized social welfare arrangements after the Great Depression. After the Progressive Era, the broader crusade for children, as noted by Chambers [1963], expanded into other family welfare areas, and the new focus was on developing noninstitutionally based services. These changes undoubtedly had some impact on services for African American children.

Some private services for the children persisted until the 1940s, but were discontinued because of inadequate funding and likely also because of increased governmental alternatives for the African American community after World War II [Axinn & Levin 1982]. Others persisted as privately supported institutions and still others were subsumed under state auspices.

For example, in Kansas City, Missouri, the Colored Big Sister Home for Girls, founded by Fredericka Douglass Sprague Perry in 1934, existed as a state-contracted private institution through the 1940s. Perry, together with the Colored Big Sister Association, began the first homefinding services for African American children in Kansas City, Missouri, because standard home placement services by the local Community Charities Chest Committee were not available to African American children. Instead, dependent young girls released from the local orphanage at age 12 were sent to the state institution for delinquents until the age of 17. Homefinding efforts eventually culminated in the establishment of a residential care facility. The Big Sister Home helped these young girls move into the community by affording access to schools, training in homemaking skills, and employment placements in private homes [Peebles-Wilkins 1989: 40].

Another example of institution-building involved the founding by Carrie Steele of an orphanage in Georgia to care for infants and children she found abandoned in the Atlanta Terminal Railroad Station where she worked as a maid. The Carrie Steele Orphan Home was constructed and chartered as a nonprofit institution in 1888 after a successful community fund-raising effort by Steele. She had previously been caring for these children in her own home at night and watching them play in the terminal by day. In 1923, the Home became a United Way-supported agency and exists today as the Carrie Steele-Pitts Home, serving about one hundred neglected, abused, abandoned, or orphaned children of all races, from six to 18 years of age [Carrie Steele-Pitts, Inc. 1988]. The Virginia Federation of Club Women turned the Virginia Industrial School over to the state in 1920; today it continues to operate as the Barrett Learning Center in Hanover County, Virginia, a public agency for juvenile delinquents of all races. Table 1 presents a chronological development of the Virginia Industrial School.

Barrett's Home School

Internal child welfare reform and services by African American clubwomen, like settlement house services provided by Lillian Wald and Jane Addams, reflected the personality traits of the founders [Kogut 1972]. Such was the case with the Virginia Industrial School for Colored Girls with its flowering, landscaped campus. Anne Firor Scott [1992: 90], noting that the Virginia Industrial School became a model school that other states tried to emulate, described a visible atmosphere of trust and hope attributable to Barrett's personality. In addition to her unique skills in facilitating a growth-promoting milieu at her home school, Barrett's skill in developing and maintaining interracial group support also contributed to the amount of financial and material resources available and the level of broad-based community endorsement for the school. Barrett's successful approach to delinquent African American girls was likely the result of a combination of her ability to effectively incorporate consultation from Hastings Hart of the Russell Sage Foundation and child welfare practices later promoted by C. C. Carstens, first director of the Child Welfare League of America.

Janie Porter Barrett was born in Athens, Georgia. She was reared as a family member in the Skinner home, where her mother was employed as a housekeeper and seamstress. Educated in mathematics and literature in this Caucasian family, she was exposed to persons of privilege and refinement and grew up with a lifestyle atypical of the African American community. Her mother later sent her to Hampton Institute in Virginia, where she was trained as an elementary school teacher. At Hampton, Barrett [1926: 361] was inculcated with patriotic, altruistic values,

TABLE 1
Chronological Development of the Virginia Industrial School

Date	Historical Development
1911	Fund-raising began
January 1913	147 acre farm site purchased for Virginia Industrial Home School for Colored Girls
May 1913	First board meeting
January 1915	First two girls admitted
November 1915	Barrett appointed superintendent
1916	First cottage built
1919	Second cottage and school building added
1920	Placed under state control, renamed Virginia Industrial School for Colored Girls
1927	Superintendent's residence built
1940	Barrett retires as superintendent
1950	Renamed Janie Porter Barrett School for Girls
1965	School is racially integrated
1970s	Renamed Barrett Learning Center

Source: Compiled from the cited primary source data in the Peabody Collection, *Leader* (1916); Hampton University and the *Virginia Welfare Bulletin* (1956).

and a sense of duty to her race, learning lessons "in love of race, love of fellow-men, and love of country." Her worldview led to the development of an industrial home school based on a philosophy of social and human development lodged in educational programming.

The Industrial Home for [Wayward] Colored Girls opened its doors in Hanover County near Richmond in 1915 on a 147–acre site purchased by the Virginia Federation of Colored Women's Clubs, an organization founded by Barrett, its first president, between 1907 and 1908 [Peebles-Wilkins 1987]. At the time the school was founded, it was estimated that about 500 young African American girls needed supervised care, training, and rehabilitation. The farmland with a farmhouse had been purchased in 1914, but the federation had been gradually raising money since 1911 and anticipated paying for the land in full after five years [Aery 1915]. Urged on, however, by the sentencing of an eight-year-old African American girl to six months in jail, "every woman gave until she could feel it" [Barrett 1926: 356]. Having raised $5,300, the federation paid for the land, chartered the school, and designated the farmhouse as Federation Cottage after the clubwomen's organization. Barrett's encounter with the judge to get custody of the eight-year-old girl gives us a glimpse of differential perceptions and the handling of dependent African American girls by the Virginia juvenile justice system.

Prior to establishing the Industrial Home, Barrett had already established a Child Welfare Department at the Locust Street Settlement. In addition to guidance for young mothers and helping children through adolescence, a committee from the Child Welfare Department had been successfully removing underage African American children from jail to alternative placements [Daniel 1931: 57–58]. A Negro reform school had been founded by the Virginia African American community as early as 1897 [Ludlow 1904], but putting African American children in jail and the lack of differential planning for dependent African American children persisted. Barrett read about the sentencing of the eight-year-old child in the newspaper and immediately appealed to the judge in Newport News, Virginia, to send the child to the Weaver Orphan Home in Hampton, Virginia, where Barrett was living. The judge, viewing the child as a criminal who was in court because African American women needed to look after their children, only reluctantly released the child into Barrett's care. Thus, Barrett [1926: 355–356] was able to "save Virginia the disgrace of making a baby like this serve a sentence."

A juvenile court was established in Newport News shortly after Barrett's encounter, but this rather dramatic example of the need for a more specialized facility for dependent African American children served to raise the consciousness of both the African American and Caucasian middle-class communities. The federation quickly recognized that the support of men and women of both races was necessary to fully realize its goals.

Some state support was necessary to supplement private fund-raising, but the Virginia state governmental system had a practice of not allowing any women—Caucasian or African American—to receive and manage funds. For the facility to be considered for a state financial appropriation, a board consisting of Caucasian women and businessmen was recommended. Barrett, however, recognized that continued and active participation by the African American community was essential to ensure the success of the girls and the home school. (For example, some of the private fund-raising was associated with donors who had been cultivated by Hampton Institute). Although organizing an interracial board in segregated Virginia was discouraged, after much persistence and with a great deal of effort, Barrett was able to organize such a board, comprising both men and women from the North and South, to obtain a small state supplement [Aery 1915: 604]. The school opened in spite of "vigorous protests" from the local Caucasian community, with Barrett stating, "Beg them to give us a chance—to try us. If the school proves objectionable, I promise to move it" [Daniel 1931: 59]. To ensure the success of her home school, she took on the position of superintendent. Board members, along with federation club members, played key roles in supporting Barrett as superintendent, raising funds, visiting similar schools in the North, enlisting community endorsement, and helping to identify homes where girls could be placed when ready for the community.

Although sources do not afford a great many details on the child welfare consultation provided to the Industrial School, the operations of the school itself shed light on the influences of the Child Welfare Department of the Russell Sage Foundation and of the standards set by the Child Welfare League of America between 1921 and 1925. The delinquency institution was expected to have social responsibilities, which included assuring that institutionalization was the last resort, providing adequate preparation for parole once children were admitted, and including investigation and follow-up in discharge planning [Harrison

1985: 590–594]. Before officially opening the home school, advice about industrial training was sought from Dr. Hastings Hart at Russell Sage. The Russell Sage Foundation cottage plan was used to create a homelike environment for the girls. The operations of the cottage system and the overall operations and goals of the industrial home for girls modeled the social responsibilities of a delinquency institution. Barrett's pioneering leadership style in relation to the delinquent is best characterized as transformational. Viewing the home school as a "moral hospital," the word *wayward*, although popular vernacular during the time, was never used by the school even though it does appear in the early media [Aery 1915: 602; An Industrial School. . . 1913; Schools for Wayward Girls 1916; Daniel 1931: 68].

Admissions and Intake

All residents were admitted to the home school on referral from the State Board of Welfare. Ultimately, all girls admitted were considered incorrigible and without other placement options in the community. In addition to Harris Barrett's cottage, the superintendent's residence and three other cottages were on the campus of the industrial home school—Federation Cottage (the farmhouse part of the initial purchase) and the Hanover and Virginia Cottages, built with additional state appropriations [Aery 1919: 473–474]. Virginia Cottage was used for the intake and admissions process. Upon arrival, each girl was assigned to Virginia Cottage for social assessment: "I require them to tell me the whole truth about their past . . . when I know everything, I understand better how to help" [Daniel 1931: 61]. Then, starting with a clean slate, a peer system with Big Sister assignments was used to help each resident learn the school's expectations. After a ten-day period of instruction about the rules and regulations, girls were given demerits for lapses in behavior, personal appearance, and work habits, and negative points were accumulated. Table 2 shows the marking system.

TABLE 2
Barrett's Behavioral Marking System (Demerits)

Behavior	*Demerits*
Escapes	All Credits
Insubordination	300–1500
Stealing	150
Lying	150
Impudence	150
Insolence	150
Disrespect	150
Disobedience	25–100
Quarreling	50
Discourtesy	10
Inattention	10
Laziness	50–200
Disorder	10
Uncleanliness	50
Fighting	150–200
Carelessness	10

Source: Barrett's Seventh Annual Report, cited by Daniel [1931: 69].

The school operated on an honor system, with each girl working toward becoming an "honor girl" wearing the "white dress," and being promoted to Federation Cottage, the highest of the cottages. Discipline at the home school was strict, with team groups consisting of ten residents assigned a team lieutenant and a captain to monitor behavior. School matrons followed up on any necessary disciplinary action. In addition to the demerit system, silences were also used as a form of discipline. A biographical account of Barrett by Sadie Daniel mentions, without giving descriptive details, a "Thinking Room" for the "development of moral strength" [Daniel 1931: 68]. One is left with the impression that the so-called "thinking room" was some form of isolation resembling "quiet rooms" used in psychodynamic forms of therapeutic treatment for children who lose control.

Preparation

The goal of the industrial home school was to help each girl gain
self-control and develop home-life skills in preparation for independent community living. The home school, like other educational programs for African American girls, was focused on
domestic sciences and household skills. Preparation for jobs accessible to African American women was a programmatic goal
and concentrated on social role adaptation in the face of racial
segregation and oppression; well into the 1950s, the majority of
African American women were employed as domestics. Educational preparation paralleled the public school curriculum
through grade eight, and the academic content was supplemented with other opportunities such as programs to promote
English-proficiency skills. Religious training, crop harvesting,
and household management were all part of the vocational education program. Applied agricultural training was instituted on
the basis of two rotating teams, one of farm girls learning to work
the farm and the other of house girls learning household management. A supply-demand approach was used because household domestics were more easily placed. Like contemporary chef
school or culinary arts training programs, the residents actually
prepared the dining table and meals. Neighbors in the community helped subsidize the school by giving the residents laundry
and sewing work. Such community services no doubt strengthened Barrett's relationship with the neighbors.

The curriculum also included appreciation for nature and
pleasurable use of leisure time, such as bird watching, plant
growing, and a range of sport, theater, and other organized recre-
ational activities. "Clean, straight living" [Barrett 1926: 357] could
be considered the hallmark of the institution. Patriotism and
responsible citizenship were stressed, even though the residents
often expressed skepticism in the face of differential treatment,
segregation, and oppression. As in the segregated public schools,
Negro History Week was observed and celebrated during the

second week of February. The purpose of this observance was to instill racial pride and to teach residents about the accomplishments of successful African American men and women.

Several other prevailing themes that characterize a humanistic but structured, kind, and caring learning environment are identifiable in descriptions of the home school's pedagogy and day-to-day operations. Highly valuing and taking pride in her education at Hampton Institute, Barrett was committed to transmitting to others the lessons she learned there. The principles of the Golden Rule were applied at the school, and behavioral expectations were applied both to personnel and to residents. As one might anticipate, attendance and staff shortages were an administrative concern. Personnel were expected to be committed, efficient, and trained, with "sane judgment, kind hearts, and the ability to direct intelligently" [Daniel 1931: 70; Davis 1920: 364]. Cooperation from residents was enlisted by not embarrassing or humiliating any of the girls. Each girl was accepted, given the chance to start over, and treated kindly ["Hampton woman honored" 1916]. Open communication and free expression were supported by impromptu "open forums" for group discussion, as requested by the residents. "Character training exercises issued by the National Association of Child Welfare (Child Welfare League)" [Daniel 1931: 67] were also used and there were group discussions and problem-solving sessions based on life course simulations.

Parole

Girls were honorably released from the institution after successful completion of parole, which was possible after two years of satisfactory performance. Home school residents could be paroled to employment situations under supervision in either African American or Caucasian homes, or to their own families. The investigation process described by C.C. Carstens was carried out by an application and screening process that eventually included investigation and approval of homes by the state welfare department. After approval and a thorough explanation of a resident's needs and the supervision requirements, a contractual agreement was signed between the Industrial School and the employer family. Each resident was required to send two dollars of her earnings back to the home school. A bank account was established for each girl. Initially, one dollar went into her bank account and the other dollar was credited to the institution until costs associated with a clothing allowance purchase for parole were recovered. Afterwards, all the money went into the resident's account and the resident left the institution with money when officially discharged. In addition to written communication between Barrett and the residents, monthly reports were required from the individual responsible for the parolee. If the resident had difficulty adjusting, more contact between the home and the school was required. Early on, Barrett began to see the need for a parole officer to do close follow-up supervision.

Paroling residents to their own homes was less frequent. Socioeconomic and environmental circumstances caused concern about the residents' vulnerability to prostitution and other avenues to illegal income. Barrett expressed the need for child welfare advocacy for low-income families as a deterrent to delinquency.

Discharge

After two years of successful parole, the residents were discharged after a graduation or closing exercises. After a 14-year period, 33% of the residents were discharged because they were no longer minors, about 42% were discharged after successful parole, 2% of the residents had died, and not even a half percent of the girls successfully ran away (see table 3).

Anecdotal accounts do suggest parole recidivism and residents with poor health status. These factors, coupled with admission during the late teens and the inability to comply consistently with the rules of the system, likely account for the 33% of the

TABLE 3
Admission Outcomes, 1915–1929 (N = 823)

Outcome	Number of Girls
Discharged after parole	343
Discharged due to majority age	272
In community school	100
Died	20
Transferred to:	
Hospitals for feebleminded	20
Piedmont Tuberculosis Sanatorium	2
State Board of Welfare	3
Ran away, still at large	4
Paroled under supervision	59

Source: Table is a modification of statistics reported in Daniel [1931: 77].

residents who stayed in the institution and were released when they became adults.

Contemporary Implications and Conclusions

This article examines one historical response by the African American community to the exclusion of African American children from turn-of-the-century child welfare services. As Barrett [1926: 355] noted:

> Rendering service, climbing to a higher plane of citizenship, and uplifting those farthest down was what the women of the Virginia Federation had in mind when they started out to establish the Virginia Industrial School. At that time there was no place except the jail for a colored girl who fell into the hands of the law, so there was no question about the need for such an institution.

Today, one of the prevailing concerns in the child welfare system involves the overinclusion of African American and other minority children in the existing forms of out-of-home care. Juvenile detention is sometimes the only available recourse for African Americans from low-income families, who should instead receive outpatient therapy, adequate child care, or sufficient family preservation services.

The considerations associated with the entrapment of minority children in out-of-home placements extend far beyond the juvenile justice system and expand to the entire child welfare system. Certainly, many of these considerations are manifestations of unemployment, poverty, the breakdown of the family structure, and other life circumstances associated with oppression and social and economic injustices. For these reasons, it is the philosophical response to oppression described in this historical account that has the greatest relevance for contemporary child welfare services.

Several prevailing themes of equal importance are noteworthy in this example of internal social reform within the African American community:

- Collective responsibility and self-development as well as external community involvement and interracial cooperation
- Description of life circumstances and advocacy for the needs of children
- Utilization of the existing knowledge base about the needs of children and quality child welfare services
- Collaborative efforts of the public and private sector to promote new service initiatives
- Employment of trained personnel for humane and skillful child welfare interventions
- Persistent and consistent concern for the quality of care
- Instilling children with values that promote responsible citizenship and social responsibility
- Development of personal and racial pride by means of programs that preserve racial heritage and promote social justice
- Dedication, commitment, and concern for others

The contemporary crisis in youth services is complicated by the increasing prevalence of drugs, gang involvement, and violent juvenile crimes. As the child welfare system continues to seek innovations, current initiatives for African American children should be informed by the past. The present account suggests that, at a minimum, quality child welfare services for the African American community should involve the training, hiring, and continued professional development of all child welfare workers by means of such opportunities as those available in the Title IV-E training grants. Communities that still have a shortage of African American and other minority social workers should develop aggressive efforts to ensure the inclusion of these workers in hiring and training efforts. Diversity training and promotion of culturally sensitive assessment and intervention strategies should be included in supervision and staff development. Social support network analysis and the inclusion of these networks in child welfare service plans are also important goals [Thompson & Peebles-Wilkins 1992; Tracy 1990]. ◆

References

Aery, W. A. (1915, November). Helping wayward girls. *Southern Workman*, 598–604. Hampton, VA: Peabody Collection, Hampton University.

Aery, W. A. (1919, October). Industrial Home School for Colored Girls at Peake in Hanover County, VA. *Southern Workman*, 473–474. Hampton, VA: Peabody Collection, Hampton University.

An industrial school for wayward girls. (1913, July 3). *New York Age*. Hampton, VA: Peabody Clipping Book 28, Huntington Memorial Library, Hampton University.

Axinn, J., & Levin, H. (1982). *Social welfare: A history of the American response to need* (2nd ed.). New York: Longman Press.

Barrett, J. P. (1926, August). The Virginia Industrial School. *Southern Workman*, 55, 352–361. Hampton, VA: Peabody Collection, Hampton University.

Billingsley, A., & Giovannoni, J. M. (1972). *Children of the storm: Black children and American child welfare*. New York: Harcourt, Brace, Jovanovich, Inc.

Carrie Steele-Pitts Home, Inc. 100 Years, 1888–1988: Share the legacy. (1988). Atlanta, GA: Author.

Chambers, C. A. (1963). *Seedtimes of reform*. Minneapolis, MN: University of Minnesota Press.

Child jailings decline in Virginia. (1976). Richmond, VA: Education and Schools Industrial, Juvenile Delinquency Clipping Files, Richmond Public Library.

Daniel, S. (1931). *Women builders*. Washington DC: Associated Publishers.

Davis, J. E. (1920, August). A Virginia asset: The Virginia Industrial School for Colored Girls. *Southern Workman, 49*, 357–364. Hampton, VA: Peabody Collection, Hampton University.

Hampton woman honored. (1916, February 23). *Amsterdam News*. Hampton, VA: Peabody Clipping Book 28, Huntington Memorial Library, Hampton University.

Harrison, D. (1985). C.C. Carstens: Permanency planning pioneer. *Child Welfare, 64*, 587–597.

Janie Porter Barrett School for Girls. (1956, February). *Virginia Welfare Bulletin, 34*(2), 9. Richmond, VA: Education and Schools Industrial, Juvenile Delinquency Clipping Files, Richmond Public Library.

Kogut, A. (1972). The settlements and ethnicity: 1890–1914. *Social Work, 17*, 22–31.

Ludlow, H. (1904). Virginia Negro Reform School. *Southern Workman, 33*, 606–616. Hampton, VA: Peabody Collection, Hampton University.

Negro Home School building to be dedicated. (1916, May 9). *Leader*. Hampton, VA: Peabody Clipping Book 28, Huntington Memorial Library, Hampton University.

Ogbu, J. (1978). *Minority education and caste*. New York: Academic Press.

Peebles-Wilkins, W. (1987). Janie Porter Barrett (1865–1948). In A. Minahan, (Editor-in-Chief), *Encyclopedia of social work 2*, (pp. 914–915). Washington, DC: National Association of Social Workers.

Peebles-Wilkins, W. (1989). Black women and American social welfare: The life of Fredericka Douglass Sprague Perry. *Affilia, 4*(1), 33–44.

Schools for wayward girls. (1916, February 6). *Chicago Defender*. Hampton, VA: Peabody Clipping Book 28, Huntington Memorial Library, Hampton University.

Scott, A. F. (1992). Janie Porter Barrett. In D.C. Hine (Ed.), *Black women in America: An historical encyclopedia*, (pp. 90–92). New York: Carlson Publishing Company.

Smith, E. P. (1991). Promoting policy change through funding withdrawal: The Race Discrimination Amendment of 1942. Presentation at Social Welfare History Group Symposium, Council on Social Work Education, Atlanta, GA, March, 1991.

Stehno, S. M. (1988). Public responsibility for dependent black children: The advocacy of Edith Abbott and Sophonisba Breckinridge. *Social Service Review*, 485–489.

Terrell, M. C. (1899). The duty of the National Association of Colored Women to the race. *Church Review* (pp. 340–354). In Mary Church Terrell Papers. Washington, DC: Moorland-Spingarn Research Center, Howard University.

Thompson, M., & Peebles-Wilkins, W. (1992). The impact of formal, informal, and societal support networks on the psychological well-being of black adolescent mothers. *Social Work, 37*, 322–328.

Tracy, E. M. (1990). Identifying social support resources of at-risk families. *Social Work, 35*, 252–258.

8

FROM INDENTURE TO FAMILY FOSTER CARE: A BRIEF HISTORY OF CHILD PLACING

Tim Hacsi

Americans have always arranged for some children to be reared by adults other than their own parents. In colonial America, children from all classes were indentured into new homes to learn a trade. In the 1850s, the Children's Aid Society began sending impoverished urban children to western states to be placed in rural homes. By 1900, some private placing agencies were making board payments to foster parents. Over the course of the twentieth century, boarding out developed into the modern family foster care system as social work gained prominence and the role of state and federal governments in child welfare grew.

Tim Hacsi, Ph.D., is Postdoctoral Fellow, Chapin Hall Center for Children, University of Chicago, Chicago, IL.

Throughout American history, some children from impoverished families have always been reared in the homes of other people, but the *ways* that they were cared for have changed. In colonial America, children from all classes were sometimes indentured to families where they were to live, work, and learn a trade; this was an especially common way of caring for orphans and other dependent children, but it was seen as appropriate for children from other classes as well. Between 1800 and 1850, orphan asylums became a widespread way of caring for children from impoverished families; at the same time, changing conceptions of childhood helped narrow the use of indenture to children from very poor families. In the 1850s, a variation on indenture, placing-out, began moving children from poor urban families to rural homes. Unlike indenture, placing-out was based on an anti-urban, anti-immigrant ideology. In the 1880s and 1890s, some agencies began to pay foster parents for boarding young children, so that the children would not be forced to work, as well as for caring for children who were difficult to live with or who had special needs. This boarding-out system gradually evolved into the modern family foster care system as government became increasingly involved in the welfare of children.

Certain underlying elements have always shaped the ways that impoverished children were treated. Parental poverty has always increased the risk of children being removed from their families and placed elsewhere, whether in other homes or institutions. Society's reluctance to provide sufficient aid to keep impoverished families together has made it necessary for private agencies and government officials to arrange care for children whose parents cannot care for them. Child abuse and neglect, much of which arises from the strains created by severe poverty, became headline news in the 1870s, and have been major public issues in recent decades.

The role of government in funding and supervising child welfare has grown gradually over the past century. Between 1900 and 1930, the gradual professionalization of social work went hand in hand with increased government involvement in child welfare to cause a shift toward the boarding-out system and away from institutional care of children. But institutional care and child placement are not opposing systems; whichever has been the dominant system has always made use of the other as a supplement. A century ago, orphan asylums often placed children with families for indenture or adoption, and in the late twentieth century, institutions and other forms of group care function as part of the out-of-home care system.

Changing conceptions of the nature of childhood have also played an important role in shaping child placement systems. In colonial America, children were viewed as miniature adults who were expected to grow up as quickly as possible. Teaching children the value of hard work and the skills of a trade was at the heart of indenture. In the early nineteenth century, a new view of childhood as a separate stage of life emerged. Childhood began to be seen as a stage of innocence that should be cultivated and nurtured; children should be allowed to be children, not turned into small adults as quickly as possible. Some reformers saw it as essential that children be removed from impoverished families in crowded cities and placed in "pure" rural settings. Today, the out-of-home care system is populated by children who are deemed neglected by standards of child care that would have seemed very strange to colonial parents.

Indenture and the Rise of Orphan Asylums

In the eighteenth century, local government officials known as the overseers of the poor were charged with distributing poor relief. These officials had the authority to indenture children from poor families in lieu of providing relief, and they did so regularly. In the colonial era, the duties of masters under indenture were spelled out in practical terms: children were to be fed, clothed, housed, and taught skills. Some children were taught to read and write, but education was not a universal component of indenture contracts. The indenture relationship was primarily economic rather than emotional or psychological in nature [Folks 1900; Kelso 1922; Mintz & Kellogg 1988].

Though many impoverished children were indentured by public officials, some parents entered into indenture agreements without any government involvement. Although used as a placement for children from low-income families, indenture in colonial America was by no means limited to children of the poor. It was commonplace for children from families that were not poor to be sent to other people's homes at the age of 13 or 14. Sometimes a formal contract of indenture was drawn up; in other cases the arrangement was informal [Mintz & Kellogg 1988; Cray 1988].

In the first few decades of the nineteenth century, an urban middle class emerged with a new conception of childhood as a distinct phase of human development. Children's characters were to be shaped not by breaking their wills as in the colonial era, but by leading them to internalize beliefs about behavior and morality [Ryan 1981]. Consequently, children stayed at home longer, and child-rearing methods changed.

By the early nineteenth century, indenture was no longer used by all classes; only children from low-income families were indentured. Public officials continued to indenture orphans, half-orphans, and other dependent children whose parents were unable to provide for them or were for some reason deemed unfit. Masters had to meet somewhat higher expectations about what to provide apprentices. For example, after Pennsylvania established free public schooling in 1834, masters were legally required to supply indentured children with "three months schooling" each year [Heffner 1913: 146]. Although still widely used, indenture was clearly on the wane by the middle of the nineteenth century. Indenture contracts were still employed on occasion in the early twentieth century, but they were a rarity, having been gradually supplanted by other child welfare services half a century earlier.

In a reaction to the cholera epidemic of 1832 and poverty in the nation's rapidly growing urban centers, numerous religious and charitable organizations founded orphan asylums. Although institutional care has often been seen as competing with indenture and other plans that place children with families, in practice the services were often used conjointly. Many orphan asylum superintendents placed small children with families where they would receive more individual attention than was possible in an asylum. Asylums also indentured older children in the hope that they would learn a trade, although by the late nineteenth century asylums were increasingly likely to provide some form of manual training within the institution itself [Porter 1984; Hacsi 1993].

Nevertheless, between 1830 and 1860 orphan asylums became the nation's predominant method of caring for dependent children. By the 1880s, however, orphan asylums were facing heavy criticism, usually accompanied by arguments favoring placing children with families. It was no coincidence that Charles Loring Brace, the most famous critic of asylums, was also the nation's most influential advocate of placing-out. Under Brace's guidance, the old concept of indenture took on a new form that shared as much with modern day family foster care as with indenture.

Placing-Out

In 1853, the idea of placing children in homes rather than institutions gained new life when Brace founded the New York Children's Aid Society (CAS). CAS's fundamental assumption was that children should be placed in rural homes rather than in institutions. Brace was anti-urban, anti-immigrant, and anti-Catholic. Like many reformers in the second half of the nineteenth century, he idealized rural America and feared urban growth. As a result, CAS's child-placing approach combined anti-institutional thought with anti-urban fears by trying to place children from urban slums in the country, usually with Protestant farmers [Brace 1893; Katz 1986].

Children came to CAS in a variety of ways. Agents swept the streets looking for street children and vagrants who did not have homes. Orphan asylums and infant asylums brought children to CAS, as did public officials. Most child-placing agencies that came into existence later found homes for their children within a day's travel of their original homes, but CAS wanted to move children as far from the city as possible. The CAS "orphan trains" became famous. Aside from the distance children traveled, these placements were similar to those made by asylums. Younger children were to be taken in and cared for as members of the family. Older children were expected to perform a considerable amount of work on the farms where they were placed. CAS avoided using indenture contracts because it considered them too binding, but older children were placed largely in response to the needs of rural western states for more farm labor. In this respect, placing-out was quite like informal indenture.

A 14- or 15-year-old child working for a living was commonplace in the late nineteenth century. Middle-class children might still be in school at that age, but working-class and impoverished children were almost always employed to help their families.

CAS's rationale for shifting children from their biological parents to new homes, however, was a dramatic departure from the ideas behind indenture. On the one hand, children had been indentured as a way to prepare them for adult life and work. Only rarely had children been indentured out of a desire to sever ties between child and parent. On the other hand, CAS's placing-out system was designed to "protect" children from the urban environment and from their own parents, who were presumed to be unworthy individuals incapable of rearing children properly. All ties between children and their biological parents were to be ended [Brace 1872].

Like orphan asylums and other nineteenth century charities designed for the poor, child-placing organizations were usually founded by individuals or groups with strong religious views; unlike orphan asylums, however, the placing organizations were almost always Protestant. Denominational groups often founded their own agencies: by the mid-1850s, for example, the Home

Missionary Society of Philadelphia, a Methodist Episcopal organization, had added placing dependent children in rural homes to its other activities [Clement 1979].

Although some Catholic groups did place children in families, they usually favored institutional care, partly because of the difficulty in finding rural Catholic homes for placement [Doherty 1910]. But the few Catholic agencies that regularly placed children in families used placing-out as a complement to Catholic orphan asylums; unlike CAS, they were not opposed to institutional care.

The desire to remove children from supposedly unworthy, perhaps even dangerous, parents created a sense of urgency among placing-out advocates. Brace's writings were suffused with a sense of impending disaster, and he was hardly alone. When Edmond T. Dooley became superintendent of the San Francisco Boys and Girls Aid Society in 1882, he actively sought out children, removing them from their own homes or taking them in off the streets, and placed them under the agency's care. Dooley's haste was so great that children were placed in families without the agency bothering to gain legal custody of them; adults who applied for children were not investigated, and placed children were not visited [Shackelford 1991].

Placing agencies usually found homes by advertising for them, but rarely bothered to screen the respondents. After children were placed, agencies maintained little or no contact with them. Even when agencies wanted to check up on placement homes, insufficient funds often kept them from doing so [Brace 1893]. Those agencies that did check on children often found that placements were not working, and that the children had to be moved. Children under the care of Pennsylvania's Children's Aid Society for more than a year, for example, often experienced four or more placements [Clement 1979].

Just as placing-out advocates had criticized orphan asylums for producing "institutional" children unprepared to function as self-reliant citizens, asylum supporters criticized placing-out agencies because they did not carefully examine the new homes they found for their children. In particular, Catholics attacked CAS for placing Catholic children in Protestant homes. In the late nineteenth century, placing agencie's methods of finding homes began to change; at least partly in response to criticism, they began to recognize that not *all* rural homes were automatically *good* homes. Some agencies' investigations of prospective homes became more thorough; neighbors and influential community members, such as ministers, were interviewed before the placing of children [Clement 1979]. Not surprisingly, the more careful the examination of prospective placement homes, the lower the rate of acceptance.

Children under the age of five who were placed were the most likely to be adopted (whether legally or de facto) by their new parents. An 1884 survey conducted by Hastings H. Hart found that children placed before the age of 12 were more likely to stay throughout the terms of their placement than were older children. Unfortunately, most placements seem to have involved older children. Of the more than 22,000 children placed in "permanent" homes by CAS between 1854 and 1900, over 17,400 (78%) were older than 10. Since most placement homes wanted children who could work to earn their keep, a disparity existed between the best age for children to be placed and the requests from potential parents [Doherty 1910; Ross 1977].

A disparity also existed between what placement agencies wanted and what the parents of the children wanted. In the late nineteenth century, placing-out (like institutional care) was often used by families to help them weather difficult times brought on by a death, serious illness, or long period of unemployment. The majority of children who entered the care of placement agencies were brought by parents or other relatives, many of whom tried to reclaim their children when the family was back on its feet. Despite the hopes of most placing-out advocates, many children returned to their families within a few years of being placed elsewhere [Hacsi 1993; Clement 1979].

In the last quarter of the nineteenth century, child abuse and parental neglect began to be recognized as important problems. During the 1870s, Societies for the Prevention of Cruelty to Children (SPCC) began to appear in eastern cities. SPCCs often removed children from abusive or neglectful homes and placed them in other homes or orphan asylums; courts granted these societies what amounted to police powers to remove children when they saw fit [Gordon 1988]. Largely as a result of the work of the SPCCs, other agencies and governments began to acknowledge the existence of child abuse and neglect. In the 1890s, Massachusetts recognized "three classes of children" in its "child-saving" work: dependent children whose main problem was poverty, neglected children, and juvenile offenders. The main problem of dependent children was their family's poverty, but neglected children were "the offspring of parents who *can*, but *do not*, provide suitably for them, and whose vicious lives render them unfit to have the care of them" [Richardson 1893: 54]. In practice, once children were in the child welfare system, "dependent" and "neglected" children were treated the same. The line distinguishing dependent children from neglected children was elusive. Though some of these parents undoubtedly were "bad" parents, most were simply impoverished.

Boarding-Out

Expectations about how much a child should work and about the relative importance of emotional ties between parent and child shaped views about how children should be treated in placement homes. Older children placed in "free" homes, like indentured children, were expected to work to earn their keep. Younger children were not expected to work; they were to be taken in for love. Ironically, placement agencies began making payments to foster families in an effort to ensure that children would not be valued exclusively for their labor.

In the 1880s, Boston's Temporary Home for the Destitute began to make board payments to families. During the 1890s, board payments completely replaced the agency's previous method of free placements [Tyor & Zainaldin 1979]. The State Primary School of Massachusetts also began experimenting with placing children under age 10 in boarding homes in 1882 [Fee 1910]. In 1893, Homer Folks wrote that another reason for boarding-out was that otherwise it might prove impossible to find homes for "children who are unattractive in appearance or who have some slight physical, mental, or moral defect or peculiarity which turns the balance against them when foster parents are making their choice" [Bremner 1971: 325].

Changing to boarding-out led placing agencies to look more closely at the situation within the placement home. After all, agencies did not want to pay people to rear children unless they were doing a good job. For example, the State Primary School checked much more closely on its placement homes where children were boarded than agencies using "free" placement homes had customarily done. In Massachusetts, no family could take in more than two children unless they were siblings, and only state wards came into the boarding system [Calkins 1886].

Between 1880 and 1920, the question of whether to pay adults who took in other people's children complicated the debate on home placement versus institutional care. When the 1899 National Conference of Charities and Corrections came out in favor of home placement over institutional care for dependent children, it did not take a stand on whether board payments should be made [Proceedings 1899]. Supporters of free placements feared that if money were paid to some foster parents, the pool of free homes would dry up. Supporters of board payment hoped to ensure that young children were not worked to earn their keep. Gradually, boarding-out won the battle, but it took more than half a century. In the South, where child welfare developments lagged, placing-out remained far more common than boarding-out in the late 1920s; in fact, orphan asylums still held far more children than placement homes [Duke 1930: 66–67].

The growing popularity of boarding-out, sometimes known as foster care, was intimately tied to the growth of the juvenile court system in the three decades after 1900. Although some dependent children had come under court supervision throughout American history, the creation of a court system specifically for minors greatly increased the number of children who became state wards. Juvenile courts spoke a great deal about maintaining families. In practice, however, they were far more prone to remove children from their parents than to try to help the family as a whole. In many states, mothers' pensions, the successor to outdoor relief and the predecessor of Aid to Families with Dependent Children, were awarded on the basis of an investigation by an officer of the juvenile court. If the officer found the mother to be unworthy of aid, as often happened, the result might be worse for the family than if the family had not sought help. In such cases, the court might remove the child to a foster home [Pelton 1989].

The growing involvement of government in child welfare, first at the state and later at the federal level, was a central reason for the expansion of foster care in the twentieth century. The rise of the juvenile court, which now plays a crucial role in the out-of-home care system, is the most obvious example, but not the only one. State Boards of Charity, which proliferated in the late nineteenth century and gained increased powers during the Progressive Era, strongly favored home placement over asylums. The 1906 Biennial Report of California's State Board of Charities and Corrections reflected most states' attitudes:

> The best place for a child is a good home. The asylums, however good work they may do, are unnatural and can not be a parent. The State should encourage the placing out of all children possible into good homes. They should be placed out at as early an age as possible, so that they

can grow up in the family and become a part of it. [Biennial 1906: 127]

Although California's state government made regular payments to orphan asylums to care for dependent children, it did not make payments to families caring for dependent children. Even though many private placing agencies had already begun to shift from free to boarding placements, the state legislature favored placing-out. The legislature was trying to save money by shifting away from asylum care, and boarding-out was far more expensive than placing-out. There were also philosophical reasons for California's shift away from asylum care; placing-out was intended to break all ties between "bad" parents and their children. In fact, the state board's next biennial report called for increasing judicial powers so that courts could "sever forever the parent's right and control over the child" if that parent was morally "delinquent," or if the parent had "abandoned" a child by failing to pay an asylum's fees, thus leaving the state responsible [Biennial 1908: 169]. The argument made half a century earlier by Brace and other reformers still had resonance for many.

When a state government became involved in placing or boarding children in homes, some manner of state regulation usually followed. As in many other aspects of child welfare, California acted well before most other states. By 1915, California was licensing and regulating, if only loosely, agencies that found placement homes for children [Biennial 1915]. By 1920, California was making payments to boarding homes, including those arranged by private agencies, so long as the children had been "committed by the juvenile courts of the state as needy" [Biennial 1918: 24].

By the 1920s, placing-out had been replaced by boarding-out in a number of cities. In New Orleans, placing-out had "ceased to be of great value except as a preliminary stage toward adoption" of small children, but boarding children with foster families was an important new development in the city's child welfare work.

It worked so well with dependent children that delinquent children were also being placed in boarding homes [Carstens 1926: 480–481]. Though placing-out still existed, it was clearly going out of vogue. In the 1920s, even CAS stopped its orphan train shipments of children to the rural West [Holt 1992].

Foster Care

By the 1930s, it was becoming clear that boarding-out was outpacing both institutional care and free placing-out. The decline of the latter methods became certain with the creation of Aid to Dependent Children (ADC, later AFDC) as Title IV of the Social Security Act in 1935. Under ADC, available federal funds that could be used to keep impoverished families together rose dramatically. As a result, many families that previously would have turned to an orphan asylum or child placement agency were able to keep their children at home. At the same time, the increasing financial involvement of state governments in the child welfare system meant that when children were removed from their homes, they were more likely to be boarded in a family than placed in an asylum. By 1950, more children were in foster homes than in institutions; by 1960, almost twice as many children were in foster care as were in institutions; and, in 1968, more than three times as many children were in foster care as in institutions [U.S. Department of Health, Education, and Welfare 1968].

In the 1940s and 1950s, as foster care expanded and the use of asylums declined, the total number of dependent children being cared for outside of their own homes stayed relatively stable, between 3.5 and 4.5 per thousand children under the age of 18 [U.S. Department of Health, Education, and Welfare 1968]. During the 1960s and 1970s, however, the foster care population exploded, reaching a peak in the late 1970s [Pelton 1989]. The most important factor driving skyrocketing foster care populations during this period was the rediscovery of child abuse.

Research during the 1950s led some physicians to conclude that large numbers of parents were abusing their children. In 1962, an article entitled "The Battered-Child Syndrome" was published in an important medical journal; in short order, the popular press was running feature articles on child abuse [Nelson 1984]. In fact, more children enter foster care due to neglect than abuse, although the lines between the two are often blurry, just as the distinction between neglect and simple poverty has never been absolutely clear.

Federal funding was an additional reason for the dramatic rise in foster care populations between 1960 and 1977. Although federal funds became directly available for foster care in urban areas in 1951, the amount of securable money became meaningful only in 1961. At that time, rules regarding AFDC payments were changed to allow payments for children in foster care whose biological families were eligible. Later amendments to the Social Security Act, Titles IV-B and XX, also made federal money available for foster care [Cox & Cox 1985]. In 1961, Title IV-A of the Social Security Act made federal matching payments available to states *only* for children placed in foster care by a court decision, whose families also meet other AFDC requirements. The availability of federal AFDC money for foster care clearly helped spur the growth of foster care caseloads. By 1976, the number of children in AFDC foster care was well over 100,000 [U.S. General Accounting Office 1977].

The most important federal legislation of recent years regarding foster care is the Adoption Assistance and Child Welfare Act of 1980. This act targets money toward preventive services and efforts aimed at reuniting families, thus attempting to shift policy away from family breakup and toward family maintenance. The argument that children should be kept with their families whenever possible, and reunited with their families as quickly as possible if they must be temporarily removed, fights against the ideology that has driven child placement since Charles Loring Brace's time. In practice, family preservation programs have been implemented in many states over the past decade, and have had mixed results. Not surprisingly, given the history of child welfare, family preservation and reunification programs are often criticized for keeping children with "unfit" parents.

Although AFDC and foster care are separate systems (aside from the federal funding sometimes available for foster care), the availability and generosity of AFDC clearly affects the number of families that come under the jurisdiction of foster care. The purchasing power of AFDC grants has dropped dramatically since 1970. In 1990 inflation-adjusted dollars, the median monthly AFDC grant for a family of three with no other income fell from $601 in 1970 to just $364 in 1990 [Johnson et al. 1991].

Under these conditions, it should be no surprise that, after dropping in the late 1970s and early 1980s, the number of children in foster care has risen rapidly over the last decade. This recent urban surge in the foster care population has other important aspects: the number of infants under one year of age in foster care has risen; in some cities, many children are born addicted to drugs, including crack. Not only are more children entering foster care but, on the average, they are staying longer. The combined effect of more admissions and lengthier stays has been a foster care population that is growing by leaps and bounds [Goerge et al. 1994].

An important additional reason for the increase in foster care caseloads has been the growing popularity of foster placement with relatives, that is, kinship care. By 1990, formal kinship foster care had become an important part of foster care services. Informal care by relatives, however, has always been used for large numbers of children without viable parents, and remains far more common. Between 1980 and 1992, the number of children being reared by their grandparents rose from two to three million, a number that dwarfs the foster care population [Tedford 1992].

Today, the foster care system serves a population whose central problem is poverty, as it always has been. Tragically, however, the children now coming into foster care are poorer, younger, and far more troubled than those in the past, and they are staying in care for longer periods of time.

Conclusion

One crucial thread in the history of child placement is the role played by state governments as they became increasingly involved in child welfare. Governments almost always preferred placing and boarding children over institutional care, took far more care than private agencies in investigating prospective foster homes, and usually made it clear that the child remained a state ward who could be removed at any time. In the twentieth century, government worked hand-in-hand with new professions, particularly social work, to shape child welfare.

One of the most dramatic differences between placing-out and today's foster care system is that foster care is usually intended to provide temporary care for children, with the hope that they can someday be returned to their parents. Whereas a century ago placing-out advocates sought to break up families, today's foster care system hopes to reunite families, so long as the home provides a safe environment for children. Or at least that is the law; in practice, old habits die hard.

In fact, the question of whether families should be kept together or children should be permanently removed from their parents remains. Current debates over whether families should receive services or lose their children echo those of the past. The questions asked by Homer Folks in 1921 are still relevant:

> Whenever the question arises of removing a child from its home, I wish that three questions might be asked and objectively answered: first, is there any real and conclusive reason why the child should not stay where it is? Second, what is lacking in his present home which we deem necessary for the child's care, and just how is that

particular thing going to be provided under our proposed plan? Third, how much will our proposed plan cost and would that sum, if used to assist the child in his own home, secure better results? [Folks 1921: 82]

These questions remain at the heart of decisions made every day by social workers; they are also at the center of debates over how to reform the foster care system. Perhaps realizing that they are very old questions, and that they have already been answered in a number of ways, can make the current debate more productive, and help the children who, through no fault of their own, enter the foster care system. ◆

References

Brace, C. L. (1872). *The dangerous classes of New York and twenty years' work among them.* New York: Wynkoop & Hallenbeck.

Brace, C. L. (1893). The Children's Aid Society of New York: Its history, plan, and results. In National Conference of Charities and Corrections (Eds.), *History of child saving in the United States.* Montclair, NJ: Paterson Smith (1971 reprint edition).

Bremner, R. H. (Ed.). (1971). *Children and youth in America: A documentary history.* Volume II: 1866–1932 (Parts 1–6). Cambridge, MA: Harvard University Press.

Calkins, A. A. (1886). Boarding out of dependent children in Massachusetts. In *Proceedings of the 13th National Conference of Charities and Correction.* Boston: George H. Ellis.

Carstens, C. C. (1926). A social audit of child welfare work as a whole in New Orleans, with special reference to community planning. In *Proceedings of the 53rd National Conference of Social Work.* Chicago: University of Chicago Press.

Clement, P. F. (1979). Families and foster care: Philadelphia in the late nineteenth century. *Social Service Review, 53,* 406–420.

Cox, M. J., & Cox, R.D. (1985). A brief history of policy for dependent and neglected children. In M. J. Cox & R. D. Cox (Eds.), *Foster care: Current issues, policies, and practices.* Norwood, NJ: Ablex Publishing Corporation.

Cray, R. E., Jr. (1988). *Paupers and poor relief in New York City and its rural environs, 1700–1830.* Philadelphia: Temple University Press.

Doherty, W. J. (1910). Placing-out of children. In *Proceedings of the First National Conference of Catholic Charities,* Washington, DC.

Duke Endowment. (1931). *Sixth annual report of the orphan section.* Charlotte, NC: Press of Presbyterian Standard Publishing Company.

Fee, J. E. (1910). Massachusetts system of boarding out children. In *Proceedings of the First National Conference of Catholic* Charities, Washington, DC.

Folks, H. (1900). *The care of destitute, neglected, and delinquent children.* Albany, NY: J. B. Lyon Company.

Folks, H. (1921). New values in the field of child welfare: In terms of conventional child-caring work. In *Proceedings of the 48th National Conference of Social Work.* Chicago: University of Chicago Press.

Goerge, R. M., Wulczyn, F. H., & Harden, A. W. (1994). *Foster care dynamics: California, Illinois 1983–1992: A first-year report from the Multistate Foster Care Data Archive.* Chicago: Chapin Hall Center for Children, University of Chicago.

Gordon, L. (1988). *Heroes of their own lives: The politics and history of family violence.* New York: Penguin Books.

Hacsi, T. A. (1993). *"A plain and solemn duty": A history of orphan asylums in America* (Doctoral Dissertation, University of Pennsylvania).

Heffner, W. C. (1913). *History of poor relief legislation in Pennsylvania, 1682–1913.* Cleona, PA: Holzapfel Publishing Company.

Holt, M. I. (1992). *The orphan trains: Placing out in America.* Lincoln, NE: University of Nebraska Press.

Johnson, C. M., Miranda, L., Sherman, A., & Weill, J. D. (1991). *Child poverty in America* Washington, DC: Children's Defense Fund.

Katz, M. B. (1986). *In the shadow of the poorhouse: A social history of welfare in America.* New York: Basic Books, Inc.

Kelso, R. W. (1922). *The history of public poor relief in Massachusetts: 1620–1920.* Boston: Houghton Mifflin Company.

Mintz, S., & Kellogg, S. (1988). *Domestic revolutions: A social history of American family life.* New York: The Free Press.

National Conference of Charities and Corrections. (1899). *Proceedings of the 26th Annual National Conference of Charities and Corrections.* Boston: George H. Ellis.

Nelson, B. J. (1984). *Making an issue of child abuse: Political agenda setting for social problems.* Chicago: University of Chicago Press.

Pelton, L. H. (1989). *For reasons of poverty: A critical analysis of the public child welfare system in the United States.* New York: Praeger.

Porter, S. L. (1984). *The benevolent asylum—image and reality: The care and training of female orphans in Boston, 1800–1840* (Doctoral Dissertation, Boston University).

Richardson, A. B. (1893). The Massachusetts system of caring for state minor wards. In National Conference of Charities and Corrections (Ed.), *History of child saving in the United States.* Montclair, NJ: Paterson Smith (1971 reprint edition).

Ross, C. J. (1977). *Society's children: The care of indigent youngsters in New York City, 1875–1903* (Doctoral Dissertation, Yale University).

Ryan, M. P. (1981). *Cradle of the middle class: The family in Oneida County, New York, 1790–1865.* Cambridge, MA: Cambridge University Press.

Shackelford, R. (1991). *To shield them from temptation: "Child-saving" institutions and the children of the underclass in San Francisco, 1850–1910.* (Doctoral Dissertation, Harvard University).

State Board of Charities and Corrections of the State of California. (1906–1922). *Biennial reports.* Sacramento, CA: Superintendent State Printing.

Tedford, D. (1992, June 22). A tough role for grandparents. *The Houston Chronicle.*

Tyor, P. L., & Zainaldin, J. S. (1979). Asylum and society: An approach to institutional change. *Journal of Social History, 13,* 23–48.

U.S. Department of Health, Education, and Welfare. (1968). *Child Welfare Statistics, 1968.* Washington, DC: U.S. Government Printing Office.

U.S. General Accounting Office. (1977). *Children in foster care institutions—Steps government can take to improve their care.* Washington, DC: U.S. Government Printing Office.

9

A HISTORY OF PLACING-OUT: THE ORPHAN TRAINS

Jeanne F. Cook

Between 1854 and 1930, the placing-out or orphan train strategy, considered to be the forerunner of modern family foster care, relocated approximately 150,000 children and youths from the city of New York to families in the Midwest. The program was designed to give children who were orphaned or from impoverished urban families an opportunity to live with rural families to increase their chances to become productive citizens as adults. This article summarizes the implementation of placing-out, including contributing social conditions, the underlying philosophy, the basic components, and professional and public perceptions. Implications of the orphan trains for current child welfare policies and practice are considered.

Jeanne F. Cook, Ph.D., LISW, is Policy Specialist, South Carolina Department of Social Services, Columbia, SC, and Part-Time Instructor, College of Social Work, University of South Carolina.

One of the central issues of poverty with which American society has struggled involves assisting people who are poor without making those people indefinitely dependent on public support. Traditionally, providing assistance to individuals whose poverty was due to circumstances beyond their control has encountered less resistance than helping other groups of people. Though children generally have been categorized as "deserving," the motivation for providing assistance to them has not always appeared to reflect that sentiment. This article examines the development, implementation, and discontinuance of placing-out programs for poor children from New York City. These programs, operated between 1853 and 1930, placed approximately 150,000 children with families for family foster care and adoption.

Placing-Out: The Orphan Train Strategy

In the mid-nineteenth century, Charles Loring Brace [1880] and the Children's Aid Society (CAS) [1893] argued that the agency's programs would fill an existing gap in services by providing for children for whom there was no room in orphanages and those for whom an orphanage was inappropriate. Brace and CAS also argued that institutional care did not prepare children for life in the community and that most children did not want to go to orphanages. Orphanages were criticized for their selective admission policies, generally made on the basis of race/ethnicity and religion; their use of harsh discipline systems; their administrative freedom to discharge children arbitrarily; their overcrowding; their inability to accommodate the growing number of children in need of care as a result of immigration and the Civil War; and the disproportionate number of immigrant children in placement [Bremner 1970; Downs & Sherraden 1983; Kitterson 1968; Letchworth 1893].

Despite the diversity of services offered by CAS, the placing-out system is the one program for which the agency and Brace are most often remembered, credited, and criticized. This was the most ambitious and controversial program undertaken by CAS. Although the concept of placing children with families to whom the children were not related originated neither with CAS nor in the United States, the agency's placing-out system was significant in several ways. It was the first extensive and systematic placing-out program initiated by a charitable organization [Wheeler 1983]. In addition, the program differed from the indenture system in which children were legally apprenticed to families and paid for their work. One policy of the CAS program was that the agency or the biological parents would retain custody of any child placed unless adoption was requested by the foster parents and legal requirements for adoption were met. Another important distinction from indenture was the program's emphasis on finding families for children as opposed to the employment arrangements common to indenture programs [Brace 1880; Children's Aid Society 1893; Langsam 1964; Nelson 1987; Young & Marks 1990].

Children were selected for the program in various ways. Some children were already participating in one of the agency's other programs. Some were referred from the courts, juvenile facilities, and other children's institutions. Some parents brought their children to the agency for placement. In addition, CAS's community agents, who worked in neighborhoods to encourage children to participate in other programs offered by the organization, also recruited children for placing-out [Children's Aid Society 1893; Nelson 1985; Wheeler 1983].

Children chosen to be placed out were considered orphaned, homeless, abandoned, dependent, or neglected. In reality, only a few were orphans, and many others had at least one living parent and housing of some sort. Unless children were actual orphans, parents were required to give their permission for the child's participation in the placement program. Children who were thought to be incorrigible, who appeared to be sickly, or who were physically or mentally handicapped were generally not accepted for participation. African American children also were excluded, possibly because of concern that the agency would be accused of practicing slavery or due to their small numbers in New York and the prejudices of both the sending and receiving communities [Children's Aid Society 1893; Fry 1974; Holt 1992; Langsam 1964; Nelson 1985; Patrick et al. 1990; Wheeler 1983; Young & Marks 1990].

After placing 207 children individually during the first year of the program, a decision was made in 1854 to send children in groups because more could be accomplished with little increase in cost or the magnitude of work. Before the initiation of a trip west for any group of children, a CAS agent visited various towns within the targeted states. The agent's tasks were twofold: promoting the children's arrival and appointing a selection committee that would be responsible for approving potential foster families and that would provide a linkage between the foster family, the child, and CAS [Children's Aid Society 1893; Langsam 1964; Nelson 1985; Patrick et al. 1990; Young & Marks 1990].

When needed, housing in one of the agency's group residences was provided for the children pending departure of the next scheduled trip to predesignated towns in the Midwest. Each child was given new clothing for the trip. A CAS agent and members of the caregiving staff accompanied each train that transported the children [Children's Aid Society 1893; Nelson 1985; Patrick et al. 1990; Wheeler 1983; Young & Marks 1990].

At each stop, the children left the train and were taken to a local community gathering place, usually a church, courthouse, or opera house. Some families had made previous arrangements to receive a particular child, but most often the children were lined up for interested adults to view and select. Children who were not chosen during this process would be transported to the next town for consideration, unless the agent tried to recruit a placement locally before the train departed [Nelson 1985; Patrick et al. 1990; Wheeler 1983; Young & Marks 1990].

CAS required that a child go with a family willingly and that the agent make a home visit before settling the placement. Families had to provide an education and proper care. In addition, either the family or the child could request an end to the placement, resulting in arrangements for an alternate family or the child's return to New York. CAS also required follow-up personal visits and correspondence with the children until they reached adulthood and were living on their own [Brace 1880; Children's Aid Society 1893; Langsam 1964; Nelson 1985; Patrick et al. 1990; Young & Marks 1990].

Between 1854 and 1930, approximately 150,000 children were placed by the CAS emigration program or one of the other organizations that modeled the CAS program. The children rode the trains to California, Colorado, Illinois, Indiana, Iowa, Kansas, Michigan, Minnesota, Missouri, Nebraska, Ohio, Texas, and Wisconsin. A small number of children were placed in southern states—Arkansas, Florida, Louisiana, North Carolina, South Carolina, and Virginia. Some children were placed within the rural areas of New York State and other northeastern states, such as Connecticut, Massachusetts, New Jersey, and Pennsylvania [Kitterson 1968; Langsam 1964; Wheeler 1983; Young & Marks 1990].

Another major New York-based emigration program was started in 1876 by the New York Foundling Home, which placed infants and preschool children in Catholic families. The Foundling Home's initiation of its program was based in part on a complaint expressed by the Catholic leadership that CAS was placing Catholic children with Protestant families in an effort to decrease the number of Catholics in the country [Kitterson 1968; Langsam 1964; Patrick et al. 1990; Wheeler 1983; Young & Marks 1990].

Public Perceptions

The community's understanding of the placing-out strategy and other CAS programs can be derived from the print media. From

1853 to the 1920s, much media attention was given to the circumstances of impoverished children in the city and the inadequacies of their parents. Descriptions of these children appeared to solicit public responses of pity and fear. For example, in "Homeless children" [1859] these children were described as born "into sin and poverty"; were identified with "tears, rage, dirt, and cruelty" during their formative years; and were likely to become "ulcers of society" unless intervention occurred. Impoverished parents of these same children were generally presented in the press as unsympathetic characters who constituted "a class from which spring mainly the great tides of wretchedness and crime."

Parents were seen as the source of their children's entry into criminality; the parents encouraged the children to contribute to the family's income by engaging in "semi-vagrant occupations" [Vagrancy among children 1881], such as selling newspapers or gathering rags and bones, or in small crimes such as stealing or begging [Our city charities 1860; Crime and charity. . . 1861]. The New York press also provided coverage of the organization, including articles that singled out the CAS placing-out program because it was accomplished "without expense to the public" [Children's Aid Society 1890] and had produced "the ripest fruits of the society's labors" [The Children's Aid Society 1902: 8]. As further evidence of the success of CAS, the press reported that "very few lapses into criminal life" were known among the children who had been placed-out [New York child saving 1895].

The Demise of the Placing-Out Program

By the latter part of the 1800s, placing-out supporters such as Jacob Riis [1894: 624, 625] acknowledged the contribution of the environment to the human problems of the poor. Riis pointed out that environmental conditions, the "influences and instincts of tenement life" and "the evil forces of the slums" contributed to poverty. Despite this recognition, both Riis and C. Loring Brace, the son of CAS's founder, concluded that saving the children by relocation was the most effective solution [New York child saving 1895].

The emigration program peaked in 1875 and began a steady decline, then ended in 1930 [Young & Marks 1990]. At the end, *Social Services Review* offered a complimentary description of the vision behind the program and the difficult times in which it had been carried out [An early adventure 1929: 75, 77, 78]. An editorial reminded readers to keep in mind "the condition of the dependent and neglected children of New York City in the days when there was almost no social work, public or private, in their behalf" and "no juvenile court to protect such a child." The editorial went on to identify Brace as "a great pioneer who had courage and faith, enthusiasm and tireless energy."

Reasons cited by some authors for the demise of the program included the initiation of new ways of coping with industrialization, the recognition of environmental factors as causes for some social problems, and the reforms of the Progressive Era, including compulsory school attendance and child labor laws. Another relevant development was the emergence of social work as a profession, which focused on new methods for working with impoverished children and families. Social workers promoted new and revised strategies, including publicly funded aid to mother-headed families to prevent the need for out-of-home care; the development of in-state family foster home programs; the promotion of temporary rather than permanent out-of-home care whenever possible; a more comprehensive approach to regulating agencies and monitoring out-of-home care resources; and the redesign of orphanages, using homelike cottages rather than large dormitories [Addams 1910; Ashby 1984; Bremner 1971; Costin 1983; Fry 1974; Hays 1957; Heale 1976b; Langsam 1964; Mangolin 1978; Minton 1893; Patrick et al. 1990; Stansell 1982; Takanishi 1978; Thurston 1930; Wheeler 1983; Wohl 1969; Young & Marks 1990].

By 1875, several states had passed laws limiting child immigration. Michigan first limited interstate placements of children in 1875 and in 1895 required the child's home state to post a bond, according to Langsam [1964]. In 1899, similar requirements were passed in Indiana, Illinois, and Minnesota. A 1901 Missouri law required that the home state's Board of Charities guarantee that the child was free from communicable or incurable diseases and was neither "vicious" nor mentally handicapped. Missouri also required that the sending state reclaim any child who became a ward of the state within five years of placement [Patrick et al. 1990].

Appraisal of the Orphan Train Approach

The effectiveness and appropriateness of placing-out as a plan for orphaned, homeless, and dependent children were widely debated during the last half of the nineteenth century. Since CAS had the largest and best known emigration program, much of the praise and criticism was directed at CAS and at Charles Loring Brace.

One of the earliest charges was the accusation from Catholics that the intent of the emigration program was the conversion of Catholic children to Protestantism. Critics alleged that this was being accomplished by placing Irish immigrant children with non-Catholic families. Other accusations were that children were being sold into slavery and that brothers and sisters, separated in placement and given the surnames of their foster parents, could meet as adults and marry without knowing they were related. Some critics charged that CAS was ridding New York City of its criminal-minded and otherwise undesirable children by sending them to unsuspecting midwestern families. Others argued that New York City was being deprived of future solid citizens because the *best* immigrant children were the ones who were being placed-out [Ashby 1984; Brophy 1972; Langsam 1964; Nelson 1985; Patrick et al. 1990; Wheeler 1983; Young & Marks 1990].

The process of screening potential families in receiving states was also criticized because of the possible hesitancy by local screening committees to deny approval to their neighbors. It was alleged that children were sometimes placed with families who abused or neglected them, or overworked them or evicted them. It was also said that bad situations went unnoticed by CAS agents, who made inadequate or infrequent follow-up contacts [Ashby 1984; Folks 1902; Langsam 1964; Nelson 1985; Patrick et al. 1990; Thurston 1930; Warner 1908; Wheeler 1983; Whol 1969; Young & Marks 1990].

Brace [1880] took the lead in defense of the emigration program. He denied charges of slavery and anti-Catholicism. He swore that both Catholics and Protestants served on the local selection committees and that children were offered homes by families of all religious faiths. He further reminded critics that older children were free to leave any placement they found unsatisfactory, since the emigration program was not indenture. Likewise, a family could request removal of any child who was deemed inappropriate. He also evaluated the accuracy of allegations of child abuse and neglect by families and of children's criminal activities. Though he reported that there was little evidence to support either concern, CAS did take steps to decrease the possibility that children would be mistreated. For example, several agents were permanently assigned to western states [Brace 1880; Brace 1894; Children's Aid Society 1893; Langsam 1964; Patrick et al. 1990; Thurston 1930; Young & Marks 1990; Warner 1908].

At the 1893 National Conference of Charities and Corrections, CAS reported that of the 84,318 children placed between 1853 and 1893, 85% had been placed successfully. Success was defined in terms of children who remained in foster homes and were not either returned to New York or placed locally in a correctional facility or orphanage. According to Thurston [1930], a similar study on placement outcomes conducted at 10-year periods between 1865 and 1905 was completed by George G. Ralph of the New York School of Social Work in 1923. The study found an increase in favorable results, that is, children who remained in placement, from the starting year to the end of the study period, but the study also noted unfavorable results for 38% of the boys and 20% of the girls by 1905.

Several retrospective studies have evaluated aspects of the emigration program strategy. Nelson [1980] concluded that Brace's plan grew from aroused public concern, had proven to be more economical than institutional care, and was the predecessor of modern family foster care. In a follow-up study, Nelson [1985] found that there was little evidence to support the belief that in-state placements were superior to the interstate placing-out program of CAS. Bellingham's [1984] study concluded that placements through CAS were generally intended to aid family economic circumstances by providing substitute caregiving or to serve as an entry into the labor force for an older child. In a later analysis of the same data, Bellingham [1986] found that (1) placements and custody transfers were initiated voluntarily with parental approval to help parents cope with structural life problems or to help older youths in transition to adulthood, and (2) placements were based on utility rather than on imposed designs of social control. Research by Ecks [1984] suggested that the arrangement for a purchase-of-service approach to out-of-home care was based on insistence within ethnic communities on family input into the religious beliefs to which foster children were exposed and the public's conviction that government officials were not the best source for determining children's values. An analysis by Holt [1992] concluded that "placing-out and the people it involved reflect the complexities of American life and growth" [p. 184], including America's expansion and the corresponding need for adequate labor to support western growth. According to Holt, the end of the placing-out program was also influenced by changes in American life, including early twentieth century social reforms, the development of social welfare theories that led to a holistic approach to serving children and families, the establishment of specialized training for working with the poor, and changes in rural regions that increased populations and decreased the need for imported labor.

The credibility of some criticisms of the placing-out program also has been confirmed, particularly in light of more current child welfare thinking. Research has indicated that sometimes siblings were separated for placement, some children were abused or neglected, approximately as many children were placed whose families were poor as children who were orphans or homeless, and some children were permanently removed from their biological families when a temporary separation would have sufficed [Langsam 1964; Patrick et al. 1990; Thurston 1930; Young & Marks 1990]. The present author conducted in-depth interviews with 25 individuals who had been placed by CAS or the New York Foundling Home during the latter decades of the placing-out program. Some of the findings have been identical to those noted by other researchers, including sibling separation, family poverty as a principal factor in some place-ments, and permanent removal from biological families in some situations in which temporary placement could have resolved the problems in the home. In addition, some participants in this study expressed concern over the quality of their placements, the lack of contact with their siblings after placement, prejudice in the communities in which some placements were made, and the failure of placement agencies to monitor some placements as promised. Some interviewees described circumstances in which they were treated by their adoptive or foster families as unpaid workers, more like slaves than family members.

Despite the identified flaws in the placing-out program, how-ever, Charles Loring Brace can be acknowledged as a pioneer who realized that the charitable services of his time were insuffi-cient to deal with the social problems of a rapidly changing society. Latter-day evaluators generally have concluded that the program was the forerunner of modern practices in child wel-fare, was well-intentioned, and can be understood best within the context of the times and environment in which the program operated [Ashby 1984; Heale 1976a; Holt 1992; Kitterson 1968; Langsam 1964; Nelson 1985; Patrick et al. 1990; Wohl 1969; Young & Marks 1990].

Conclusion

Some recent observers have noted similarities between the social problems of Brace's day and the current problems of urban America, which are resulting in an increasing reliance on out-of-home care [Cordasco 1971; Lindemann 1990; Mangolin 1978; National Child Welfare Resource Center 1991; Patrick et al. 1990]. Hartman [1990] identifies several problems, including those of an escalating number of low-income and/or homeless families and children, children damaged by alcohol and other drugs, and HIV-affected families.

Cordasco [1971], Lindemann [1990], Mangolin [1978], and Patrick et al. [1990] suggest that some past strategies may have implications for contemporary urban poverty and child welfare concerns, including Brace's pragmatic philosophy of reducing poverty through education, work, and change of environment. For example, one recent controversial proposal concerning diminishing adoptive and out-of-home care resources would reestablish an orphanage system in which a child's placement in institutional care would be permanent, regardless of the child's age at the time of placement [Ford & Kroll 1990; Research on effects of orphanages. . . 1990; Shaffer 1990; Stark 1990]. Another proposal surfaced during a 1991 child welfare teleconference on orphan trains held by the National Child Welfare Resource Center [1991]. One participant commented on the likely increase in the number of children worldwide who would be orphaned by AIDS. He suggested that the time might be right to initiate a modernized orphan train placement system for children.

Others conclude that current beliefs about poverty and some strategies to address it are not far removed from those of Brace's time. They have noted that the removal of children from mothers deemed to be neglectful or negligent and the existence of modern day orphan *planes* used to transport children from impoverished families in other countries to the United States for adoption are similar to the historic models [Kitterson 1968; Stansell 1982; Wexler 1990].

The past can be a vital resource by enabling us to measure change, generate policy options, and select policy for the future in light of the context of environment and time period [Mandilbaum 1977]. Historical study gives us a cultural context, including values and beliefs, on which past policies were based [King & Sterns 1981]. In view of current proposals for return to historical arrangements, an examination of these strategies may be particularly critical. As Abbott [1938: vii] pointed out, "For an understanding of our present situation and how the obstacles to progress may be overcome, it is necessary to know the road we have traveled, the wrong turns that have been made because objectives were not clearly defined and because of fear to try a new road even when it was clear that the old one was only a cul-de-sac." ♦

References

Abbott, G. (1938). *The child and the state: Legal status in the family, apprenticeship, and child labor* (Vol. 1). Chicago: University of Chicago Press.

Addams, J. (1910). *Twenty years at Hull House.* New York: The McMillan Company.

An early adventure in child-placing: Charles Loring Brace. (1929). *Social Services Review, 3,* 75–97.

Ashby, L. (1984). *Saving the waifs: Reformers and dependent children, 1890–1917.* Philadelphia: Temple University Press.

Bellingham, B. (1986). Institution and family: An alternative view of nineteenth-century child saving. *Social Problems, 33*(6), S33–S53.

Bellingham, B. W. (1984). *Little wanderers: A socio-historical study of the nineteenth century origins of child fostering and adoption reform, based on early records of the New York Children's Aid Society* (Doctoral dissertation, University of Pennsylvania).

Brace, C. L. (1880). *The dangerous classes of New York, and twenty years' work among them.* (3rd ed). New York: Wynkoop & Hallenbeck.

Brace, E. (Ed.). (1894). *The life of Charles Loring Brace.* New York: Charles Scribner's Sons.

Bremner, R. H. (1970). (Ed.). *Children and youth in America: A documentary history* (Vol. I: 1600–1865). Cambridge, MA: Harvard University Press.

Bremner, R. H. (1971). (Ed.). *Children and youth in America: A documentary history* (Vol. II: 1866–1932). Cambridge, MA: Harvard University Press.

Brophy, A. B. (1972). *Foundlings on the frontier.* Tucson, AZ: University of Arizona Press.

Children's Aid Society. (1893). The Children's Aid Society of New York: Its history, plans, and results. In National Conference of Charities and Corrections (Eds.), *History of child saving in the United States* (pp. 1–36). Montclair, NJ: Patterson Smith (1971 reprint edition).

Children's Aid Society: The record of a year of its good work. (1890, November 26). *The New York Times*, p. 9.

Cordasco, F. (1971). Charles Loring Brace and the dangerous classes: Historical analogies of the urban black poor. *The Kansas Journal of Sociology, 7* (3, 4), 142–147.

Costin, L. B. (1983). *Two sisters for social justice: A biography of Grace and Edith Abbott.* Chicago: University of Illinois Press.

Crime and charity among the children. (1861, October 11). *The New York Times*, p. 5.

Downs, S. W., & Sherraden, M. W. (1983). The orphan asylum in the nineteenth century. *Social Service Review, 57,* 272–290.

Ecks, J. A. (1984). *Understanding the New York system of foster child care: A sociological interpretation* (Doctoral dissertation, Rutgers University).

Folks, H. (1902). *The care of destitute, neglected and dependent children.* New York: The Macmillan Company.

Ford, M., & Kroll, J. (1990). *Challenges to child welfare: Countering the call for a return to orphanages.* St. Paul, MN: The North American Council on Adoptable Children.

Fry, A. P. (1974). The children's migration. *American Heritage, 26*(1), 4–10, 79–81.

Hartman, A. (1990). Children in a careless society. *Social Work, 35,* 483–484.

Hays, S. P. (1957). The shock of change. In F. R. Bruel & A. D. Wade (Eds.), *Readings in the history of social welfare policy and services* (pp. 94–100). Chicago: The University of Chicago.

Heale, M. J. (1976a). Patterns of benevolence: Associated philanthropy in the cities of New York, 1830–1860. *New York History, 57*(1), 53–79.

Heale, M. J. (1976b). From city fathers to social critics: Humanitarians and government in New York, 1790–1860. *The Journal of American History, 63*(1), 21–41.

Holt, M. I. (1992). *The orphan trains: Placing-out in America.* Lincoln, NE: University of Nebraska Press.

Homeless children. (1859, March 5). *The New York Times,* p. 2.

King, G. B., & Sterns, P. N. (1981). The retirement experience as a policy factor. *Journal of Social History, 14,* 589–625.

Kitterson, R. H. (1968). *Orphan voyage.* New York: Vintage Press.

Langsam, M. Z. (1964). *Children west: A history of the placing-out system of the New York Children's Aid Society, 1853–1890.* Madison, WI: University of Wisconsin.

Letchworth, W. P. (1893). The history of child-saving work in the state of New York. In National Conference of Charities and Corrections (Eds.), *History of child saving in the United States.* (pp. 154–203). Montclair, NJ: Patterson Smith (1971 reprint edition).

Lindemann, H. (1990, December 15). Farms for the homeless. *The New York Times,* p. 26.

Mandilbaum, S. (1977). The past in service to the future. *Journal of Social History, 11,* 193–205.

Mangolin, C. R. (1978). Salvation versus liberation: The movement for children's rights in a historical context. *Social Problems, 25,* 441–452.

Minton, S. E. (1893). Family life versus institutional life. In National Conference of Charities and Corrections (Eds.), *History of child saving in the United States.* (pp. 37–53). Montclair, NJ: Patterson Smith (1971 reprint edition).

National Child Welfare Resource Center. (1991, April 9). *Orphan trains* (Teleconference). Portland, ME: University of Southern Maine.

Nelson, K. E. (1987, December). *Charles Loring Brace: His life up to the founding of the New York Children's Aid Society.* Paper presented at the Annual Meeting of the American Historical Association, Social Welfare History Group, Washington, DC.

Nelson, K. E. (1980). *The best asylum: Charles Loring Brace and foster family care* (Doctoral dissertation, University of California Berkeley).

Nelson, K. E. (1985). Child placing in the nineteenth century: New York and Iowa. *Social Service Review, 59*(1), 107–120.

New York child saving: Many serious problems are necessarily involved. (1895, May 26). *The New York Times,* p. 16.

Our city charities: The Children's Aid Society. (1860, April 7). *The New York Times,* p. 2.

Patrick, M., Sheets, E., & Trickel, E. (1990). *We are a part of history: The story of the orphan trains.* Santa Fe, NM: The Lightning Tree.

Research on effects of orphanages available. (1990, Fall). *Adoptalk,* 1, 12.

Riis, J. A. (1894, January). A Christmas reminder of the noblest work in the world. *Forum,* 624–633.

Shaffer, D. (1990, September 4). Group considers opening orphanage-type homes. *Saint Paul Pioneer Press,* pp. 1A, 8A.

Stansell, C. (1982). Women, children, and the uses of the streets: Class and gender conflict in New York City, 1850–1860. *Feminist Studies, 8,* 309–335.

Stark, R. H. (1990, Spring). A return to the orphanages is a step backwards. *Caring, 7,* 16.

Takanishi, R. (1978). Childhood as a social issue: Historical roots of contemporary child advocacy movements. *Journal of Social Issues, 34*(2), 8–28.

The Children's Aid Society. (1902, December 19). *The New York Times,* p. 8.

Thurston, H. W. (1930). *The dependent child.* New York: Columbia University Press.

Vagrancy among children. (1881, July 17). *The New York Times,* p. 6.

Warner, A. G. (1908). *American charities* (3rd Ed.). New York: Thomas Y. Crowell.

Wexler, R. (1990, December 15). Misguided 'orphan trains' idea rolls on. *The New York Times,* p. 26.

Wheeler, L. (1983). The orphan trains. *American History Illustrated*, *18*(8), 10–23.

Wohl, R. R. (1969). The country boy myth and its place in American urban culture: The nineteenth century contribution. *Perspectives in American History*, *3*, 77–156.

Young, P. J., & Marks, F. E. (1990). *Tears on Paper: Orphan train history*. Springdale, AR: Just Us Printers, Inc.

Zietz, D. (1959). *Child welfare: Principles and methods*. New York: John Wiley & Sons, Inc.

10

FROM FAMILY DUTY TO FAMILY POLICY: THE EVOLUTION OF KINSHIP CARE

Rebecca Hegar and Maria Scannapieco

The proportion of children in out-of-home care who are placed in the homes of relatives has increased rapidly and substantially. This article presents a range of definitions and ways of conceptualizing kinship care, and traces how care by relatives has evolved from a matter of family duty to one of social policy. Within the broader context of kinship care, the article emphasizes the experiences of children and families of color.

Rebecca Hegar, D.S.W., is Associate Professor and Associate Dean, University of Maryland School of Social Work, Baltimore, MD. Maria Scannapieco, Ph.D., is Assistant Professor, University of Maryland School of Social Work, Baltimore, MD.

193

T he increasing number and proportion of children in out-of-home care placed in the homes of relatives are among the most important child welfare trends of the decade [Berrick et al. 1994; Center for the Study of Social Policy 1990]. This article describes historical and recent developments in kinship care and discusses policy implications. It considers a range of definitions and ways of conceptualizing kinship care and applies the broadest of these when exploring the experiences of persons of color.

Overview of Kinship Care

Definitions of Kinship Care

The term *kinship care* has been recently used by the Child Welfare League of America (CWLA) Commission on Family Foster Care, which, in cooperation with the National Foster Parent Association, developed goals and recommendations promoting relatives and friends as placement resources for children in out-of-home care [CWLA 1994; Takas 1992]. The movement toward kinship care is congruent with the earlier work of Stack [1974], who documented the importance of extended kinship networks in the African American community. The term *kin* usually includes any relative, by blood or marriage, or any person with close family ties [Takas 1993]. Billingsley [1992: 31] refers to the "close family ties" category as relationships of appropriation, meaning "unions without blood ties or marital ties." He writes that "people can become part of a family unit or, indeed, form a family unit simply by deciding to live and act toward each other as family." It is kinship in this broad sense that informs the statement by the Child Welfare League of America [1994: 2]: "Kinship care may be defined as the full-time nurturing and protection of children who must be separated from their parents by relatives, members of their tribes or clans, godparents, stepparents, or other adults who have a kinship bond with a child."

Some definitions of kinship caregiving concern both informal and formal child placement with relatives. Takas [1993: 3] notes that "Kinship care includes both private kinship care (entered by private family arrangement) and kinship foster care (care provided for a child who is in the legal custody of the state child welfare agency)."

Other authors prefer the terms *kinship caregivers* for those who provide private care and *kinship foster parents* for those whose care falls within the formal child welfare system [Berrick et al. 1994]. The majority of empirical research has been conducted with "kinship foster parents" [Berrick et al. 1994; Iglehart 1994; Thornton 1991]. In this article, we consider kinship care in the broadest sense when reviewing its historical context. In discussions of research and of social policy, we focus on the narrower meaning most commonly encountered in those contexts, which is out-of-home care provided by relatives to children in the custody of state child welfare agencies.

Demographic Trends

Although social policy and social work practice emphasize permanency planning and family preservation, the foster care census is skyrocketing. Due in part to a 333% increase in the number of children reported as abused or neglected during the past 15 years, the number of children entering out-of-home care since 1982 has increased dramatically [Merkel-Holguín 1993]. This increase in the out-of-home care population has been accompanied by a decrease in the number of foster parents, from 147,000 in 1984 to 100,000 in 1990 [National Commission on Foster Family Care 1991].

The increasing number of children in care and the declining pool of traditional foster families, along with recognition of the benefits of family care, are among the forces that have led to a growing use of kinship care. More than 31% of all children in state custody are placed with extended family members, according to a recent U.S. Health and Human Services report based on data from 29 states [U.S. Department of Health and Human Services 1992].

In certain states, the percentage of foster children in kinship homes ranges even higher than the national average, exceeding the number of children in nonrelative family foster homes [Gleeson & Craig 1994]. For example, 51% of all Illinois children in out-of-home placement are in kinship care [Wulczyn & Goerge 1990]. California, which serves 20% of the nation's children in out-of-home care, places over 50% of these children with relatives [Berrick 1992]. Two-thirds of that state's increase in placements from 1984 to 1989 involved children placed with providers related to the children [California Child Welfare Strategic Planning Commission 1991 (cited in Berrick 1992)].

Urban centers have seen the largest increase in kinship placements. The number of children in formal kinship care in New York City, for example, increased from 151 in 1985 to 14,000 in 1989 [Thornton 1991], and a more recent count shows a total of 23,591 [Takas 1993]. In Philadelphia, which began making kinship placements only a few years earlier, kinship homes constituted 67% of the total number of family foster homes by 1992 [Takas 1992].

In addition, many children live in informal kinship care and are not included in studies of the out-of-home care system. As many as 1.3 million American children live with kin in homes where neither parent is present. Among these are three-quarters of a million children receiving Aid to Families with Dependent Children in the homes of their kin—10% of the total AFDC rolls [National Commission on Family Foster Care 1991].

Historical Context of Kinship Care

Early History

The voluntary fostering of children in the homes of relatives or friends is a tradition found in regions as diverse as medieval Europe and twentieth century Africa [Eastman 1988; Isiugo-Abanihe 1984]. Strengthening kinship ties was and continues to be one goal of voluntary fostering [Isiugo-Abanihe 1984]; as a cultural practice it implies no loss or deficit in the child's immediate family.

Until the time of the industrial revolution and the corresponding growth of social institutions in Europe and the United States, there were few alternatives for children whose parents died or became unable to care for them. Under the English Poor Law, grandparents became responsible for their grandchildren in cases of dependency [Trattner 1984]. Children were also subject to the Poor Law resort to alms and workhouses, forced apprenticeship, or emigration. England developed wardship as a legal mechanism that placed other dependent children, usually heirs to property, in the care of relatives or other adults. Many more undoubtedly lived without legal formalities with family members acting from affection and/or a sense of family duty.

First the family—and second the larger ethnic community—were the residual lines of defense against social problems [see Wilensky & Lebeaux 1965]. It was only later, during the eighteenth and nineteenth centuries, that orphanages were established, primarily in response to epidemics and wars that decimated whole communities and kinship networks, making family care of children impossible. Most of these early institutions were founded by religious and ethnic groups to serve children from their own communities.

Children of Color in the U.S. Placement System

Several factors worked to exclude African American children from the early orphanages, and from the private placing-out societies that introduced formal foster care in the late 1800s. The most obvious factor was slavery. If their parents died or were incapacitated, or if they or their parents were sold, slave children often were cared for within the slave community. Even after the end of slavery, the emerging formal institutions for dependent children served few African American children for more than a century, although there were exceptions.

This pattern of exclusion and underservice was attacked in the 1920s and 1930s by Chicago social workers who advocated for and established public child welfare agencies [Stehno 1988]. Evidence of a similar pattern of racial and religious discrimination was the basis for a lawsuit brought in 1973 by the American Civil Liberties Union to force New York City's private foster care agencies to accept proportionate shares of African American children from Protestant, non-Christian, and nonreligious backgrounds [Wilder 1988].

Throughout the twentieth century, family and community self-help, sometimes centered on the church, continued to provide for dependent African American children [Billingsly 1992; Gray & Nybell 1990; Martin & Martin 1985; Stack 1974]. Some authors observe that helping patterns seen in African American families echoed earlier African traditions that were not successfully obliterated by slavery and the American experience [Martin & Martin 1985].

For the range of reasons sketched above, care of African American children was accomplished primarily by less formal arrangements within their own communities until expansion of public foster care services in the 1930s and federal funding in 1961 improved access to formal child placement [Stehno 1988]. Even after better access was attained, however, the tradition of care within the extended family remained strong [Downs 1986; Gray & Nybell 1990]. For example, one study reports that the proportion of African American children in "informal adoptions" has increased in recent years, from 13.3% living with extended family members in 1970 to 16.5% in 1989 [cited in Billingsly 1992: 30].

Other ethnic minorities, particularly Latinos and Native Americans, have also experienced difficulties within formal child welfare structures. Outside of the major population centers, there were not enough child-caring agencies until after 1935, when the Social Security Act first provided states with grants-in-aid to establish public child welfare services in rural areas. Children

located away from major population centers were often un-
derserved by private children's institutions and child-placing
organizations.

Early in the history of the French and Spanish territories, Catholic children needing care were taken in at missions and convents,
and the first separate children's institution in what is now the U.S.
was founded by Ursuline sisters in New Orleans in 1727 [Trattner
1994]. For many French, Spanish and, later, Mexican American
children, however, the extended family was the only, as well as the
culturally preferred, resource. Contemporary observers note the
continued importance of care of children by relatives [Delgado &
Humm-Delgado 1982] and within the family-extending institution
of *compadrazgo* (coparenting) [Vidal 1988].

Much as African American history has been uniquely shaped
by slavery, the Native American experience has been shaped by
U.S. policy toward conquered peoples. Some early mission work
with Native Americans had involved taking children from their
families to be reared in a different cultural environment. That
goal was later furthered by the Bureau of Indian Affairs, particularly by the founding of Indian Boarding Schools [Johnson 1981].
In a pattern unique in the history of North America, many Native
children were placed in institutions, rather than being left to the
care of family, kinship network, and ethnic community. This
pattern of placement outside the culture became one impetus
behind passage of the Indian Child Welfare Act of 1978, the first
U.S. policy document to state an explicit preference for kinship
placement. Despite a history of Native children being intentionally removed from their kinship circles, kinship care has continued to be a central aspect of Native culture [Shomaker 1989].

Federal Child Welfare Policy and Kinship Care

The federal government was slow to involve itself in child placement matters, even after the establishment of the U.S. Children's
Bureau in 1912. The Social Security Act of 1935 first offered states
matching money for rural child welfare services, but it was not

until the amendments of 1961 that federal funds were available to pay foster care costs for AFDC-eligible children who came into state custody. Although federal policy was unclear, many states interpreted the 1961 amendments as precluding foster care payments to relatives, leaving those who provided care for related children dependent on lower AFDC grant rates or without any reimbursement at all [Killackey 1992]. It was at this time that a two-tier system of payment became formalized in many states, with kinship homes occupying the lower tier.

The out-of-home care population grew during the 1960s and early 1970s, and by 1977 an estimated 395,000 children were in care [Shyne & Schroeder 1978]. Many factors probably contributed to this phenomenon: new awareness of child abuse and the enactment of mandatory reporting laws; increasing numbers of single-parent families due to divorce, desertion, and single mothers keeping their babies; and civil rights advances that made it more difficult for public welfare agencies to avoid serving minority clients. That out-of-home care for AFDC-eligible children was one service for which federal funds were available surely fueled the rate of placement.

Not long after the permanency planning movement in the 1970s became a force to reduce the swelling rolls of children in care, several federal child welfare policy shifts began to encourage placements with relatives. As noted above, this idea was first embodied in the Indian Child Welfare Act of 1978 in response to the unique history of Native American child placement outside the extended family and tribe. In the Act, a prioritized list of placement alternatives lists relatives at the top, requiring agencies to keep Native American children in kinship homes whenever possible.

The next policy event to promote kinship care came in 1979, when the U.S. Supreme Court ruled in *Miller v. Youakim* [1979] that for purposes of federal foster care payments, relative homes meeting foster home licensing standards were eligible for the same reimbursement as nonrelative homes. Like many states,

Illinois, where the case originated, had prohibited relative caregivers from receiving the higher foster care rates.

Along with the *Miller* decision, passage of P.L. 96–272 in 1980, with its emphasis on placement within the most family-like setting possible, contributed to increased use of kinship foster homes. This policy focus has been accompanied over the last decade and a half by complementary social patterns and forces. The number of children in care was lowered during the 1970s by permanency planning initiatives, only to rise again in the mid-1980s, fueled by high rates of family disruption and intractable urban problems—street violence, drug abuse, and eventually, the AIDS epidemic. This most recent rise in the number of children in care has been accompanied by a decline in the number of available nonrelative foster families, due in part to the rise in two-worker families, geographic mobility, and other sociological trends. The imbalance of more children for fewer homes has resulted in crises in many urban child welfare departments.

Although trends promoting formalized kinship care are apparent, child placement practice remains quite uneven across U.S. jurisdictions and regions. For example, many relatives who provide care to children in state custody still do not receive the same payments and services as nonrelative foster parents [Gleeson & Craig 1994; Scannapieco & Hegar, in press]. States are obligated under *Miller* to pay the foster care board rate only to relatives of AFDC-eligible children in state custody whose homes meet all licensing or approval requirements. Many kinship homes do not do so because of housing conditions, crowding, or background problems such as prior child protection or criminal records.

Kinship Care Research and Policy Issues

Overview of Research

To make informed policy choices concerning kinship care, it is important to consider what the recent but growing body of research suggests about the children, their caregivers, and agency plans and services. Children in kinship care tend to be young, with a mean age of seven or eight [Berrick et al. 1994; Dubowitz et al. 1990, 1993; Gabel 1992; Task Force 1990; Wulczyn & Goerge 1990]. They are more predominately African American than the population in traditional foster care [Berrick et al. 1994; Iglehart 1994]. Typical reasons for placement are neglect [Dubowitz et al. 1990, 1993; Iglehart 1994; Wulczyn & Goerge 1990] and substance abuse [Berrick et al. 1994; Gabel 1992; Task Force 1990; Thornton 1991].

Between 36% [Iglehart 1994] and 50% [Dubowitz et al. 1990] of children in kinship care perform below grade level; they have been found to score at least one standard deviation above the norm on the Behavior Problem Index (BPI) [Berrick et al. 1994], and 35% are reported to have an overall Child Behavior Checklist score in the clinical range [Dubowitz et al. 1990]. Iglehart [1994] reports that 33% of the children have behavioral problems serious enough to be noted in the case record, but that an even larger proportion of children in traditional foster care have similar problems.

Maternal grandmothers and aunts are the predominate kinship caregivers, and their age averages about 50 [Berrick et al. 1994; Dubowitz et al. 1990, 1993; Gabel 1992; Task Force 1990; Thornton 1987, 1991; Wulczyn & Goerge 1990]. Most have completed high school [Berrick et al. 1994; Dubowitz et al. 1990; Gabel 1992], while nonrelative foster mothers average more education [Berrick et al. 1994]; most are not currently married [Berrick et al. 1994; Dubowitz et al. 1990; Gabel 1992], in contrast to nonrelative foster mothers [Berrick et al. 1994]. Approximately 48% of kinship caregivers are employed out of the home [Berrick et al. 1994; Dubowitz et al. 1990, 1993], and many live in poverty [Task Force 1990].

Levels of monitoring of the welfare of children in kinship care are lower than in other foster homes [Berrick et al. 1994; Iglehart 1994], and 91% of kinship caregivers have received no training during the previous year [Berrick et al. 1994]. Berrick and colleagues [1994] found, however, that kinship caregivers are very satisfied with their agency workers. One study found kinship homes significantly underrepresented among confirmed cases of maltreatment [Zuravin et al. 1993].

Relative placements are very stable [Berrick et al. 1994; Dubowitz et al. 1990, 1993; Iglehart 1994], significantly more so than other foster placements [Goerge 1990], and kinship caregivers express a commitment to the children in their care and a willingness to care for them as long as needed [Berrick et al. 1994; Dubowitz et al. 1990; Thornton 1991]. The majority, however, see no need to adopt or assume guardianship of children who are already related to them [Berrick et al. 1994; Iglehart 1994; Thornton 1991]. Although return to parental custody is the reported goal in 33% [Dubowitz et al. 1990] to 61% of the cases [Task Force 1990], reunification rates are lower than in traditional foster care [Berrick et al. 1994; Dubowitz et al. 1990, 1993; Gabel 1992; Task Force 1990; Thornton 1991; Wulczyn & Goerge 1990]. Given the serious problems of many parents and the stability of kinship care, the Task Force [1990: 42] notes, "While this goal is laudatory, it is not realistic in many of the cases."

Policy Issues in Kinship Care

Kinship care has evolved from a matter of family duty to one of family social policy. Further, demographics suggest that kinship care will grow in the future, probably faster than other types of care. Findings about the long-term nature of many kinship placements also emphasize the need to assess its strengths and limitations; although some children spend a few weeks or months in relative placements, many more have come to kinship homes to stay because their parents have been rendered unfit by substance abuse, have died of AIDS, are in prison, or are otherwise absent. This reality highlights a basic philosophical contradiction. Should kinship care be considered one type of out-of-home care, temporary by definition, requiring the same reunification efforts as are made with other families with children in care? Or can the placement of a child with a close relative in itself meet the goal of permanency, much as the goal of eventual "independent living" shows acceptance that some older children will remain in care until adulthood? When relatives are able to assume guardianship or pursue adoption, kinship care clearly becomes a permanent placement, but, for reasons discussed below, many caregivers need the continued support the state offers foster parents.

To assess the desirability of the trend toward kinship care, it is necessary to examine the balance sheet on kinship homes, what they offer and where the problems lie. Foremost from a child-centered perspective, kinship care offers children familiar care-givers in a time of family crisis. Due to prevailing patterns of kinship and residence, this most often means placement within a familiar racial or ethnic community. Whereas traditional foster care programs are often criticized for failure to recruit homes from among ethnic minorities of color, kinship care recognizes and takes advantage of historical patterns of family caregiving in those communities. The long-term nature of many placements makes the cultural continuity offered by kinship care all the more important. Kinship care also frequently allows siblings to continue their family relationship.

From the perspective of those who fund public child welfare services, a further advantage concerns cost differentials. When kinship caregivers are licensed (or certified or approved) as foster parents, the services and board payments they receive are comparable to those given other foster care homes. However, the absence of recruitment costs and lower placement turnover probably make kinship foster care a somewhat less expensive alternative to administer. In addition, many jurisdictions do not require all relative caregivers to be licensed. In those situations, the monthly cost of care provided to the children is considerably less than if they were in unrelated family foster homes or in other types of placements, although the longer stays in kinship homes also must be considered. In addition to savings due to the lower costs of finding kinship caregivers and less frequent re-placement of children, costs are also less for caregiver training, supervision, board rates, and other services and allowances. The conclusion that kinship care is, in many cases, a less expensive option for the state is surely one reason for its growth during the last 20 years of constrained spending for social services.

Do these fiscal advantages come at the expense of good child placement practice? If kinship care is sometimes cheaper, is it as good as other placement options? Although the available research is somewhat contradictory, it suggests that children in kinship care probably average about as many medical, educational, and emotional problems and needs as those in other foster homes, while they and their families receive fewer services from the state. Kinship caregivers themselves are clearly more stressed by health problems, unemployment, single-parenthood, and low incomes than traditional foster parents. This difference in personal and social resources highlights one of the most disturbing aspects of the kinship care picture: children living in poverty or near-poverty, lacking adequate financial and social support from the state that assumed responsibility for their care. Because a disproportionate share of African American children are placed in kinship care, as compared to traditional family foster care, they are most likely to experience these conditions.

Kinship care's evolution has produced a situation that is in many ways anomalous. The foster care board rate is not intended to support the caregiver, just to defray the costs of caring for the child. This rate of reimbursement is granted to foster families, who average higher levels of education, employment, and income than do kinship caregivers. At the same time, many kinship caregivers are left in poverty by the same board rate or even lower AFDC payments. In addition to the single board rate for all children of a given age, other aspects of foster care services also tend to be "one size fits all," for example, number of hours of required training and mandated minimum frequency of agency contact. Perhaps discrete goals of temporary and long-term kinship care would help define the different levels of service required in different situations. In addition, a more flexible menu of benefits and services offered to both traditional and kinship foster parents might better meet the needs of children in their care. Surely families need different types and amounts of training, and some might prefer to decline reimbursement for some expenses or trade for others not now covered. Certainly, the lowest income families should not be left to rear children in state-sanctioned poverty. Unfortunately, increased board rates and flexibility in benefits are unlikely policy developments in a child welfare system overwhelmed by more basic needs and problems.

Underlying any discussion of kinship care, as well as of traditional family foster care, is the issue of what society offers families in return for rearing children. Concern that relatives qualify for more support than parents leads some to question whether the availability of kinship foster care actually encourages parents to acquiesce to state placement, for example, by failing to work for reunification with their children [Takas 1992]. In the United States, care of children is not a social utility carrying publicly sponsored benefits (e.g., child-rearing allowances, health coverage, respite care) for whoever performs the task. If parents, kinship caregivers, and foster parents were equally eligible for such benefits and services, many troublesome questions about kinship care leading to unnecessary state custody or leaving foster children in poverty would be moot. By whatever means and models of delivery, children in kinship care deserve families with the resources to meet their basic and developmental needs. Of course, so do all our children. ◆

References

Adoption Assistance and Child Welfare Act of 1980. Public Law 96–272.

Berrick, J. D. (1992). *A comparison of kinship foster homes and foster family homes: Implications for kinship foster care as family preservation.* Washington, DC: Child Welfare League of America North American Kinship Care Policy and Practice Committee.

Berrick, J. D., Barth, R. P., & Needell, B. (1994). A comparison of kinship foster homes and foster family homes: Implications for kinship foster care as family preservation. *Children and Youth Services Review, 16*(1–2), 33–64.

Billingsley, A. (1992). *Climbing Jacob's ladder: The enduring legacy of African-American families.* New York: Simon & Shuster.

Center for the Study of Social Policy. (1990). *The crisis in foster care.* Washington, DC: The Family Impact Seminar.

Child Welfare League of America. (1994). *Kinship care: A natural bridge.* Washington, DC: Author.

Child Welfare League of America. (1992). *Report of the CWLA North American Kinship Care Policy and Practice Committee, draft #3.* Washington, DC: Author.

Delgado, M., & Humm-Delgado, D. (1982). Natural support systems: Source of strength in Hispanic communities. *Social Work, 27,* 83–89.

Downs, S. W. (1986). Black foster parents and agencies: Results of an eight state survey. *Children and Youth Services Review, 8,* 201–218.

Dubowitz, H., Tepper, V., Feigelman, S., Sawyer, R., & Davidson, N. (1990). *The physical and mental health and educational status of children placed with relatives—Final report.* Prepared for the Maryland Department of Human Resources and the Baltimore City Department of Social Services. Baltimore: University of Maryland School of Medicine.

Eastman, K. S. (1988). Gambian fostering. *Journal of International and Comparative Social Welfare, 4*(2), 72–81.

Gabel, G. (1992). Preliminary report on kinship foster family profile. New York: Human Resources Administration, Child Welfare Administration.

Gleeson, J. P., & Craig, L. C. (1994). Kinship care in child welfare: An analysis of states' policies. *Children and Youth Services Review, 16*(1–2), 7–32.

Goerge, R. M. (1990). The reunification process in substitute care. *Social Service Review, 64,* 422–457.

Gray S. S., & Nybell, L. M. (1990). Issues in African-American family preservation. *Child Welfare, 69,* 513–523.

Iglehart, A. P. (1994). Kinship foster care: Placement, service, and outcome issues. *Children and Youth Services Review, 16*(1–2), 107–121.

Indian Child Welfare Act of 1978. Public Law 95–608.

Isiugo-Abanihe, U. C. (1984). Child fostering and high fertility interrelationships in West Africa. *Studies in Third World Societies, 29,* 73–100.

Johnson, B. B. (1981). The Indian Child Welfare Act of 1978: Implications for practice. *Child Welfare, 60,* 435–446.

Killackey, E. (1992). Kinship foster care. *Family Law Quarterly, 26,* 211–220.

Martin, J. M., & Martin, E.P. (1985). *The helping tradition in the black family and community.* Silver Spring, MD: National Association of Social Workers.

Merkel-Holguín, L. (1993). *The child welfare stat book 1993.* Washington, DC: The Child Welfare League of America.

Miller v. Youakim, 440 U.S. 125, 99 S. Ct. 957 (1979).

National Commission on Family Foster Care. (1991). The significance of kinship care. In *A blueprint for fostering infants, children, and youths in the 1990s.* Washington, DC: Child Welfare League of America.

Scannapieco, M., & Hegar, R. L. (in press). Kinship care: Two case management models. *Journal of Child & Adolescent Social Work.*

Shomaker, D. J. (1989). Transfer of children and the importance of grandmothers among Navajo Indians. *Journal of Cross-Cultural Gerontology, 4*(1), 1–18.

Shyne, A., & Schroeder, A. W. (1978). National study of social services to children and their families. Rockville, MD: Westat.

Stack, C. (1974). *All our kin: Strategies for survival in a black community.* New York: Harper & Row.

Stehno, S. M. (1988). Public responsibility for dependent black children: The advocacy of Edith Abbott and Sophonisba Breckinridge. *Social Service Review, 62,* 485–503.

Takas, M. (1993). *Kinship care and family preservation: A guide for states in legal and policy development* (unpublished manuscript). Washington, DC: American Bar Association Center on Children and the Law.

Takas, M. (1992). Kinship care: Developing a safe and effective framework for protective placements of children with relatives. *Children's Legal Rights Journal, 13*(2), 12–19.

Task Force on Permanency Planning for Foster Children, Inc. (1990). *Kinship foster care: The double-edged dilemma*. Rochester, NY: Author.

Thornton, J. L. (1991). Permanency planning for children in kinship foster homes. *Child Welfare, 70*, 593–601.

Trattner, W. I. (1994). *From poor law to welfare state: A history of social welfare in America* (5th ed). New York: Free Press.

U.S. Department of Health and Human Services, Office of the Inspector General (1992). *State practices in using relatives for foster care*. Washington, DC: U.S. Government Printing Office.

Vidal, C. (1988). Godparenting among Hispanic Americans. *Child Welfare, 67*, 453–459.

Wilder v. Bernstein, 645 F. Supp. 1292 (S.D.N.Y. 1986), affirmed, 848 F.2d 1338 (2d Cir. 1988).

Wilensky, H. L., & Lebeaux, C. N. (1965). *Industrial society & social welfare*. New York: Free Press.

Wulczyn, F., & Goerge, R. M. (1990). *Public policy and the dynamics of foster care: A multi-state study of placement histories* (research report to the U.S. Department of Health and Human Services, Office of Assistant Secretary for Planning and Evaluation). New York: New York State Department of Social Services and Chicago: Chapin Hall Center for Children, University of Chicago.

Zuravin, S., Benedict, M., & Somerfield, M. (1993). Child maltreatment in family foster care. *American Journal of Orthopsychiatry, 63*, 589–596.

11

ADOPTION AND DISCLOSURE OF FAMILY INFORMATION: A HISTORICAL PERSPECTIVE

E. Wayne Carp

Adoptive parents have recently sued child-placing organizations for wrongful adoption, a legal term for fraudulently misrepresenting or neglecting to give adoptive parents a child's medical or family history. This article presents a historical perspective of adoption agency policies on disclosing to adoptive parents the medical and social history of the children they have adopted or are seeking to adopt.

E. Wayne Carp, Ph.D., is Associate Professor of History, Department of History, Pacific Lutheran University, Tacoma, WA.

During the past decade, adoptive parents have challenged adoption agencies' right to withhold the medical and social history of an adopted child and the child's biological family by bringing lawsuits alleging the tort of wrongful adoption. This civil action is a recent legal development. The first successful wrongful adoption lawsuit, *Burr v. Board of County Commissioners*, took place in 1986. The tort of wrongful adoption permits adoptive parents to sue adoption agencies and collect monetary damages if the agencies deliberately conceal, intentionally misrepresent, or negligently fail to disclose the health status or family background of an adopted child [DeWoody 1993; Connelly 1991; Dickson 1991; Maley 1987; Goldenhersh 1992]. Since then, courts in at least five states have upheld wrongful adoption suits against child-placing institutions [Woo 1992; Goldenhersh 1992]. A Massachusetts jury in 1991, for example, awarded an adoptive couple $3.8 million because the state's Department of Social Services withheld the information that the adopted child was developmentally disabled and his biological mother was schizophrenic [Lambert & Moses 1991]. In response to these lawsuits, adoption agencies have claimed that they were following standard social welfare procedure in withholding an adopted child's medical and social history from the adoptive parents.

But have adoption agencies always withheld an adopted child's medical and social history from adoptive parents? The material that follows suggests that the answer is no. It describes the historical development of adoption agencies' policies on disclosing medical and social history to adoptive parents and also seeks to explain why wrongful adoption lawsuits did not occur until recently and why they will probably die out in the next decade. Using a variety of sources, including the adoption case records of the Children's Home Society of Washington (CHSW or Society), annual reports of child-placing institutions, articles in popular magazines, statements by professional social workers, and survey research by the Child Welfare League of America (CWLA), this article argues that adoption agencies' release of medical and social history to adoptive parents has been cyclical in nature.

During the first half of the twentieth century, a majority of adoption agencies disclosed all the facts in a child's case record to adoptive parents. Beginning in the 1950s, however, adoption agencies increasingly restricted disclosure of negative medical and social history to adoptive parents, partly in an effort to protect adopted children from social stigma and partly to accommodate adoptive parents' reluctance to discuss the matter with their children. In the past two decades, child-placing institutions have returned to a more open disclosure policy as a result of changes in the type of children available for adoption, the increasing flexibility of adoptive parents' attitudes toward special-needs children, and the impact of the adoption rights movement.

Adoption Agencies, Adoptive Parents, and Postadoption Contact

Twentieth century adoption literature documents that, to paraphrase a familiar adage, adoptive parents have been evaluated but not heard. Before the Second World War, policy recommendations and advice for evaluating adoptive parents' qualifications to adopt a child abounded in social work journals, adoption agency newsletters, and popular magazines. Professional social workers worked tirelessly to establish standards concerning the adoptive parents' mental and physical qualities, financial security, emotional stability, and religion. They called for extensive home studies, worried about the proper number of references to require, and debated whether the probationary period should be one year or less [Slingerland 1919; Hewins & Webster 1927; Sargent 1935; Clothier 1942]. Yet the paucity of any discussion of postadoption contact in social work literature before the 1950s is striking. If one relied only on professional publications, one would conclude that social workers did not expect to become deeply involved with adoptive families after an adoption was legalized, and deliberately curtailed their involvement as a natural step in "normalizing" the family [Cole & Donley 1990]. But the confidential adoption case records of CHSW, a voluntary, nonsectarian, child-placing agency, reveal a different picture of postadoption contact prior to the Second World War. It shows that then, as now, adoptive parents needed help with their children as they matured. What is less well known is that adoptive parents found a welcoming and cooperative staff when they returned to the agency. CHSW provides an example of an adoption agency that was eager to provide adoptive parents with advice and counsel and, upon request, disclosed fully their children's social and medical background.[1]

How representative was CHSW? Corroborative evidence from the Child Welfare League of America and geographically diverse child placement agencies, such as those in Illinois, New York, Minnesota, Ohio, and Florida, lends strong support to the view that the Society's policies were not unique. Rather, they were representative of professional adoption agencies' attitudes and practices [Carp 1992]. In evaluating CHSW's representativeness, it must be kept in mind that most adoption agencies' records are sealed by law, and most agency officials refuse to give researchers access to them. Scholars are invited to test this article's representativeness by conducting research at their local adoption agencies. Unless adoption agency officials permit researchers access to the case records, historians and social workers may never obtain the data they need.

CHSW, Adoptive Parents, and Postadoption Contact

Table 1 details the variety of reasons why adoptive parents contacted the Society during the years 1895 to 1988. In most cases, the contact was unexpected, primarily because the Society never prepared or encouraged adoptive parents to seek postadoption contact. Nor did many adoptive parents, who preferred to remain anonymous and not be reminded of or forced to reveal the child's

TABLE 1
Types of Requests Initiated by Adoptive Parents to the Children's Home Society of Washington (1895–1988)

Type of Request	#	%
Birth Certificate	33	42
Medical/Social History	33	42
Counseling or Advice	11	14
Other	2*	2
Total	79	100

*Includes one request for the Society's newsletter and one request for a copy of the adoption papers.

adoption, welcome the idea of returning to the agency. Without pressure from outside the home—employers, school authorities, haphazard birth registration—or from within—the child's illness, delinquency, or desire for biological family information—adoptive parents would have never returned to the Society.

Given the social and psychological pressures discouraging contact, it is not surprising that only 15% of all adoptive parents contacted the Society for counsel, advice, and help. They asked Society officials for advice on how to tell their child about the adoption, how to obtain lost adoption papers, and how to find employment for the child. They asked caseworkers to intervene with school authorities, employers, and even with perspective spouses. In one remarkable case, an adoptive mother who objected to her son Jack's impending marriage to a woman named Martha asked a CHSW caseworker to break up the couple. Though the caseworker refused, she counseled the boy about "the seriousness of marriage, but hesitated to mention Martha, fearing for the confidence Jack had in the Organization if he felt that they were making inquiries into his personal life." Nevertheless, on her own initiative, the caseworker elicited damaging family information about Martha from local school authorities and turned it over to Jack's mother.[2]

Adoptive parents also asked Society officials to act as intermediaries between their adopted children and biological parents.
Most commonly, they asked for help when their child manifested
behavior problems, especially those due to difficulty in school,
promiscuity, or in the words of one adoptive couple, "reverting
to type."[3] When an adoptive father wrote complaining that his
daughter was "necking with some soldier in Tacoma," he received a reply from a CHSW caseworker inviting him to the
Seattle office where she would "be glad to talk to him about his
difficulties and if this [was] impossible, that our visitor in his area
could see him there."[4] Similarly, it was not unusual for adoptive
parents, fearing their children were headed for reform school or
prison, to ask CHSW caseworkers to talk to them.[5]

In addition to requesting help, 42% of adoptive parents returned to obtain a birth certificate for their adopted children,
which they never received from the Society.[6] Due to the haphazard nature of state and county birth registration during the early
decades of the century, birth certificates of children born in hospitals were often issued to biological parents, who seldom turned
them over to the Society. The lack of a birth certificate was of little
consequence until the adopted child, now grown to young adulthood, needed a passport, wanted to enlist in the armed services,
or was applying for defense-plant work or a civil service position. Adoptive parents, acting on behalf of their children, then
contacted the Society requesting a birth certificate. Some parents
were panic stricken; having kept the child's adoption a secret,
they hoped to obtain a birth certificate that would not reveal the
facts about the child's birth.[7]

Another 42% of adoptive parents contacted the Society to
receive their children's medical history and information about
the social background of the biological parents.[8] They were particularly interested in records of infant inoculation, childhood
eye or stomach problems, and in such inheritable diseases as
diabetes or heart trouble. Because most people in the early decades of the century believed that mental illness was inherited,

adoptive parents also queried the Society about this issue [Haller 1963; Cravens 1978]. When Mrs. X's adopted daughter, Janice, was committed to a mental institution, for example, she wrote CHSW requesting "all the information possible in regard to the girl's ancestry, especially her parents."[9] Similarly, Mr. and Mrs. Y asked the Society, after their son was sent to a special school, "if the mental deficiency was inherited" from their son's biological family.[10] When requesting the child's social history, adoptive parents frequently asked for all the information in the file concerning the biological parents. They also made requests for specifics of the adopted child's past, including his or her nationality, religion, and the whereabouts of biological siblings.[11] Oftentimes, adoptive parents contacting the Society for social history acted at the request of their child who wanted "to know about his heritage" or desired to locate his or her biological parents.[12]

CHSW's Disclosure Policy

Although never formally codified during the first half of the twentieth century, CHSW's disclosure policy can be reconstructed from case records and Society correspondence. From these sources, it is clear that CHSW caseworkers were instructed to cooperate with and help adoptive parents who contacted the agency with a request for a birth certificate, advice or intervention, or medical and social history. As one adoptive mother reminded CHSW officials: "The Society told me [that] at any time I wished to know more about the child they would gladly let me know as they had all the records."[13] Consequently, when adoptive parents requested a birth certificate for their child, CHSW caseworkers promptly provided them with the information necessary for acquiring one.[14] Many adoptive parents were visibly relieved after 1939 when they were told that the state Department of Birth Registration would issue them a birth certificate that made no reference to the adoption, bearing only the names of the adoptive parents and the new name of the child [Session Laws 1939]. In addition to help in procuring birth certificates, Society officials counseled adoptive parents about how to tell their children about the adoption and on how to obtain copies of lost adoption papers. Society caseworkers also promptly came to the aid of adoptive parents who requested help getting their adult child a job or a marriage partner. Moreover, Society officials, at the behest of adoptive parents, intervened with school officials and often counseled troubled adopted youths.[15]

Society officials also willingly complied with adoptive parents' requests for medical and social information. They diligently searched case records for adopted children's medical ailments and dutifully reported their findings to adoptive parents. When adoptive parents requested the social history of their child's biological parents, Society officials responded by giving them identifying and nonidentifying information. Thus, when Mrs. A. wrote a letter requesting the social history of her adopted son, Henry, for example, a Society caseworker replied by sending her the first and last name and address of the boy's biological father as well as the names of his brothers and sisters. Similarly, Society officials gave adoptive parents information pertaining to their child's nationality and religion.[16] Oftentimes, the adoptive parents' initial request for social history also expressed a desire to locate their child's biological family. Caseworkers cooperated in acting as neutral intermediaries to facilitate reunions between adopted children and their biological parents.[17]

Representativeness of CHSW's Disclosure Policy

How representative of other adoption agencies was CHSW's disclosure policy? Scattered anecdotal evidence in popular magazines suggests that the policy of full disclosure was widespread. As one informed commentator reported, "the best child-placing organizations wish the prospective parents to be as fully informed as possible as to the child's history. Not only is this history usually of great assistance . . . in the intelligent bringing up of the child, but in after life, when the child realizes that he is adopted, he should be allowed to know the facts concerning his forebears" [Willsie 1919: 35]. Similarly, *The New York Times Magazine* reported that it was standard practice for adoption agencies to review the child's history with the adoptive parents, including "his health, his psychometric tests, and as much as is known of his heredity. Parents are told everything about background except the identity of the child's natural parents" [MacKenzie 1940: 7].

Fortunately, we do not have to rely solely on anecdotal evidence. Several social work studies done in the 1930s and 1940s survey adoption agencies' disclosure policies. These studies establish that from 50% to 70% of agencies observed a disclosure policy that encouraged giving adoptive parents much of the medical and social history in a case record. A 1937 survey of 30 child-placing organizations, for example, found that they were evenly divided between telling prospective adoptive parents as little as possible of a child's background, particularly material of an unfavorable nature, and revealing everything except the biological parents' identity [Lippman 1937]. A decade later, a larger survey of 55 CWLA member adoption agencies found that 70% told adoptive parents everything in the case record except identifying information [Child Welfare League of America 1947: 48]. These studies indicate that CHSW's open disclosure policy was typical of a large majority of child-placing agencies before the 1950s, although its practice of revealing identifying information to adoptive parents appears to be more liberal than that of most other institutions.

Factors Influencing Disclosure Policy

Adoption agencies instituted a fairly open disclosure policy toward adoptive parents' requests for medical and social history for four reasons. First, during the early decades of the twentieth century, it was not a difficult task: there was not much family information to give to adoptive parents because of the incompleteness of adoption records, which rarely contained extensive medical or social background information. Second, before World War II, a majority of adopted children were older children with memories of their biological parents, so that in many cases adoption workers were simply telling adoptive parents what the adopted child already knew. Thus, adoption agencies were not the only source for information about the biological parents, alleviating the pressure on them to disclose negative information. Third, adhering to an ideal of full disclosure to adoptive parents was consistent with other social work ideals to provide biological mothers and adult adopted persons with family information upon request. Recent research has revealed that, for a variety of reasons, adoption workers routinely disclosed identifying and nonidentifying family information to all adult adopted clients who requested it [Carp 1992]. Finally, child-placing officials, influenced by the turn-of-the-century eugenics movement, were especially cognizant of the need to give adoptive parents medical and social history if there was any hint of mental illness in the child's background. As Watson [1918: 113], chair of the Philadelphia Conference on Parenthood, cautioned, "No child that is of diseased and no child of feeble-minded parents should be placed in any home for adoption until the [adoptive] parents know the full facts of the case." The Child Welfare League of America codified this ideal:

> Children with special handicaps of a physical nature or related to personality or behavior, and those whose heredity suggests that difficult problems may arise, should be placed for adoption only when the adoptive parents thoroughly understand the child's condition and needs. [1932: 23]

Challenges to the Disclosure Policy

CWLA's standard of full disclosure went unchallenged until the publication of Gallagher's *The Adopted Child* [1936: 116–125].

Gallagher, a volunteer adoption worker, criticized adoption agencies' liberal disclosure policies and advocated instead that child-placing institutions withhold from adoptive parents all information about the child's biological family. Gallagher thought that adoptive parents who could honestly plead "we know nothing of your social background nor who your father or mother were, nor why you were not brought up by them but given to us for adoption" were "fortunate indeed." In Gallagher's view, adopted children were better off not knowing anything about their origins than having their curiosity aroused by fragments of unreliable testimony that social workers had collected from unmarried mothers, relatives, and neighbors. She recommended that when the child asked for information about his or her biological family, the adoptive parents should simply answer, "We do not know and you can never know," assuring her readers that the child would accept this statement "as he accepts many things about which he has a normal curiosity that cannot be satisfied" [Gallagher 1936: 117]. For Gallagher, if adoption caseworkers did not tell the adoptive parents anything about the child's biological parents, the child could not be scarred by false or wrong information.

In responding to Gallagher, professional social workers reasserted their commitment to the social work ideal of full disclosure to adoptive parents. They universally condemned Gallagher, especially for her advice to withhold from adoptive parents information about their child's past. In a typical book review, Sophie van S. Theis [1936], America's foremost authority on adoption at the time and then secretary of the Child Placing and Adoption Committee of the New York State Charities Aid Association, rejected Gallagher's concept of child welfare and concluded that the book held "no value for social workers." Other social workers, in direct opposition to Gallagher's position, advocated giving parents information about their adopted children. Writing in the *Bulletin of the Child Welfare League of America*, George J. Mohr [1936], president of the American Orthopsychiatric Association, stated that there was "no alternative but to fully advise prospective adoptive parents of all favorable and unfavorable known factors that might influence the subsequent development of the child." In 1942, the influential psychiatric social worker Florence Clothier [1942: 271] concurred, writing that adoption workers had an obligation to reveal to prospective adoptive parents all pertinent information, including genetic and medical history.

Conversely, professional social workers expected adoptive parents to tell their children about the adoption and eventually convey to them the medical and social history concerning the biological family. Indeed, as early as 1927, the Pennsylvania Children's Home Society refused to consent to an adoption if the prospective adoptive parents were unwilling to tell the child of it [Hewins & Webster 1927]. By 1954, a survey of 270 adoption agencies revealed that 98% made adoption revelation a prerequisite for prospective adopters to be considered for child placement [Schapiro 1956]. Social workers universally agreed that the best method of adoption revelation was for adoptive parents to tell their children of the adoption often and at an early age, usually before five [Hewins & Webster 1927].

Adoptive Parents' Response

How did adoptive parents respond to adoption agencies' injunctions to tell their children of the adoption and to share the biological family's social history with the children? The evidence suggests that most adoptive parents concealed the fact of adoption from their children and never discussed the social history of the child's biological parents. As early as 1927, reports came back to child-placing institutions such as the Illinois Children's Home & Aid Society [1927] that adoptive parents were permitting their children "to grow up in ignorance of the fact of adoption." Clients of CHSW confided to their case worker that they had never told their ten-year-old adopted son that he was adopted and wished "it were possible for the boy never to be told the truth."[18] During the Second World War, adoptive parents' failure to tell their children of their adoptive status was frequently brought to light when boys being inducted into the army needed birth certificates attesting to their United States citizenship. They were referred to adoption agencies, much to their surprise and dismay [Raymond 1955]. In the three decades after the war, adoptive parents appeared to have become more forthcoming about telling. Jaffee and Fanshel [1970: 312] discovered in a follow-up study of 100 adoptive families that 93% of the parents had informed their children of their adoption. Yet the study also revealed that "only 12% of the families had shared with their children the true facts of adoption as they knew them," that is, facts about the biological parents.

Origins of Agencies' Restrictive Policies

In the 1940s and early 1950s, perplexed social workers searched for the reasons that adoptive parents were reluctant to reveal the fact of adoption or discuss the child's background. One of the first investigations was the study of 28 adoptive families conducted by Hutchinson [1943], a professor of social work at Columbia University's School of Social Work. Hutchinson discovered that although adoptive parents readily promised adoption agencies that they would tell their children about their adoptions, they often postponed telling. Adoptive parents who were "less confident, less mature" feared that they would lose the children's love if they told them of their adoptions. Some adoptive parents especially feared the social history questions the children would ask about their biological families. Others deliberately "forgot" the background information the adoption agency provided and preferred to tell the child they knew nothing about the biological parents [Lockridge 1947: 152]. Similarly, Raymond [1955] reported that adoptive parents voiced resentment at social workers for burdening them with the social history of the biological family. According to Raymond [1955: 80], "They wish they had not been given so much concrete information about their child's background. This information, they felt, had been of no positive help to them in any direction, and made them feel uncomfortable about having to evade some direct questions when they would have preferred to say truthfully, 'I don't know.' "

By the early 1950s, in the wake of an upsurge in out-of-wedlock births and the increasing application of psychoanalytic concepts to child-placing, social workers revived Gallagher's plea to withhold from prospective adoptive parents all information about the child's biological family. They did so to ease adoptive parents' discomfort in discussing the issue, to relieve them of the burden of possessing information they were not "mature" enough to absorb, and to avoid stigmatizing the adopted child. The first indication of a change in attitude occurred in 1954 when psychiatric social worker Kohlsaat and psychiatrist Johnson [1954: 92], both of the Mayo Clinic, argued in *Social Casework* that "because of the possibility of neurotic character traits in the adoptive parents, they and the child must be protected by keeping from them any knowledge about the child's background." On the one hand, they feared that adoptive parents, "hostilely envious of those who can bear children," would use negative information as a "cudgel" when angered by their child's misbehavior. On the other hand, Kohlsaat and Johnson asserted, any criticism of the adopted child's biological parents, especially if it had to do with illegitimacy, would prevent the resolution of the Oedipus complex and be devastating to the child's self-esteem. To avoid these problems, they recommended that all confidential information about the biological family be cleared through a few selected adoption agency supervisors, who would then certify the baby's adoptability to the caseworker. By insulating the caseworker from any knowledge of the biological family's background, Kohlsaat and Johnson believed that the adoptive parents would accept the caseworkers attitude that "I know this to be a fine baby because my investigating chief and consultants have so agreed;

that is enough for me" [1954: 94]. Kohlsaat and Johnson labeled prospective adoptive parents who demanded knowledge of the child's past as "very anxious, narcissistic, and unconsciously sadistic" [1954: 93].

Like Gallagher's, Kohlsaat and Johnson's views were quickly denounced by adoption workers. Three social workers responded to the Kohlsaat and Johnson article in a subsequent issue of *Social Casework*. One noted that Kohlsaat and Johnson's basic assumption that adoptive parents were neurotic and could not be trusted was "alien to our long-standing belief in the basic integrity of people, and faith in the potential strength of the parent-child relationship" [Readers' comments 1954: 259]. All objected strongly to the idea of completely withholding biological family information from adoptive parents. Yet all of the social workers advocated not full but "selective and positive" disclosure of the biological family's background because adoptive parents should not "be burdened with irrelevant history or particular psychopathology" [Readers' comments 1954: 261].

The controversy over whether or not adoption workers should disclose biological family information to the adoptive parents revealed the fissure dividing the social work profession, but the dispute between total disclosure and total withholding had ended. The debate had now shifted to how much family information should be withheld. The results of a 1954 CWLA survey of 257 adoption agencies confirmed this trend. Although agencies were still evenly divided on the question of disclosing family background information, in practice those agencies claiming "complete disclosure" qualified their answers by stating they gave only "selected background material" or left out "sordid or irrelevant details" [Schapiro 1956: 86–87]. No longer did adoption agencies view the ideal of conveying family information as obligatory. Even those agency authorities favoring full disclosure justified the practice only to forestall adoptive parents from returning to the agency or receiving false information from unreliable sources.

Agency authorities defended the practice of giving adoptive parents only favorable information about the biological parents because it would help them "to assist the child in building his own positive image later."[19] In addition, agency officials reasoned, the sharing of irrelevant or unverified information was of little benefit to the parent-child relationship and "may cause real damage in arousing anxiety and apprehension."[20] One example was incest. Many agency officials believed that it was "doubtful that knowing about incest in the child's background [was] helpful to parents" and thus did not share such information with them.[21] One unidentified agency official enunciated what was becoming the standard justification for withholding information from adoptive parents: "We should be honest, but when we don't tell, we know why we aren't telling. The agency bears a responsibility not to share things which will work harm upon a child. In that sense we are dishonest."[22]

Although both policies—full and selective disclosure—were applied on a case-by-case basis, adoption authorities were tilting toward not being "overmeticulous in presenting all the negatives."[23] In January 1955, CWLA sponsored a National Conference on Adoption at which Kohlsaat and Johnson's extreme view that "nothing should be told to adoptive parents regarding the child's background" resurfaced. When some conference participants disagreed, a consensus was reached that "agencies should select pertinent facts helpful to the adoptive parents and child" and withhold facts that were prejudicial or stigmatizing. The conference report noted that there was considerable disagreement on what information was "dangerous or not necessary to share."[24] Ultimately, policy was left to the discretion of the adoption agencies, which increasingly chose to reveal to adoptive parents only favorable family information or none at all. The selective viewpoint was endorsed in CWLA's revision of its *Standards* [1959: 27], which instructed member agencies not to give adoptive parents "information which is not relevant to the child's development and would only arouse anxiety."

Self-help adoption manuals of the 1950s provided a rationale for the agencies' selective disclosure policy and implicitly supported adoptive parents' reluctance to respond to their children's request for biological family information. They suggested that without such "sordid details" adoptive parents could, "with true peace of mind," honestly plead ignorance when their children asked questions about their biological families [Raymond 1955: 80]. Similarly, Ernest and Francis Cady's *How To Adopt a Child* [1956] gave adoptive parents concrete examples of the type of information that should be withheld from children, including incest, biological fathers in prison, and "incorrigible" mothers. In the latter case, the Cadys suggested that it might be kinder to the children to imply that the biological mother was dead. *The New York Times Magazine* noted that although professional adoption workers did not approve of such falsehoods, some adoptive parents believed that it was "simpler and kinder to say that the natural parents were dead" [Barclay 1958].

Current Agency Disclosure Policies

In the past two decades, adoption agencies have, unknowingly, returned to the more open disclosure policy of the early twentieth century. They have changed their stance because of three principal reasons: differences in the population of children coming into the adoption system, changes in adoptive parents' attitudes, and demands by adoption rights activists for open records. Adoption experts have increasingly recognized that as the population of adopted children has changed from one in which healthy Caucasian infants predominated to one in which children are often older, from a minority background, or possessing special needs, adoptive parents must be given all the medical and family information concerning the child [Feigelman & Silverman 1983; Barth & Berry 1988; Cole 1990]. In addition, many adoption officials have come to realize that they need not fear, as they once did, that adoptive parents will reject children with special needs. Whereas 30 years ago most adoptive parents demanded a physically and mentally perfect child, today more are willing to accept older or disabled children who might once have been thought unadoptable [Barth & Berry 1988; Groze et al. 1992]. Finally, the demand of adoption rights activists in the early 1970s to open all adoption records has found support among a significant number of social workers, thus raising further doubts about adoption agencies' policy of withholding information from adoptive parents [Wertkin 1986].

By 1978, all of these circumstances caused CWLA to again revise its *Standards* and eliminate completely the section on withholding adverse information from adoptive parents [1978: 47–48]. In addition, the 1978 *Standards*, reaffirmed in 1988 [CWLA 1988: 37–38], recommended that CWLA's member agencies give adoptive parents the child's developmental, medical, and genetic history, as well as nonidentifying information about the biological parents. Reinforcing adoption agencies' voluntary compliance, many state legislatures responded to adoptive parents' demands that adoption agencies release family information. In the following decade, that is, roughly 1978 to 1990, at least 21 states enacted mandatory disclosure statutes requiring adoption agencies or intermediaries to provide adoptive parents with information about the child's health, education, and family background [Dickson 1991; DeWoody 1993]. As "wrongful adoption" suits receive more publicity from the media [CBS 1992], additional states will undoubtedly enact similar legislation.

Conclusion

Where, then, does this leave "wrongful adoption" suits? In light of the research presented here, it is clear that adoption agencies' disclosure policies have been cyclical in nature. Only for a short period during the twentieth century—the mid-1950s to approximately the early 1980s—did adoption agencies withhold negative medical and social information from adoptive parents.

Moreover, it is only in the short period, roughly the early 1970s—in which restrictive disclosure policies coincided with a dramatic change in the character of adopted children—that the basis for "wrongful adoption" suits emerged. In the future, it is safe to predict, the incidence of wrongful adoption suits will decline radically and be viewed as a poignant oddity in the history of adoption. ◆

Notes

1. The Children's Home Society of Washington's adoption case records are located at the Children's Home Society of Washington, Adoption Resource Center, 3300 N.E. 65th Street, Seattle, WA 98115. They run consecutively from 1895 to 1973 and contain data on postadoption contact through 1988. I have sampled one out of ten of the Society's 21,000 case records. This study's sample consists of 79 cases or about 15% of all postadoption contact by adoption triad members.

2. Children's Home Society of Washington Case Record 2462. (Hereafter cited as CHSW CR). All names of CHSW clients used in this article are fictitious. Despite the Society caseworker's interference, Jack and Martha eventually married.

3. CHSW CR 5012.

4. CHSW CR 4942.

5. This paragraph is based on the following CHSW CR: 16652, 2462, 3512, 4302, 4842, 4942, 5802, 8242, 3432, 3512.

6. CHSW CR 1732, 2462, 2542, 2672, 2842, 2862, 3052, 3312, 3362, 3432, 3672, 3682, 4012, 4302, 4442, 4542, 4782, 4942, 5362, 5532, 5592, 5802, 5812, 6162, 6632, 6722, 6842, 7092, 7102, 8022, 8112, 8242, 8692.

7. See for example, CHSW CR 1732, 2053, 4442.

8. CHSW CR 322, 1372, 1662, 2202, 2462, 2542, 2772, 3032, 3172, 3542, 3862, 4462, 4542, 4592, 4742, 4782, 4942, 5012, 5802, 7082, 7582, 8112, 8632, 8662, 9082, 12214, 12312, 12522, 12643, 13334, 16334, 16433, 16583.

9. CHSW CR 3032.

10. CHSW CR 3862. See also CHSW CR 5852.

11. CHSW CR 2462, 2772, 3862, 4542, 7082, 9082, 2202, 3542, religion 4742, 4592.

12. CHSW CR 2772. See also CHSW CR 1842.

13. CHSW CR 12.

14. CHSW CR 1732, 2462, 3312, 3672, 3682, 4442, 4542, 5812.

15. CHSW CR 6542, 16652, 2462, 3512, 4302, 4842, 6402, 16433, 16652.

16. CHSW CR 322, 962, 1112, 1842, 2772, 3172, 3542, 3862, 4462, 4602, 4742, 4782, 4942, 5012, 8112, 8632, 9082, 12312, 12522, 16583.

17. CHSW CR 1842, 5752, 5802.

18. CHSW CR 4342. See also, CR 882, 1732, 2232, 2842, 4042, 4442, 4462, 5582, 6632.

19. Child Welfare League of America, "Agency Adoption Practices: Abstracts from the Preliminary Report of the Survey of the Child Welfare League of America." (June 1955): 41. Child Welfare League of America Records, Box 16 (7), Social Welfare History Archives, University of Minnesota.

20. Ibid., 42.

21. Ibid., 42–43.

22. Ibid., 43.

23. Ibid.

24. Ibid.

References

Barclay, D. (1958, November 9). Chosen children: A fresh look. *The New York Times Magazine*, p. 60.

Barth, R. P., & Berry, M. (1988). *Adoption and disruption: Rates, risks, and responses.* New York: Aldine De Gruyter.

CBS Evening News, November 11, 1992.

Cady, E., & Cady, F. (1956). *How to adopt a child*. New York: Whiteside & William Morrow.

Carp, E. W. (1992). The sealed adoption records controversy in historical perspective: The case of the Children's Home Society of Washington. *Journal of Sociology and Social Welfare, 19,* 27–58.

Child Welfare League of America. (1932). *Standards for institutions caring for dependent children*. New York: Author.

Child Welfare League of America. (1947). *Report on adoption practices, policies, and procedures*. New York: Author.

Child Welfare League of America. (1959). *Standards for adoption service* (rev. ed.). New York: Author.

Child Welfare League of America. (1978). *Standards for adoption service* (rev. ed.). New York: Author.

Child Welfare League of America. (1988). *Standards for adoption service* (rev. ed.). Washington, DC: Author.

Clothier, F. (1942). Placing the child for adoption. *Mental Hygiene, 26,* 257–274.

Cole, E. S. (1990). A history of the adoption of children with handicaps. In L. M. Glidden (Ed.), *Formed families: Adoption of children with handicaps* (pp. 51–58). New York: Haworth Press.

Cole, E. S., & Donley, K. (1990). History, values, and placement policy issues in adoption. In D. M. Brodzinsky & M. D. Schechter (Eds.), *The Psychology of Adoption* (pp. 273–294). New York: Oxford University Press.

Connelly, S. M. (1991). The need for disclosure laws: A survey of the wrongful-adoption cause of action and statutory remedies for adoption fraud. *Review of Litigation, 10,* 793–821.

Cravens, H. (1978). *The triumph of evolution: American scientists and the heredity-environment controversy, 1900–1941*. Philadelphia: University of Pennsylvania Press.

DeWoody, M. (1993). Adoption and disclosure of medical and social history: A review of the law. *Child Welfare, 72,* 195–218.

Dickson, J. H. (1991). The emerging rights of adoptive parents: Substance or specter? *UCLA Law Review, 38,* 917–990.

Feigelman, W., & Silverman, A. R. (1983). *Chosen children: New patterns of adoptive relationships*. New York: Praeger.

Gallagher, E. G. (1936). *The adopted child*. New York: Reynal & Hitchcock.

Goldenhersh, J. (1992). Adoption agency may be held liable for misrepresentations to adoptive parents. *Family Law Reporter, 18,* 1223–1224.

Groze, V., Haines-Simeon, M., & McMillen, J. C. (1992). Families adopting children with or at risk of HIV Infection. *Child & Adolescent Social Work Journal, 9,* 409–426.

Haller, M. H. (1963). *Eugenics: Hereditarian attitudes in American thought*. New Brunswick, NJ: Rutgers University Press.

Hewins, K. P., & Webster, L. J. (1927). *The work of child placing agencies* (Children's Bureau Publication No. 171). Washington, DC: U.S. Government Printing Office.

Hutchinson, Dorothy. (1943). *In quest of foster parents: A point of view on homefinding*. New York: Columbia University Press.

Illinois Children's Home & Aid Society. (1927). Safeguarding adoption. *Homelife for Children, 14*(4), 11.

Kohlsaat, B., & Johnson, A. M. (1954). Some suggestions for practice in infant adoptions. *Social Casework, 35,* 91–99.

Jaffee, B., & Fanshel, D. (1970). *How they fared in adoption: A follow-up study*. New York: Columbia University Press.

Lambert, W., & Moses, J. M. (1991, October 30). Couple gets $3.8 million in adoption suit. *The Wall Street Journal*, p. B6.

Lippman, H. S. (1937). Suitability of children for adoption. *American Journal of Orthopsychiatry, 7,* 270–273.

Lockridge, F. (1947). *Adopting a child*. New York: Greenberg.

MacKenzie, C. (1940, November 10). A boom in adoptions. *The New York Times Magazine*, p. 7.

Maley, J. R. (1987). Wrongful adoption: Monetary damages as a superior remedy to annulment for adoptive parents victimized by adoption fraud." *Indiana Law Review, 20,* 709–734.

Mohr, G. J. (1937). Adoption. *Child Welfare League of America Bulletin, 16*(8), 1, 4–5.

New York State Charities Aid Association. (1934). *State Charities Aid Association News, 23*(1), 2.

Raymond, L. (1955). *Adoption . . . and after.* New York: Harper and Row.

Readers' Comments. (1954). *Social Casework, 35,* 259–262.

Schapiro, M. (1956). *A study of adoption practice* (Vol. 1). New York: Child Welfare League of America.

Sargent, H. D. (1935). Is it safe to adopt a child? *Parents' Magazine, 10,* 10, 26.

Session laws of the state of Washington. (1939). Chap. 133, Sect. 1. Olympia, WA: State Law Printing.

Slingerland, W. H. (1919). *Child placing in families: A manual for students and social workers.* New York: Russell Sage Foundation.

Theis, S. (1936). Book review. *Survey, 72,* 320.

Watson, A. E. (1918). The illegitimate family. *Annals of the American Academy of Political and Social Science, 77,* 103–116.

Wertkin, R. A. (1986). Adoption workers' views on sealed records. *Public Welfare, 44,* 15–17.

Woo, J. (1992, July 9). Adoption suits target agencies for negligence. *The Wall Street Journal,* p. B1.

Willsie, H. (1919). When is a child adoptable? *The Delineator, 95,* 35–37.

12

FROM "OPERATION BROWN BABY" TO "OPPORTUNITY": THE PLACEMENT OF CHILDREN OF COLOR AT THE BOYS AND GIRLS AID SOCIETY OF OREGON

Patricia M. Collmeyer

This article traces the history of adoption practices for children of color at the Boys and Girls Aid Society of Oregon. Research utilizing the casefiles and archives of the agency revealed that during the study period (1944–1977), 466 children of color were placed with adoptive parents of the same race or of a different race. The children included Asian Americans, Native Americans, and African Americans.

Patricia Collmeyer, M.A., M.Ed., is an independent scholar who serves as the archivist/historian of the Boys and Girls Aid Society of Oregon. The author wishes to thank Marie Lanser Beck for her helpful comments and to acknowledge the cooperation and support of many former and present staff members of the Boys and Girls Aid Society of Oregon, especially Allan Neubauer.

235

In 1899, a mother in Portland, Oregon, relinquished her 20-day-old daughter, Lena, to Mr. and Mrs. Mow with the hope that they would "adopt, educate and raise my girl baby." The Mows cared for Lena for nearly two years until one June day when she was abruptly removed from their home by three policemen. The newspaper reported that the officers "tried to gain admittance into the living apartments of the Mow family, but Mrs. Mow refused to open the door. The warrant was read to her through the door, and the detectives kicked the door in, and took forcible possession of the child" ["Another child" 1901].

The authorities surrendered Lena to the Boys and Girls Aid Society of Oregon (BGAS) for placement with another family. William T. Gardner, who was then superintendent of the agency, opposed having the Mows "associating with or influencing the behavior of" Lena ["She says Young" 1901] because the child was Caucasian and the Mows were Chinese. Gardner strongly disapproved of this transracial placement. His attitude, and the subsequent adoption of Lena by a Caucasian family, directly contradicted the wishes of Lena's biological mother, who had personally placed her daughter with the Mows.

In 1982, Lena, age 83, returned to the offices of the Boys and Girls Aid Society of Oregon. Although unable to remember anything of her early years in Portland's Chinatown, she did muse about how things might have been. "In this day and age Chinese people probably could adopt me. It must have been a sad time to have strange men come and take me from my parents" [BGAS 1982].

The question of transracial adoption posed problems in turn-of-the-century Portland and continues to be a controversial issue nearly 100 years later. The Boys and Girls Aid Society of Oregon has sought homes for children of color for many years, but the adoption practices of the agency have changed over time. In its efforts to attract adoptive families, the agency pioneered new practices. The agency's efforts also reflected the influence of broader societal factors such as public acceptance of adoption and community attitudes towards racial groups.

The Boys and Girls Aid Society

The Boys and Girls Aid Society of Oregon, a private, nonsectarian, child welfare agency, was founded in 1885 by prominent citizens of Portland for the purpose of rescuing homeless, neglected, or abused children of Oregon [BGAS Flyer 1895]. Although removed from the large urban areas of the country, Portland was not immune from the problems plaguing American cities at the end of the nineteenth century. Truancy, parental alcoholism, youthful vandalism, and child abandonment threatened the fabric of this new western city. The agency's founding members sought alternatives for children caught in the midst of family turmoil.

From its earliest days, the agency believed that children were best served within a family environment, and sought to place children in boarding or adoptive homes rather than in institutions. By the 1940s, the work of the agency emphasized adoption, however, BGAS remained a multiservice agency, providing maternity services to unwed mothers and foster boarding-home care for children.

In 1944, Stuart Stimmel became the director of BGAS. A graduate of the Columbia University School of Social Work, Stimmel proved to be a perfect match for the agency. He held the conviction that each child deserved the "security of a permanent family. For children who have lost their original families this can best be accomplished through adoption by parents who are able to make that deep personal commitment which every child needs to know has been made to him" [Stimmel 1961–1977]. As a vocal supporter of the American Civil Liberties Union, Stimmel viewed the child's need for a permanent home as a civil rights matter.

Although childless himself, Stimmel aided thousands of children during his 33-year tenure at the agency. His dynamic leadership and vision spurred the agency to pioneer such adoption practices as direct infant placement, a condensed prelegalization period, single-parent adoptions, and the adoption of special-needs children. Stimmel, a lawyer and member of the Oregon State Bar Association, advocated changes in adoption law to reaffirm that adoption was "as final and as binding as biological parenthood" [Stimmel 1961–1977].

The agency's efforts to find homes for children were productive. Adoptions rose from an average of 69 per year in the 1940s to 158 in the 1950s. During the 1960s, adoptions averaged 204 per year, and BGAS became the largest adoption agency in Oregon. Despite this success, Stimmel realized that children of color, for whom the agency had difficulty finding permanent homes, required special attention.

The agency served children from a wide range of backgrounds. It obtained adoptive homes for children from Oregon's Native American population as well as for children of Asian ancestry, placing the majority of these children with Caucasian families. In 1962, Stimmel described these early efforts: "Since World War II we have experienced little difficulty in finding good adoptive homes for children of Oriental or Indian ancestry . . . . We have consistently placed Negro and part-Negro children in adoption but it has been difficult to find enough good adoptive homes for all the children who need loving parents" [Stimmel 1961–1977].

"Operation Brown Baby"

Portland was often an entry point for Asians from Pacific Rim countries. As well, with the availability of shipyard work during World War II, the state's small African American population jumped by 300%.[1] To meet the challenge of finding homes for a growing number of children from these populations, Stimmel developed a program to put his agency in closer contact with communities of color. In 1956, Mark Smith, a prominent African

American, was named to the Board of Trustees of the agency. As administrator of the civil rights division of the Oregon Bureau of Labor, Smith brought to the board the respect of the African American community and the ability to champion children's rights. For the next decade, Smith, in partnership with Stimmel, reached out to the African American community.

At the same time, Stimmel hired the agency's first African American staff member. Kathryn Bogle, also a much-loved, active member of Portland's African American community, gave the agency a respected liaison to Oregon's African Americans. Stimmel also cultivated friendships with other prominent African Americans, among them Edwin Berry, the founder of the Portland Urban League. These bridges to communities of color were instrumental in expanding the agency's services to meet the needs of an increasing number of children of color. In 1955, the number of placements of these children doubled the number of the previous year.

As the agency's programs became better known to communities of color, the number of children referred to the agency also increased. By early 1957, more children of color were under the care of the agency than ever before, but they were also waiting longer for adoptive placement.[2] To recruit additional adoptive families of color, Bogle and two other staff members addressed the Portland Urban League about the agency's adoption program, hoping to enlist support and "dispel many misconceptions" [BGAS board minutes, February 27, 1957].

By May 1957, the agency was ready to launch a new program to recruit homes for children of color. Bogle named this special project "Operation Brown Baby" and personally directed many of the program's initiatives. She approached many of her friends about adopting a child, asked African American ministers to identify adoptive family candidates, and personally visited prospective adoptive parents.

These efforts paid off. Placements of children of color rose from 12 in 1955 to 33 in 1959. Although "Operation Brown Baby" concentrated on finding homes within the African American community, other non-Caucasian placements increased correspondingly (see figure 1).

A Second Recruitment Campaign for Children of Color

By 1961, however, the number of placements for children of color dropped to 15, and the agency revitalized its efforts to recruit minority homes, especially for African American children. In contrast to the focus of the "Operation Brown Baby" program, Stimmel added a new element to this campaign [BGAS Board Minutes January 11, 1961]: "To meet the problem [of the lack of adoptive homes for African American and part-African American children] every effort would be made to learn of Caucasian families as well as Negro families who might be interested and able to provide good permanent homes." Although children of mixed racial background had been placed previously in Caucasian homes, the board noted that "there had never been any specific attempt to encourage white families to apply to the Society to adopt Negro children."

Stimmel designed a plan to educate the board about other agencies' efforts to develop transracial adoption programs. He provided them with details of the Montreal Children's Centre's program,[4] with magazine articles showcasing Caucasian families with African American children,[5] and with the writings of Judge Justine Wise Polier of the New York City Domestic Relations Court and also president of the board of Louise Wise Services.[6]

Anticipating a later generation's celebration of cultural diversity, Judge Polier warned of the consequences of "the arrogance or ignorance that withholds appreciation from cultural values other than our own." The attitude of cultural superiority manifested itself in the field of service to children as "a theory that proclaims that *adults can only like children who look like themselves and have backgrounds similar to their own* [emphasis added]." She called upon professional workers to remove limitations and to

FIGURE 1
Non-Caucasian Placements (1955–1959)

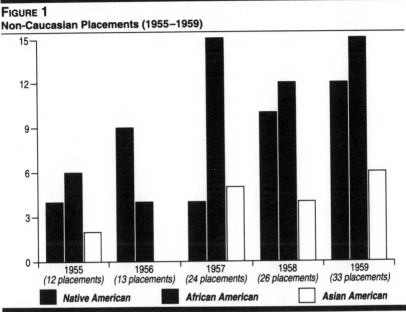

commit themselves "to provide *equal service to all children* [emphasis added] and their parents" [Polier 1960]. In Portland, Oregon, Stimmel heeded Judge Polier's call with a determination honed by many years of commitment to the cause of civil rights. He wanted all children, regardless of racial heritage, to have the chance for a permanent, loving home.

Stimmel anticipated some public disapproval but also believed that society might be more receptive to transracial adoption because of the burgeoning civil rights activities at the time. At a board meeting in January of 1961, he cited the "indignation of many people toward Southern violence to prevent school integration" as indicative of "a more favorable climate for public consideration of this matter" [BGAS Board Minutes 1885–1977].

Following the board meeting, Stimmel notified the staff of the board's endorsement. He also wrote ministers throughout the state, asking for help in locating potential adoptive families "of all racial backgrounds." Stimmel cautioned the ministers that "in the absence of special help, many healthy, intelligent children

will be deprived of permanent, loving homes solely because of
the color of their skin. They will be condemned to growing up in
an institution or in a series of temporary foster homes" [Stimmel
1961–1977].

Throughout 1961, the agency's staff members developed the
program. Their report, "A Study of Information for Recruitment of
Negro Adoptive Applicants," encapsulated the findings of recent
research and studies[7] and suggested ways to develop a three-phase
program in Oregon: (1) to attract the interest of adoptive parents; (2)
to hold adoptive parents' interest, gain their trust, and guide them
through the study process; and (3) to find the right child for the
specific family, "giving due consideration to cultural factors"
[BGAS Negro Adoptive Home Committee 1961–1962].

The agency reviewed its intake policies in light of the concerns of some African American adoptive applicants. When studies revealed that African American applicants felt "fearful" of
legal involvement, the agency suggested that "we relieve them of
some of this by providing legal services" [BGAS Negro Adoptive
Home Committee 1961–1962].

The Negro Adoptive Home Committee

The Negro Adoptive Home Committee, formed in the fall of 1961
by members of the agency's adoption division, developed an
11-point program to stimulate interest in the adoption of African
American children. Several of the committee's points highlighted
ways to publicize the need for minority adoptive families, among
them radio advertisements, newspaper and magazine articles,
poster displays, and strategically placed brochures. Direct contact would be made through African American community leaders and civic, religious, and fraternal organizations. The final
point was to "plan for, and develop non-Negro homes for Negro
children" [BGAS Negro Adoptive Home Committee 1961–1962].

The committee organized an informal evening for African
American parents who had previously adopted African Ameri-

can children, "to ask them their ideas and advice as to how we might attract more applicants and serve them better." Members of 12 adoptive families attended this meeting. Mark Smith, now the first African American president of the board, stated that the agency wanted honest suggestions about ways to improve the adoption process for African American applicants. He advised the group that "since they knew what adoption through this agency is like, they would be in the best position to help." During an "animated discussion," the group identified some problems in the adoption process, including the amount of "red tape" involved, the length of the adoption process, and, as one man acknowledged, the "reluctance [of some adoption applicants] to share intimately with the agency information about their personal lives." The group also made encouraging suggestions, such as hosting a panel discussion meeting, holding meetings in more convenient locations, and concentrating more of the agency's publicity "on the fact that Negro and other minority children are also available and that Negro families are actually adopting such children" [BGAS Negro Adoptive Home Committee 1962].

The renewed efforts to find more adoptive homes for children of color were successful, but, in contrast to the results of "Operation Brown Baby," only the number of African American placements increased (see figure 2).

A Third Attempt

By 1967, after another decline in the total number of placements of children of color (only nine in 1965 and 11 in 1966), the agency launched a third recruitment campaign. The Minority Adoption Resource Committee met "to pool ideas towards more concerted recruitment in the Negro community" [BGAS Interagency and Minority Placement Files 1972–1977]. Building on the success of previous campaigns, the committee made several proposals: (1) approach African American families who had successfully adopted in the past; (2) meet with prominent members of the

FIGURE 2
Non-Caucasian Placements (1961–1963)

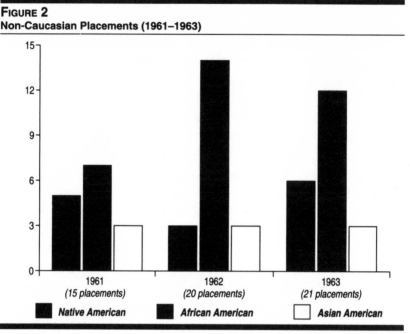

African American community; (3) place publicity in strategic
centers "where a concentration of Negro employees and participants might be expected" [BGAS Interagency and Minority
Placement Files 1972–1977].

The agency again added more staff and board members of
color to help with its campaign. Stimmel also hired Charles Olds
as associate state director. Olds was the previous director of the
Children's Home Society of Minnesota, whose placement efforts
for children of color had been discussed in Harriet Fricke's article
"Interracial Adoption: The Little Revolution" [1965].

The agency sought to educate the community about the need
for more homes for children of color. A local television station
developed a documentary, *Run, Jimmy, Run*, that featured two
Caucasian Portland families who had adopted African American
children, and cited the work that the agency was doing in the field
of transracial adoption. The agency subsequently reprinted the television show as a 16mm film, which was then distributed to other

child-welfare agencies.[8] Stimmel later estimated that millions of people had viewed this film [Adoption agency. . . 1972].

On April 21, 1968, *The Oregonian* noted that "because of an increasing trend toward interracial adoptions, The Boys and Girls Aid Society of Oregon will place focus on the subject at its 83rd annual meeting," and the newspaper acknowledged that "emphasis has been given by the society to finding more adoptive homes for children of Negro background and enlisting white couples to adopt such children." The featured speaker of the evening chose "The Interracial Family" as his topic,[9] commending families who had adopted transracially for "playing an important part in the forward motions being made on racial relations" [Minority group. . . 1968].

"Opportunity"

In October 1968, BGAS distributed flyers to administrators of adoption agencies throughout the country announcing a new program that would "give impetus" to the transracial adoption movement. Noting that "Negro families are adopting, often in greater proportion to their number than white families," the agency acknowledged that "there just aren't enough such families to meet the needs of the children." Citing its own successes and those of several other agencies, the agency affirmed its "conviction that interracial adoption of black children is at least *a partial solution* [emphasis added] to the problem of the lack of opportunity for these children." To assert its belief that adoption provided the best chance for a permanent, loving home for all children who needed families, the agency christened the program "Opportunity," hoping to help other agencies build successful transracial adoption programs [BGAS Opportunity Memo 1967–1977].

The agency received support for this program from within the African American community. In 1972, Stimmel noted that "outstanding champions of the rights of black people, like Whitney Young and countless others, strongly supported the development of interracial adoption from its very beginning. Young had applauded families who were helping "spur the color-blindness growing in this country" [Young 1968] by opening their homes to children of other races. Hesitant agencies were pressured to abandon adoption practices that smacked of segregation [Stimmel 1961–1977].

The media noted the agency's contributions to the increased number of transracial adoptions. In August 1969, an Associated Press article featured the "Opportunity" program. On August 28, 1969, the Huntley-Brinkley News broadcast a report about the agency and about transracial adoption.

Heightened national exposure prompted families from across the country to write to the agency for information. The agency encouraged contact with local agencies, but some agencies in other states reported having difficulties placing children of color, primarily African American children, within their own borders. During the early 1970s, therefore, the agency began placing children of color from as far away as New York, Tennessee, Ohio, Montana, and Indiana with Caucasian families in Oregon. In 1972, the agency staff placed 20 out-of-state African American children.[10]

Recognizing a need to understand national minority adoption trends, the "Opportunity" program began a survey of adoption practices of other agencies. The survey had two purposes: first, "to see how many blacks are placed with white families and [second] to prod reluctant agencies by showing them other agencies do it with no ill effects" [Transracial adoption. . . 1971]. Although transracial adoptions were the subject of this survey, the increased publicity about placements of children of color had another effect. Stimmel noted, "It focused the spotlight on the needs of black children and has stimulated efforts on all sides to increase the number of adoptions [by] black families . . . . Prior to the publicity given to interracial adoption, the number of black children being adopted by black families had risen very slowly" [Stimmel 1961–1977].

Although the "Opportunity" program studied the adoption of African American children in particular, it also generated information about adoptions of children of color in general. In 1969, the program reported that there were "two significant findings . . . first, that children of black ancestry represent about half of all the non-white children placed, even though Negroes represent 90% of the non-white population; and, second, that 23% of the children of black ancestry placed by the agencies went to white families" [BGAS "Opportunity" 1969].

The "Opportunity" program's annual survey kept child welfare agencies across the country aware of the growing numbers of transracial adoptions, but it may also have contributed ultimately to the decline of this practice. With the greater publicity about transracial adoptions came a growing unrest among some segments of society about the merit of such placements. In 1972, at its first annual meeting, the National Association of Black Social Workers (NABSW) issued a strong statement in opposition to transracial adoption, contending that rather than be placed with Caucasian adoptive families, "black children should remain in foster homes and institutions" [Furor over . . . 1972]. Reaction to the NABSW statements was swift and sharp, from African Americans and Caucasians.

Dr. James Curtis, an African American psychiatrist, described it as "the most destructive position that could be taken," echoing the credo of Stimmel and many other child welfare professionals that children deserve permanent, loving homes. Dr. Julia Makarushka, a Caucasian psychologist, added in agreement, "I think that all things being equal, it is better for a black child to be in a black family than a white family. But often the alternative to a white family is the destructive setting of a foster home or an institution. These are not conducive to raising strong, healthy black children" [Furor over. . . 1972].

Nevertheless, the NABSW statement did have a chilling effect on the number of children adopted transracially. "Opportunity" program's survey demonstrated the extent to which such placements declined (see figure 3).

By September 1973, Stimmel reported on the difficulty of freeing children for transracial adoptions: "We talk to other [out-of-state] agencies, and they say they have black children that need homes. We say we can place them. Then they ask if we can guarantee black homes. When we say no, they respond that they are under pressure to secure only black homes for black children" [Group said. . . 1973]. Stimmel added that the agency could place an additional 100 out-of-state African American children if only the agencies would release them for adoption by Caucasian families. The actual adoption figures for the agency reflect these difficulties (see figure 4). The peak years for Asian American placements were 1959, 1967, and 1968. The most Native American placements came in 1969; African American adoptions peaked in 1971.

As the agency grappled with the evolving dynamics of African American adoptions, changes were imminent for Native American placements as well. The Indian Child Welfare Act of 1978 gave Indian tribes exclusive jurisdiction over adoption placement for children eligible for tribal membership. Between 1944 and 1977, the agency's Native American placements accounted for the largest number of transracial adoptions (132) and the highest percentage of transracial placements for any minority group (94%). After 1977, fewer Native American placements were handled by the agency than before.

Stimmel's Retirement

Stimmel retired from the agency in 1977, having assembled a staff in accord with his progressive views. After his retirement, however, the agency's focus was no longer on adoption. The yearly totals of adoptive placements plummeted from a high of 263 in 1968 to a low of 56 in 1974. The agency continued to place children of color, but the "Opportunity" program came to an end. Many other agencies

FIGURE 3
African American Children Adopted Transracially (1969–1975)

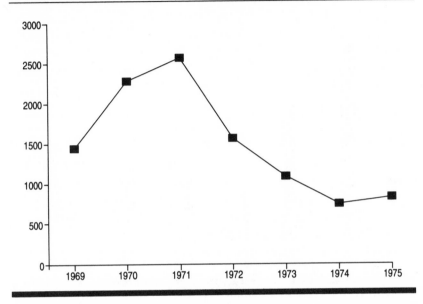

stopped making transracial placements or made them quietly. After 1977, BGAS continued to develop other programs for children, but the days of such concentrated attention on adoption and placements of children of color were over.

Conclusion

Beginning in 1944, BGAS emphasized programs that encouraged adoptive placement of children in need of permanent homes. A dedicated staff, dynamic leader, and committed board of trustees converged to introduce innovative, nontraditional adoption practices. An increase in the number of children of color, coupled with a growing consciousness of the civil rights of all people, challenged the agency to develop solutions to a growing need for adoptive homes for children of color.

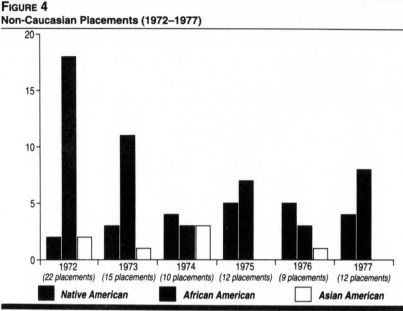

Figure 4
Non-Caucasian Placements (1972–1977)

Children from three principal non-Caucasian groups—Asian American, Native American, and African American heritage—received assistance from the agency. Finding homes for Asian American and Native American children was not difficult; however, most of these children were placed outside their own racial group. Ninety-four percent of Native American placements were transracial, as were 65% of Asian American placements.

Adoption of African American children often required intensive recruitment of adoptive families because transracial placements for African American children were not widely accepted for much of the period of this study. Between 1944 and 1977, the agency inaugurated three intensified drives to secure more adoptive homes for African American children: "Operation Brown Baby," "The Negro Home Adoption Committee," and "Opportunity." With each program, the agency built on the success of the previous one, adding new elements as it moved from an emphasis primarily on adoption of African American children by same race parents to a broad, multiracial appeal.

"Operation Brown Baby," the successful 1957 recruitment campaign, resulted in a dramatic increase in the number of new African American adoptive homes. A second major drive in 1961 met with somewhat similar results. The agency understood that when African American families were sought out, they would adopt. But other factors resulted in an increase in the number of available children. During the 1950s, as the minority community learned that social agency resources were available to them, they began turning to agencies more readily in time of need. The number of African American children waiting for adoption began growing at a faster rate than did the number of available homes.

The size of Oregon's African American population seriously constrained the agency's efforts to find homes for African American children. The number of families who were financially, emotionally, and physically able to adopt a child was finite. Two successful recruitment campaigns demonstrated the great effort and interest of Oregon's African American community to help children find homes. Fifty-eight percent of African American children placed by the agency went to African American adoptive families, a testament to the willingness of Oregon's African American families to answer the agency's call. But the agency was waging a losing campaign.

The number of children needing families was increasing far too quickly. Many of these children did not come to the agency from within the African American community alone. Fifty percent of the children identified as African American in this study had Caucasian mothers. Could the small African American community of Oregon ever have been able to absorb this growing number of children? Was that ever a fair expectation?

Beginning in 1967, the agency's emphasis on placements for children of color turned to transracial adoptions. Fifty percent of the agency's total Asian American, 82% of the African American, and 44% of the Native American transracial placements were made during the last 10 years of this study.

The heightened consciousness of civil rights injustices and the growing societal acceptance of transracial adoption, augmented by the agency's commitment to finding homes for children of color through the "Opportunity" program, certainly encouraged growing numbers of people to consider transracial adoption. Stimmel and the community leaders who supported him, along with many families both within and outside communities of color, shared a common belief that children have a fundamental right to a permanent, loving home. They believed that denying children homes solely because of their race or the race of the adoptive parents violated their civil rights.

Afterword

Nearly 100 years after Lena was separated from her Chinese family, controversy still surrounds the question of transracial adoptive placements. The growing number of children in the foster care system—estimated at 462,000 in 1993—has spurred new debate about the question of race and adoption. Finding homes for children of color, a major objective of BGAS in the 1950s and 1960s, continues to challenge social workers as the demand for adoptive parents for these children outstrips the supply of loving homes.

In a 1994 article, "Update . . . On Transracial Adoption," Ann Sullivan, Adoption Program Director of the Child Welfare League of America (CWLA), states that for children who have been separated from their family of origin, "adoption offers the best opportunity to establish an alternative permanent family relationship," a reaffirmation of Stimmel's basic tenet. Sullivan also acknowledges that "there seems to be some level of agreement that same race, same culture placements offer children the best opportunity for a genuine connection to their own heritage."

The "Update" lists the "keys to an effective adoption program that facilitates the timely adoption of African American and Latino children" by same race, same culture families. CWLA's recommendations embrace many of the elements of the program developed by BGAS nearly 40 years ago: an ongoing recruitment program, child-specific recruitment efforts, an ethnically diverse board and staff with close ties to the community, flexible office hours, accessible office locations, realistic eligibility requirements, and a flexible fee structure. This summary, however, omits one important element of BGAS's program. Non-Caucasian (and, in particular African American) families who had previously adopted through the agency gave substantial help to the agency in developing the program and, most importantly, in identifying potential adoptive families. The agency successfully used these "experienced adopters" to learn how to recruit families more effectively.

Despite the agency's ongoing efforts to locate families, despite the willingness to bend age, income, or marital status requirements, despite the dedication of staff members and board members, the agency found that there were not always enough families of color for the number of minority children available for adoption. Certainly the small populations of color in Oregon (especially the African American population) limited the agency's ability to find same-race/same-culture homes for children of color. Under these circumstances the agency made the choice that the *timely* placement of children—of all races—was its overriding principle.

The Boys and Girls Aid Society of Oregon chose to give children of color the same opportunity for early, permanent, adoptive placement that the agency provided the Caucasian children it placed. For some children, transracial placement provided the best chance for the nurturing family that Stimmel viewed as every child's right. The 1988 CWLA *Standards for Adoption Services* confirm this opinion: "Children in need of adoption have a right to be placed into a family that reflects their ethnicity or race. Children should not have their adoption denied or significantly delayed, however, when adoptive parents of other ethnic or racial groups are available" [Section 4.5]. ◆

Notes

1. Although the African American population in Oregon rose by over 300% in the 1940s, the state remained predominantly Caucasian. The 1950 U.S. Census recorded a total population of people of color in the state of only 1.6%.

2. These facts were cited at a review of the minority placement program at the May 28, 1958, Board of Trustees meeting.

3. The number of minority placements used in this study is based on a search of the "Minority Adoption" file box, which lists non-Caucasian adoptions processed between 1944 and 1972, and the "Service Statistics" reports for 1973-1977. For the purposes of consistency within this study, if a child was identified as having any racial heritage other than Caucasian, that racial designation was applied to the child. The same criterion was also applied to the status of the adoptive parents. If either parent was identified as belonging to a racial group other than Caucasian, the couple was given that group's designation. The accuracy of the figures, however, is predicated on the information supplied to the agency by the biological mother or father and the adoptive parents. There may have been instances in which racial background was unknown or inaccurately reported to the agency. In the cases when two or more minority group designations applied to one child or adoptive family, the pattern set by the agency (in the established file box) was maintained. For example, if a child of both Asian and Native American heritage was identified by the agency as a Native American child, that designation was maintained in this study. Similarly, if the adoptive mother was African American and the adoptive father was Native American, and the agency identified them (in their records) as being an African American family, that designation was maintained in this study.

4. Muriel McCrae, the director of Children's Services Centre in Montreal, described her agency's transracial adoption program when she was the featured speaker at the BGAS Annual Meeting in 1962.

5. See "Our Negro Daughter" *Ebony* (May 1960), and "We Adopted A Negro Child" *MacLean's* (November 19, 1960).

6. This article is based on a paper first presented at the National Conference on Social Welfare, Child Welfare League of America meeting, Atlantic City, NJ, on June 9, 1960.

7. The bibliography of reading material that accompanied this study lists writings/research by David Fanshel, Martha Perry, Mildred Hawkins, and Phyllis Dunne, among others.

8. Within a year of the release of *Run, Jimmy, Run*, 48 agencies in 23 states had bought or rented the film.

9.   The speaker was Dr. Richard Frost, chairman of the political science department at Reed College, Portland, OR.

10. The agency's work with out-of-state agencies also resulted in more placements of sibling groups and special-needs children. Of the 20 children placed in 1972, 15 were African American, four were Caucasian, and one was Korean. The children ranged in age from four months to nine years. Three of the children were categorized as "hard to place" and had been "waiting for some time to be adopted." One sibling group of two girls had been waiting for two years, with part of that time spent in an institution ["Opportunity Interstate Adoption Program," n.d.].

References

Another child rescued. (1901, June 25). *The Morning Oregonian*, p. 7.

Adoption agency places New York baby in Portland home. (1972, December 16). *The Oregonian*, p. B1.

Bogle, K. (1993, June 24). Taped interview by author. BGAS Archives, Portland, OR.

Boys and Girls Aid Society of Oregon. (1944–1977). Adoption casefiles. BGAS Archives, Portland, OR.

Boys and Girls Aid Society of Oregon. (1895). Flyer. BGAS Archives, Portland, OR.

Boys and Girls Aid Society of Oregon. (1972–1977). Interagency and minority placement files. BGAS Archives, Portland, OR.

Boys and Girls Aid Society of Oregon. (1885–1977). Meeting minutes of the Board of Trustees. BGAS Archives, Portland, OR.

Boys and Girls Aid Society of Oregon. (1944–1972). Minority adoptions file box. BGAS Archives, Portland, OR.

Boys and Girls Aid Society of Oregon. (1961–1962). Negro adoptive home committee files. BGAS Archives, Portland, OR.

Boys and Girls Aid Society of Oregon. (1967–1977). Opportunity files. BGAS Archives, Portland, OR.

Boys and Girls Aid Society of Oregon. (1982, Winter). Quest for roots uncovers dramatic tale . . . with a happy ending. *Newsletter*, p. 6. BGAS Archives, Portland, OR.

Fricke, H. (1965). Interracial adoption: The little revolution. *Social Work, 10,* 92–97.

Furor over whites adopting blacks. (1972, April 12). *The New York Times,* p. 38.

Group said fighting mixed race adoptions. (1973, September 18). *The Oregonian,* p. C7.

Hodges, V. (1993, October 19). Taped interview by author. BGAS Archives, Portland, OR.

Hutchinson, F. (1993, November 30). Interview by author.

Minority group adoption praised as courageous race relations step. (1968, April 24). *The Oregonian,* p. B7.

Mogran, M.E. (1993, September 20). Taped interview by author. BGAS Archives, Portland, OR.

Neubauer, A. (1992, October 6). Taped interview by author. BGAS Archives, Portland, OR.

Olds, C. (1993, September 23). Taped interview by author. BGAS Archives, Portland, OR.

Polier, J.W. (1960). Attitudes and contradictions in our culture. *Child Welfare, 39,* 1–7.

Rosacker, M. (1993, October 14). Taped interview by author. BGAS Archives, Portland, OR.

Royer, C. (Author and narrator). (1968). *Run, Jimmy, Run* [16mm film]. KOIN TV production.

She says Young is bad. (1901, July 6). *The Morning Oregonian,* p. 8.

Stimmel, E.R. (1993, October 26). Interview by author.

Stimmel, S. (1961–1977). Correspondence about interracial adoption files. BGAS Archives.

Sullivan, A. (1994). "Update . . . On Transracial Adoption." *Children's Voice, 3,* 4–5+.

Transracial adoption placements triple. (1971, July 16). *Eugene Register Guard,* p. A15.

U.S. Bureau of the Census. (1963). *U.S. census of population: 1960, vol. I, Characteristics of the population, part 39, Oregon* (p. 26). Washington, DC: U.S. Governement Printing Office.

Young, W. M., Jr. (1968). Tell it like it is. *Social Casework, 49,* 207–212.

13

FACTORS AND EVENTS LEADING TO THE PASSAGE OF THE INDIAN CHILD WELFARE ACT

Marc Mannes

The Indian Child Welfare Act (P.L. 95–608), became law on November 8, 1978. This article examines historical and contemporary forces and events, paying particular attention to the actions of key organizations and individuals, that led to passage of this landmark piece of child welfare legislation.

Marc Mannes, Ph.D., is Child Welfare Program Specialist, U.S. Children's Bureau, Washington, DC.

The year was 1968 and members of the Devils Lake Sioux Tribe of North Dakota were concerned about the treatment of American Indian children by local county welfare officials. The children were routinely removed from their families and placed in foster homes and for adoption with non-Indian couples. To make matters worse, all of these actions were carried out without consultation with either tribal officials or the Indian community [U.S. Senate Hearings 1974]. Although many other tribal groups had experienced similar treatment but had not chosen or had felt powerless to respond, the Devils Lake Sioux Community decided to challenge these actions. They requested assistance from the Association on American Indian Affairs (AAIA) in New York, founded in 1923 to defend the rights of American Indians and Alaskan Natives and to promote social, economic, and civic equality for their communities. AAIA's decision to become involved set in motion a chain of events that ultimately resulted in the passage of the Indian Child Welfare Act (ICWA) a decade later. The circumstances and activities that led to the passage of the ICWA can be understood in the context of relevant historical background and contemporary factors, issues, and activities.

The Effect of European Conquest on American Indian Children and Families

American Indian children are "born into two relational systems, a biological family and a kinship network such as a clan or band" [Blanchard & Barsh 1980: 351]. Traditionally, American Indian and Alaskan Native children were "protected in a society in which child-rearing was a community affair, in which behavioral expectations and discipline were clearly structured and in which children were highly valued" [Cross 1986: 285]. The impact of European contact with, and eventual dominance of, American Indians was so profound that it affected every aspect of traditional American Indian society, including child-rearing and family relations. Modes of economic production and exchange, political expression, and social reproduction between the two societies differed so radically from each other that traditional parent-child relationships were thrown into disarray, and the continuity and utility of kinship and other indigenous family systems were destabilized [Coontz 1988].

A Legacy of Policies and Practices Affecting American Indian Children and Families

The actions by county welfare officials in North Dakota that prompted the Devils Lake Sioux to contact AAIA were the latest manifestations of ongoing practices by federal and state governments and private organizations that resulted in the breakup of American Indian families and the placement of their children in various forms of out-of-home care. From the earliest days of the American republic, one of the primary intents of federal Indian policy was to eradicate the "Indianness" in young people. As far back as 1819, the Civilization Fund Act provided education for Indian youths for the purpose of "introducing among them the habits and arts of civilization" [Prucha 1975: 33].

Later, the placement of Indian children in boarding schools served a similar purpose. These schools were a tool of federal policy designed to sever parent-child relationships and bring about assimilation. Instead of being returned to the family during school vacations, young American Indians were placed in the homes of Caucasians under what was known as the "outing system" [Meriam 1928]. Moreover, when parents would not willingly send their children away, federal government employees would engage in the practice of "kid catching," forcibly taking the children to distant schools [Coolidge 1977].

In contemporary times, certain child welfare policies and practices may not have been overtly assimilationist, but the consequences were the same. In 1958, the Bureau of Indian Affairs (BIA) and the Child Welfare League of America (CWLA) established the Indian Adoption Project (IAP) to provide adoptive placements for American Indian children whose parents were deemed unable to provide a "suitable" home for them. Since few American Indian families actively sought or were encouraged to adopt American Indian children, the IAP emphasized transracial placements [Office of Human Development 1976]. A decade later, approximately 395 Indian children had been adopted by Caucasian parents, often with tribal approval. Over half were living with families in eastern states, far from their people and cultures.

With funding from the U.S. Children's Bureau, Fanshel [1972] showed that the adoptions appeared to meet the young child's physical and emotional needs and that adoptive parents appeared satisfied. Fanshel, however, acknowledged that problems could surface as the children entered adolescence, and he questioned the appropriateness of these placements. Joseph H. Reid, former executive director of CWLA, noted in the foreword to Fanshel's [1972] research that the interest shown by Caucasian families in adopting American Indian children prompted states to promote in-state adoptions of these children by Caucasian families. Although this change kept American Indian adopted children closer to their geographical roots, it still kept them separated from their cultural roots. During the early 1970s the Standing Rock Sioux, Sisseton-Wahpeton Sioux, three affiliated tribes of the Fort Berthold Reservation, and the Oglala Sioux Tribes passed resolutions demanding an end to removal practices, especially when they involved transracial placements [Unger 1977].

A study conducted by AAIA in 1969 and presented at the 1974 U.S. Senate Hearings on Indian Child Welfare showed that in most states with large American Indian populations, roughly 25% to 35% of Indian young people had been separated from their families, and that Indian children were much more likely to experience out-of-home placement than non-Indian children. Differential rates of Indian adoptive placement varied by as much as 19 times the rate for non-Indian adoptions in Washington State to 1.3 times the rate in Arizona; differential rates of foster home placement varied from 15.7 times greater in South Dakota to 2.6 times greater in Arizona. The relatively low differential placement rates for Arizona have to be considered in the context of the large percentage of Indian children placed in boarding schools. Table 1 summarizes the differential rates determined by AAIA's 1969 study.

Subsequent studies by AAIA in 1974, and again in 1976 at the request of the American Indian Policy Review Commission (AIPRC), found similar disparities in placement rates. A task force submitting a final report to AIPRC also confirmed the large percentage of Indian children in non-Indian family foster care and adoptive placements [Task Force Four 1976]. Extreme poverty, prejudice, discrimination, and cultural misunderstanding were cited by Indian advocates as the reasons for both higher placement rates and transracial placements [Unger 1977].

Policy and Practice Consequences for American Indian Children and Parents

The consequences to both parents and children of breaking up American Indian families were first noted by Meriam et al. [1928] over 60 years ago:

> In relieving them [Indians] of the care of their children the government robs them of one of the strongest and most fundamental of the economic motives, thereby keeping them in the state of childhood [p. 576] . . . The effects of early deprivation of family life are apparent in the children. They too are the victims of an arrested development. [p. 577]

Coontz [1988] reminds us that families play critical roles in socializing youngsters in the culture they are born into, defining their eventual place in the social order, and helping shape and mediate all family members' definitions of themselves as indi-

TABLE 1

Differential Rates of Placement of American Indian Children in Out-of-Home Care Based upon 1969 AAIA Study

State	Adoptive Placement	Foster Care
Arizona	1.3	2.6*
Minnesota	5.0	4–5
South Dakota	7.5	15.7
Washington	19.0	9.6
Wisconsin	17.8	14.0
Oklahoma	4.7	3.7**

*Does not take into account the size of the boarding school population.
**Considers only state figures. The differential rates would probably be higher if private agency data were included.

viduals. Cumulatively, assimilationist, removal, and transracial placement policies and practices have been extremely damaging to the viability of American Indian and Alaskan Native culture and corrosive to Indian youngsters' development of strong personal identities. They have also undermined the establishment and maintenance of positive behavioral dynamics and healthy emotional relationships among family members [U.S. Senate Hearings 1974].

Promoting Understanding of Indian Child Welfare Problems and Building Support for Action

AAIA staff members quickly learned that the circumstances in North Dakota were being repeated in other jurisdictions. They initiated public awareness and information activities and also established communication with officials of the U.S. Department of Health, Education and Welfare and the BIA, and with members of Congress, to convey the magnitude and implications of the child removal and placement problems, clarify how destructive these actions were for Indian children and families, and request governmental investigation and responses [U.S. Senate Hearings 1974].

On July 16, 1968, at a press conference at the Overseas Press Club in New York City, AAIA Executive Director William Byler and a delegation of Devils Lake Sioux described the plight of their families and children [U.S. Senate Hearings 1974]. Byler noted in his opening statement that "as sad and as terrible as the conditions are that Indian children must face as they grow up, nothing exceeds the cruelty of being unjustly and unnecessarily removed from their families" [U.S. Senate Hearings 1974: 95].

In addition to the press conference, a mechanism for regular communication of information was deployed. After using its general newsletter for several years to generate and disseminate information, in 1974 AAIA began to publish "Indian Family Defense," a newsletter devoted exclusively to Indian child welfare concerns [Unger 1977]. This sent a steady flow of Indian child welfare information into public policy and professional channels.

Responding to the Problems

Developing Tribal Government Child Welfare Capacity

In one of its initial efforts, AAIA helped the Devils Lake Sioux community establish a tribal child welfare board that would make formal recommendations to the tribal judge on child welfare cases [U.S. Senate Hearings 1974]. Discussions involving AAIA employees, federal agency staff, and tribal leaders considered how Indian child welfare problems could be alleviated by building the capacity of tribal governments to meet the needs of children and families [Center for Social Research and Development 1975; Office of Human Development 1976]. Developing a governmental infrastructure for child welfare was seen as essential because many tribal governments lacked basic elements such as children's codes.

In general, tribal government has endured a long history of federal judicial doctrine, derived from two U.S. Supreme Court decisions that solidified tribal self-governing capacity but limited sovereignty. In *Cherokee Nation v. Georgia* [1831], the Court defined the legal and governmental status of the Cherokee Nation (and subsequently applied it to other tribes) as a "domestic dependent nation." In *Worcester v.Georgia* [1832], the Court established that the U.S. Congress had plenary power over Indian affairs.

Despite the sanctioning of limited sovereignty, the modern expression of tribal government remained relatively dormant for a century until 1934, when the passage of the Wheeler-Howard Act (Indian Reorganization Act) included encouragement for tribes to adopt a constitution and bylaws [Cohen 1982]. With the proliferation of federal programs as a result of the 1960s war on poverty and the Great Society initiatives, tribal governments increasingly administered human service oriented projects [Mannes 1990]. AAIA staff members, federal officials, and advocates explored how tribal governments could build on this process to provide child welfare services.

Encouraging Tribal/State Cooperation

Some federal bureaucrats viewed the resolution of Indian child welfare problems as not just contingent on developing a tribal infrastructure, but also dependent on facilitating an effective intergovernmental relationship between each state and the federally recognized American Indian or Alaskan Native tribal government(s) residing within its boundaries. In the early 1970s, a number of different entities were providing services to Indian children and families, and the mix of providers varied greatly from one locale to another [Office of Human Development 1976]. State and county governments, federal agencies such as the BIA and the Indian Health Service, private agencies, and certain tribes were all serving Indian people living either on reservations or in urban areas. The number of players complicated the possibility of cooperation.

In 1970, the federal Social and Rehabilitative Services Agency (SRS), the organizational unit within which the U.S. Children's Bureau was housed at the time, instructed state child welfare agencies to follow the directives contained in tribal court orders that involved Indian children on reservations. It also reaffirmed the SRS position that federal child welfare financial assistance programs should be administered statewide and include reservations [Office of Human Development 1976].

Jurisdictional and Legal Complexities

Implementation of the 1970 SRS instruction was stymied for several reasons. States lacked respect for tribal court decisions. Although Indian child welfare cases could be brought before a tribal court, the range of decision options available to the tribal judge was quite limited. Many tribal governments had little or no capacity to actually deliver basic child welfare services, and tribal courts were often dependent on state-based services. State courts and welfare departments were unwilling to honor or give "full faith and credit" to tribal court orders because they saw tribal governments as lacking the ability to maintain effective "separation of powers" [Office of Human Development 1976]. For example, state officials believed that tribal administrative processes, judicial deliberations, and decision-making were not structurally insulated from legislative and political practices. The potential intrusion of politics into tribal judges' decisions was noted as a major impediment to impartiality. With most tribal judges lacking legal training and few tribal judicial codes addressing children's issues, tribal court actions lacked legitimacy in the eyes of state officials. Consequently, tribal court orders were mostly ignored and tribal courts were often not informed by the state/county agency of cases where they ought to have jurisdiction, or when placement decisions and actions affecting Indian children and families were made by state courts. Also, states' inability to tax Indian lands and income made them resist covering the costs of providing any social services on federally recognized tribes' reservations located within their borders [Office of Human Development 1976].

Disagreements over "spheres of authority" in delivering child welfare services and challenges by states regarding the licensing of Indian family foster homes, group homes, and institutions on reservations thwarted many initial tribal responses to Indian families and children [Office of Human Development 1976]. Rulings by attorneys general in Arizona set forth a legal rationale against providing child welfare services on reservations based on the inherent sovereignty of tribal governments [Center for Social Research and Development 1975]. In 1959 and 1970, the attorneys general determined that because of tribal sovereignty the state had no authority to directly license reservation-based child welfare entities or license an intermediary such as a tribal council or the BIA to actually provide services on a reservation [Center for Social Research and Development 1975].

The passage of Public Law 83–280 created the basis for additional legal complexities in North Dakota. Passed by Congress in 1953, the law reduced the range of tribal government sovereignty by permitting certain states to assume criminal and civil jurisdiction over reservations contained within their boundaries [Cohen 1982]. In 1963, when North Dakota assumed civil jurisdiction under P.L. 83–280, it determined that its authority could be applied only with tribal or individual Indian consent. Following this limited interpretation of state authority in response to the federal law, the North Dakota Supreme Court decided in 1963 that there was no basis for a positive ruling on a petition to terminate the parental rights of Indian parents living on the reservation, since the parents had not consented to the state's assumption of jurisdiction [Center for Social Research and Development 1975].

Certain states' use of judicial doctrine and legal interpretations to justify not serving Indian people, and evidence suggesting federally funded child welfare services were unavailable to reservation Indians on the same basis as they were to other state citizens, raised questions as to whether the states were in conflict with prevailing federal statutes and regulations and were engaged in unconstitutional practices. Although Title IV-A (involving financial assistance and AFDC-foster care) appeared to support services being provided uniformly throughout a state, Title IV-B (child welfare services) and Title XX (social services) seemed to permit some degree of variation of programs and services [Center for Social Research and Development 1975]. Prevailing case law, based on the principle of equal protection, made it clear that Indian people were fully entitled to these benefits [Center for Social Research and Development 1975].

In *Dandridge v. Williams* [1970], the U.S. Supreme Court determined that state classifications among people for social welfare based on nationality or race are "inherently suspect" and must pass a "strict scrutiny" test that demonstrates that the classification is essential to meeting a compelling state interest. The key legal issue became: Did a state's refusal to provide services and to license child welfare agencies or foster homes on reservations, based on arguments such as tribal sovereignty and the failure of Indians to pay state taxes, demonstrate a "compelling state interest" [Office of Human Development 1976]?

Determining that little progress had been made on its 1970 Program Instruction, SRS produced another in late 1974. This instruction required states to collaborate with tribes when reservation children were involved, and called on the states to develop special licensing standards for Indian foster homes and day care facilities [Office of Human Development 1976]. Lacking enforcement mechanisms, these federal policy statements had little impact. The ineffectiveness of these executive agency actions probably fueled greater interest in and support for a legislative response.

Legislative Action

Setting the Stage

Senate oversight hearings to address Indian child placement matters were eventually held during the Second Session of the 93rd

Congress on April 8th and 9th of 1974 [U.S. Senate Hearings 1974]. Senator James Abourezk from South Dakota, Chairman of the Subcommittee on Indian Affairs, ran the hearings and served as patron. American Indian witnesses recounted their personal stories. The following exchange between Margaret Townsend of Fallon, Nevada, whose children were removed and placed in a family foster home, and Senator Abourezk, was indicative of the tone and substance of personal accounts.

> Senator Abourezk: Is there anything else that you would like to say to the committee?
> Mrs. Townsend: I think that most Indian women are overwhelmed by people who think their children should be taken away from them and they don't really stand up to anybody and they don't have anybody to tell.
> Senator Abourezk: Does this happen to a lot of other Indian people in your community?
> Mrs. Townsend: Oh, yes; it does. They just think it is the right thing for the welfare to be doing and they just never say or have anything to say. They just let them do whatever they want to, let them adopt them out or whatever.
> [U.S. Senate Hearings 1974: 43–44]

The themes raised by Margaret Townsend were echoed by other witnesses. Cheryl DeCoteau of Sisseton, South Dakota, explained how she was asked by the state welfare staff to place her unborn child for adoption. The story of Don James Morrison, relayed by Mel Sampson, conveyed the anguish of an Indian youth living with Caucasian adoptive parents. Betty Jack, who chaired the Board of Directors of the American Indian Child Development Program in Wisconsin, told the committee about how her children were removed by state authorities. Mental health professionals gave detailed testimony on the psychological and social toll associated with extensive out-of-home placements, and the cumulative impact on tribal culture [U.S. Senate Hearings 1974].

Passage of the Legislation

Under the direction of staff attorney Bertram Hirsch, AAIA had produced a set of recommendations for Congress that were entered into the 1974 Senate Hearing records. Blanchard [1977] noted that Senator Abourezk asked AAIA to prepare an Indian child welfare bill, which he then introduced on August 27, 1976 as S. 3777, the Indian Child Welfare Act of 1976. The bill was referred by the Senate Committee on Interior and Insular Affairs to the Subcommittee on Indian Affairs, where it died. On April 1, 1977, Senator Abourezk resurrected and reintroduced essentially the original bill as S. 1214 [U.S. Senate Report 1977]. Public hearings were held in August, 1977, and the testimony of witnesses affirmed that the problems detailed during the 1974 hearing remained unsolved.

Opposition to S. 1214 was raised by members of the Church of Jesus Christ of Latter-Day Saints (LDS) and the federal Departments of the Interior and of Health, Education and Welfare [U.S. Senate Report 1977]. The LDS Church was concerned that certain portions of the private placement section of the bill would eliminate their LDS Indian Student Placement Program. The program placed LDS Indian children between the ages of eight and 18 for at least one school year with an Anglo-Mormon family to receive "educational, social, and leadership opportunities that were lacking on the reservation" [U.S. Senate Report 1977: 200]. A number of witnesses, including American Indian members of the LDS Church who lived with these families, attested to the virtues of the program. This testimony was in marked contrast to a state-of-the-field study of Indian child welfare conducted during 1975 and 1976, which questioned the benefit of Indian student participation in the LDS program [Office of Human Development 1976].

The federal departments believed that S. 1214 was not needed because another national child welfare bill, S. 1928 (which after many changes ultimately became the Adoption Assistance and Child Welfare Act of 1980), then being proposed by the Carter administration, addressed the same matters. The Senate committee disagreed with the federal agencies' positions, noting that S. 1928 did not support funds for Indian tribes to operate child welfare programs, and failed to recognize the sovereignty of tribal courts, jurisdictional problems, and placement preferences [U.S. Senate Report 1977].

A substitute bill incorporating a number of amendments was reported to the full Senate on November 3, 1977, and was passed by the Senate the next day. In the House, S. 1214 was referred to the Committee on Interior and Insular Affairs, and its Subcommittee on Indian Affairs held hearings on the bill. In addition to written comments and testimony regarding S. 1214 presented at the House hearings, a set of recommendations had been provided by AIPRC's Task Force Four, which had examined Indian child placement issues. S. 1214 was amended and a substitute bill was introduced by Representative Morris Udall of Arizona as H.R. 12533 [U.S. House of Representatives Report 1978].

Several major differences between the Senate and House versions of the Indian child welfare bill are worth noting. The House bill affirmed Congressional authority over Indian child welfare in response to questions of constitutionality raised by the U.S. Department of Justice. The underlying principle of H.R. 12533 was based on what was in "the best interest of the Indian child," even though the principle was acknowledged as being vague. The House version replaced the ambiguous term and concept of "placement" with "child custody placement" and delineated four specific legal proceedings constituting a "child custody placement": foster care placement; parental rights termination; preadoptive placement; and adoptive placement [U.S. House of Representatives Report 1978].

Representative Ron Marlenee of Montana was concerned that H.R. 12533 had not been sufficiently circulated to states, juvenile judges, public and private welfare agencies, and Indian tribes,

and that as a result, the proposed legislation had not been subjected to thorough review and analysis [U.S. House of Representatives Report 1978]. Also, according to Representative Marlenee,
groups such as the Montana Department of Social and Rehabilitation Services and the National Council of State Public Welfare
Administrators, who had seen the bill and had questions about
funding and jurisdiction, had not been given sufficient time to air
their questions. This dissenting view had minimal effect on the
movement of the proposed statute, and on June 21, 1978, the full
House Committee on Interior and Insular Affairs chose to mark
up H.R. 12533 instead of S. 1214 [U.S. House of Representatives
Report 1978]. On October 14, 1978 the House passed H.R. 12533,
and on the following day the Senate accepted the House version.

The Indian Child Welfare Act (ICWA) became Public Law
95–608 on November 8, 1978. Title I of the legislation affirmed
tribal governments' authority to assume jurisdiction over child
custody placement proceedings involving reservation children
and also required state courts to transfer jurisdiction for Indian
children living off-reservation to tribal courts. Title II appropriated funds to the Bureau of Indian Affairs for grants to tribal
governments and off-reservation Indian organizations for child
welfare programs that would protect children, serve families,
and preserve tribal culture. The other two titles set forth record-
keeping and information procedures and called for a study to
determine how the lack of local day schools might be contributing to the breakup of Indian families [U.S. House of Representatives Report 1978].

A Postscript to the Indian Child Welfare Act's Passage

According to Kessel and Robbins [1984], the ICWA generated
controversy and misunderstanding within the social service
community that undermined its intended impact. Fischler [1980]
argued that the passage of the ICWA jeopardized American Indian children because placement priorities emphasized parental

and tribal rights at the expense of child protection; for example, a high standard of evidence was required to document harm to a child. American Indians and Alaskan Natives saw things differently. For Blanchard and Barsh [1980], the ICWA had addressed the fundamental issue of cultural preservation.

> With enactment of the Indian Child Welfare Act, the federal government responded affirmatively to the petition of American Indians that their way of life be allowed to continue. At issue is not tribal right versus individual right, but rather the right of a people to maintain a culture that has provided them meaning in this world from the beginning of time. [p. 354]

In 1985, the Administration for Children, Youth and Families and the BIA funded a national study of Indian child welfare as affected by the implementation of the ICWA [Plantz et al. 1988]. The study revealed that public agencies and state courts in many jurisdictions were complying with the ICWA's various requirements. Several states had passed complementary state Indian child welfare legislation and had negotiated jurisdictional and service agreements with tribes. Public agencies appeared to be providing Indian children with the permanency and case review safeguards spelled out in the Adoption Assistance and Child Welfare Act of 1980. But public agencies were cited for still not providing Indian placements for many Indian children in out-of-home care, and the federal government was faulted for its limited efforts to convey performance standards and monitor and enforce compliance.

The study also identified a continuing excessive placement rate for American Indian and Alaskan Native children. Data indicated that placements for American Indian children had increased about 25% since passage of the ICWA, and that tribes administering child welfare programs seemed to be the major contributors to the increasing flow of Indian children into out-of-home care. Mannes [1993] suggests this is, in part, a result of the first generation of post-ICWA programs emphasizing culturally appropriate placements at the expense of placement prevention and/or family preservation efforts. Nevertheless, a review of case records of several tribes indicated that they were following good standards of casework practice, and that principles of permanency were being adhered to [Plantz et al. 1988].

In regard to the act itself, Title II has shifted during the past several years from funding discretionary grants to distributing funds on a formula basis. Tribes may not receive a level of support commensurate with their degree of need, but they no longer have to compete with one another, and have overcome the problem of having child welfare programs available one year and gone the next.

Societal identification and conceptualization of child welfare problems and the sanctioning of specific child welfare responses change over time, and these shifts can have important implications for Indian child welfare. One can only speculate what the impact of apparently eroding public opposition to transracial adoptions and the recently passed Multiethnic Placement Act (P.L. 103–382) might have on a future reauthorization of the ICWA. As Gordon [1988] asserts, an ever-changing mix of social moods, economic forces, legislative enactments, and political movements determines the answers to questions such as: What is labeled as unacceptable family behavior? What aspects of family problems are to be addressed? and What will be the form and substance of society's interventions? The responses to American Indian and Alaskan Native children and families by the second generation of post-ICWA programs will be largely shaped by how these questions are answered. ♦

References

Blanchard, E. (1977). The question of best interest. In S. Unger (Ed.), *The destruction of American Indian families* (pp. 57–60). New York: Association on American Indian Affairs.

Blanchard, E. L., & Barsh, R.L. (1980). What is best for tribal children? A response to Fischler. *Social Work, 25*, 350–357.

Center for Social Research and Development, University of Denver. (1975). *Legal and jurisdictional problems in the delivery of SRS child welfare services on Indian reservations (CD–01526)*. Washington, DC: U.S. Department of Health, Education and Welfare.

Cohen, F. (1982). *Handbook of federal Indian law*. Charlottesville, VA: Michie, Bobbs-Merrill.

Coolidge, D. (1977). "Kid catching" on the Navajo Reservation: 1930. In S. Unger (Ed.), *The destruction of American Indian families* (pp. 18–21). New York: Association on American Indian Affairs.

Coontz, S. (1988). *The social origins of private life: A history of American families 1600–1900*. New York: Verso.

Cross, T. L. (1986). Drawing on cultural traditions in Indian child welfare practice. *Social Casework, 67*, 283–289.

Fanshel, D. (1972). *Far from the reservation: The transracial adoption of American Indian children*. Metuchen, NJ: The Scarecrow Press, Inc.

Fischler, R. S. (1980). Protecting American Indian children. *Social Work, 25*, 341–349.

Gordon, L. (1988). *Heroes of their own lives: The politics and history of family violence*. New York: Viking Penguin, Inc.

Kessel, J. A., & Robbins, S. P. (1984). The Indian Child Welfare Act: Dilemmas and needs. *Child Welfare, 63*, 225–232.

Mannes, M. (1990). *Leadership in administering Indian human services*. Las Cruces, NM: New Mexico State University.

Mannes, M. (1993). Seeking the balance between child protection and family preservation in Indian child welfare. *Child Welfare, 72*, 141–150.

Meriam, L., Brown, R. A., Cloud, H. R., Dale, E. E., Duke, E., Edwards, H. E., McKenzie, F. A., Mark, M. L., Ryan, W. C. Jr., & Spillman, W. J. (1928). *The problem of Indian administration*. Baltimore: Johns Hopkins University Press.

Office of Human Development. (1976). *Indian child welfare: A state-of-the-field study (OHD 76–30095)*. Washington, DC: U.S. Department of Health, Education and Welfare, Children's Bureau.

Plantz, M. C., Hubbell, R., Barrett, B. J., & Dobrec, A. (1988). *Indian child welfare: A status report—Final report of the survey of Indian child welfare and implementation of the Indian Child Welfare Act and section 428 of the Adoption Assistance and Child Welfare Act of 1980.* CSR Incorporated and Three Feathers Associates (105–82–1602). Washington, DC: U.S. Department of Health and Human Services, Administration on Children, Youth and Families, U.S. Department of the Interior, Bureau of Indian Affairs.

Prucha, F .P. (1975). *Documents of United States Indian policy.* Lincoln, NE: University of Nebraska Press.

Task Force Four: Federal, State, and Tribal Jurisdiction. (1976). *Final report to the American Indian Policy Review Commission.* Washington, DC: U.S. Government Printing Office.

Unger, S. (1977). *The destruction of American Indian families.* New York: Association on American Indian Affairs.

U.S. House of Representatives Report, No. 95–1386. (1978). *Establishing standards for the placement of Indian children in foster homes to prevent the breakup of Indian families and for other purposes.* Washington, DC: U.S. House of Representatives Committee on Interior and Insular Affairs.

U. S. Senate Hearings (1974). *Problems that American Indian families face in raising their children and how these problems are affected by federal action or inaction.* Washington, DC: U.S. Senate Subcommittee on Indian Affairs of the Committee on Interior and Insular Affairs.

U.S. Senate. (1977). *The Indian Child Welfare Act of 1977.* Report No. 95–597. Washington, DC: U.S. Senate Select Committee on Indian Affairs.

14

THE CITIZENS' COMMITTEE FOR CHILDREN OF NEW YORK AND THE EVOLUTION OF CHILD ADVOCACY (1945–1972)

Mary Jean McDonald

The emergence and development of child advocacy is often described as a by-product of the social activism of the 1960s. The civil rights movement and the antipoverty programs of that decade sparked a new citizen movement whose emphasis on local democracy shifted traditional political alignments and created a more favorable context for successful advocacy in behalf of unrepresented groups, including children. This article presents a longer historical perspective and describes the evolution of modern child advocacy in the immediate post-World War II era. It examines the history of a nonprofit child advocacy organization, the Citizens' Committee for Children of New York, Inc., formed in 1945, and describes the changing content and meaning of child advocacy, as well as the types, strategies, and goals of organizations themselves.

Mary Jean McDonald, Ph.D., is Adjunct Professor of History, Montclair State University, Upper Montclair, NJ.

In a discussion paper entitled "Philanthropy in a Liberal Education," Payton [1991] described the functions of advocacy as articulating the failures of the government and the marketplace, as well as pointing out the inconstancies, inefficiencies, and other weaknesses of philanthropy itself. Advocacy, according to Payton, endows philanthropy with a social conscience. Those who study the activist role of philanthropy thus have an opportunity to explore what Geertz [1983: 36–54] called "the social history of the moral imagination."

Yet it is precisely this historical perspective that is overlooked by those who seek to understand advocacy. The emergence and development of advocacy has usually been described as a by-product of the social activism of the 1960s, especially of the civil rights movement [Jenkins 1987]. This article suggests that advocacy has a longer and more interesting history, taking as its starting point the premise that an examination of that history can tell us much about the current effectiveness and impact of advocates on children's welfare.

This work is part of a larger study that traces the evolution of child advocacy within the context of the post-1945 welfare state. It focuses on the Citizens' Committee for Children of New York, Inc. (CCC), which, soon after its incorporation in 1945, emerged as the most influential group concerned with New York City's children [Kahn et al. 1972]. A small, elite, nonprofit organization, CCC functioned as what we might today call a policy advocacy group, pursuing investigatory fact-finding and research, publishing reports and bulletins, establishing guidelines, and making policy and program recommendations. Most of this work was carried out by volunteer members, both lay and professional, and a small core staff. From its very beginning, CCC defined itself as an "advocate for children," although the term had not yet come into common use.

By the mid-1960s, changes in the broader currents of child welfare reform, as well as the emergence of a nascent child advocacy *movement*, challenged CCC's predominant position, and forced the group to reevaluate its advocacy program, strategies, and goals. Although it could be argued that the rise and fall of groups like CCC is simply a fact of organizational life—that groups unable to adapt to new political and social circumstances and attract new blood will inevitably ossify—CCC's history raises other important advocacy issues.

As advocates themselves have admitted, "precious little energy has been expended documenting and analyzing the experiences of child advocates" [Bing & Richart 1987]. Child advocacy has little recorded institutional memory on which to rely. This article seeks to correct that imbalance by exploring the changing content and meaning of child advocacy through the postwar decades. It assesses CCC's impact on the child, as well as the strategies it used, and suggests reasons for its influence. Finally, it examines briefly the changes in nonprofit child advocacy brought about by the different social, racial, and political realities of the 1960s. By documenting CCC's advocacy efforts and identifying the ingredients of its success, as well as its shortfalls, it is hoped that this article will provide instruction and inspiration to others trying to correct government inaction or indifference toward children.

Advocacy within the Postwar Context

Since at least the early nineteenth century, various individuals and groups have tried to improve the lot of poor children, particularly child laborers. In England in 1802, Sir Robert Peel obtained the passage of a bill in Parliament restricting the employment of apprentices to 12 hours a day [de Schweinitz 1943]. Seventeen years later, Peel and Robert Owen succeeded in passing a law forbidding the employment of children under nine years of age and restricting the work of children under age 16 to 12 hours a day [de Schweinitz 1943].

In this country, too, social activists have long articulated the interests of children. Americans, however, have demonstrated a more persistent uneasiness about the use of public intervention in behalf of children. Well into the nineteenth century, children's laws were based, at least in theory, on the doctrine of nonintervention [Sobie 1987]. Not until the advent of the child-saving era of the late nineteenth century did reformers succeed in wrenching some aspects of child welfare out of parental hands and making it subject to public authority.

Influenced by the humane motives that inspired the Society for the Prevention of Cruelty to Animals, early leaders of the child protection field took an active role in publicizing children's needs and campaigining for better legislation to safeguard children's interests. By 1890, a host of reform campaigns emerged, including compulsory education laws, new schools, vocational schools, and restrictions and controls on child labor, all of which became the subjects of municipal and even state regulation [Muncy 1991]. When President William H. Taft signed the bill that created the U.S. Children's Bureau in 1912, the active participation of the state in protecting and aiding children seemed assured. The mission of the bureau was defined in terms that today would be summarized as "advocacy for children from a federal vantage point" [Kahn et al. 1972: 17].

By the mid-twentieth century, government had assumed a degree of responsibility for children unprecedented in U.S. history. Public institutions such as schools and juvenile courts enlarged their functions and intervened more directly into areas long reserved to parents [Kahn et al. 1972]. Aid to Dependent Children (ADC), for example, established as part of the Social Security Act of 1935, guaranteed a basic level of assistance for fatherless children. As a result of the expanding role of government in educating children, protecting them, and providing them with services, a nationwide industry of child-serving institutions emerged. Schools, health and mental health clinics, state institutions for delinquents, and social service programs for low-income and troubled families all formed part of the postwar public sector [Bing & Richart 1987].

Historian Samuel Hays [1987] linked the postwar expansion of government activity to a new, nonmaterial phase of consumption, characterized by quality-of-life concerns and demands for more and better services from the government. The times called for a "qualitative liberalism" dedicated to bettering the quality of people's lives and opportunities, including children [Matusow 1984]. Postwar child advocacy reflected this revolution in expectations. Defined as "intervention on behalf of children in relation to those services that impinge on their lives" [Kahn et al. 1972: 63], child advocacy was based on the conviction that mere "child saving" was no longer sufficient. As Kahn et al. [1972: 32] note,

> the step from child protection to child advocacy thus represents a shift from provision of substitute care and intervention into family life to intervention into or action vis-a-vis institutions other than the family as they affect children.

Still, as more public agencies became involved in child welfare, it was uncertain whether they were benign or even effective. Bureaucracies charged with serving children were fraught with problems, including the potential abuse of authority, the lack of neutrality of bureaucrats, the lack of adequate resources, and inertia [Bing & Richart 1987]. Someone had to regulate the regulators [Kahn et al. 1972]. CCC members viewed this newly necessary task as theirs, along with mediating and advocating in behalf of dependent children and their families, and helping them negotiate their way through New York City's thickening maze of services and bureaucracies.

Thus, in many ways, the growth of the welfare state and the emergence of child advocacy were reciprocal processes. As advocates, CCC members proceeded on the premise that children and their parents had specific rights and needs and that prevailing circumstances required that they be given support to assure access to entitlements, benefits, and services. The conviction that children needed more than protection and traditional services was complemented by members' belief that the scope of government responsibility and intervention had to be expanded in order to ensure the maximum development of every child.

The Citizens' Committee for Children: Strategies, Methods, and Goals

By the mid-twentieth century, then, the term "child advocate" most accurately described those who worked in behalf of children *outside* government. Immediately upon CCC's formal incorporation in 1945, members voted not to accept any public funding, which, they feared, might compromise the integrity of the group's advocacy work. Members relished their self-proclaimed politically neutral status as experts and volunteers. Nevertheless, from the outset the group relied on what it regarded as its three primary assets—prestige, expertise, and political influence—to shape child welfare policy in New York. Made up of both lay and professional members who shared a homogeneous class, ethnic, and religious base, CCC was descended from a long line of Manhattan-bound, elite organizations of limited membership [Sayre & Kaufman 1950]. Most members were Caucasian, Jewish, and upper- or upper-middle class. The majority had come from urban areas, either Chicago or New York, where the professionals among them earned degrees in medicine, psychiatry, law, education, and social work. They were, in short, a collection of politicians, philanthropists, and public servants united by a genteel reform tradition that instilled in them the notion that civic participation was not only a privilege but a duty.

Virtually all members began their careers (either volunteer or professional) during the New Deal, and some had been active during the Progressive Era. A typical career synopsis is that of Helen Hall, a longtime CCC board member. Born in 1892, she worked in 1916 to organize the first mothers' pensions program in Westchester County, New York. In 1933 she succeeded Lillian Wald as head of the Henry Street Settlement, and one year later became a member of Franklin Roosevelt's Advisory Council to the Committee on Economic Security, the group that wrote the Social Security Act [Hall 1971].

Charlotte Carr, CCC's first executive director, was born in 1890 and began her social work career as a matron in an orphan asylum after graduating from Vassar in 1915. Described as a "large woman with impressively browed eyes," so forceful that she was once called a "feminine counterpart of John L. Lewis," Carr became assistant director of the New York State Labor Department's bureau of women in industry in 1923. Ten years later she was appointed Secretary of Labor of Pennsylvania. From 1935 through 1937, she served as executive director of the Emergency Relief Bureau in New York City under Fiorello La Guardia, but gave up that post in 1937 to head Chicago's Hull House after Jane Addams' death [McDonald 1993].

The career profiles of these and other CCC members suggest a continuum of reform activity dating from the early twentieth century and extending well through the postwar era. CCC members represented a hybrid group of reformers, one which looked back to earlier reform periods, especially the New Deal, yet also embraced a postwar liberal ideology. That ideology, closely associated with what one historian has termed "New York liberalism," encompassed an assurance of basic services, a mild redistribution of wealth, and the principle of racial tolerance in public life [Bender 1992]. Like child welfare reformers before them, CCC members were guided by a strong faith in the disinterested benevolence of the state, which they embraced as a source of regulation and planning. They formed part of a generation of activists who had promoted the establishment of public agencies devoted to dependent and neglected children during the New Deal, and who tried to preserve for the postwar years the reform values of that earlier era. Indeed, their prescriptions for improving child welfare services often proved even more aggressively statist than those of either the Progressive Era or the New Deal.

Throughout the 1940s and early 1950s, CCC emphasized expert, professional reform and a top-down, bureaucratically oriented approach to child welfare reform, characterized by efforts to rearrange the structure or organizational apparatus of New York City's government. Ideally, the group envisioned some central point of reference, some agency or unit charged with responsibility for knowing what happened to each child as he or she moved through the chain of existing child welfare services, and for stimulating improvement and/or expansion of services as required. A perennial plank in the group's advocacy platform, for example, was the creation of a city planning commission for children that would develop a "master plan" for children, led by a director with the status of a city commissioner [Carr 1946; CCC 1946; CCC 1953a]. The group also advocated the creation of a localized city children's bureau that would emulate the federal bureau by promoting research and data collection as a basis for sound planning for children.

By the early 1950s, CCC's advocacy achievements and political influence led one observer to refer to the group as "the single most effective civic organization in the city, as far as city hall was concerned" [Lowell 1991]. The group owed much of its effectiveness to Trude Lash, CCC Executive Director from 1952 through 1972. Lash insisted on the importance of establishing a solid empirical, public relations, and organizational base for CCC's advocacy program. She tried to steer the group toward coherent, concrete issues that would bring tangible benefits to New York City's children. Her determination to follow issues and victories through to implementation enhanced CCC's in-depth strength, and contributed to the appearance of omnipresence and momentum.

CCC's accomplishments during the late 1950s and 1960s appeared all the more conspicuous because they occurred during an era that Gilbert Steiner called the "quiet time" in child welfare [Steiner 1976: 145]. According to Steiner, child welfare services during the period between the Second World War and the Great

Society meant services to a relatively small group of neglected children, or those living outside their own homes. The dominant concerns of the child welfare community revolved around preventive services designed to keep a child's home intact, and foster care and adoption work [Steiner 1976].

CCC's concerns, in contrast, encompassed a wide variety of issues. From its very beginning in 1945, for example, CCC repeatedly spoke out against racial discrimination in New York City's foster care system and offered consistent support for civil rights in general [Bernstein 1991; CCC 1953b]. The group became one of the first to highlight postwar demographic changes occurring in New York City and the continuing increase of children of color in need of foster care [CCC 1955; CCC 1954]. During the early 1950s, a CCC subcommittee became one of the first groups in the nation to address the "treatment and rehabilitation of adolescent narcotic drug addicts" [CCC 1952]. From the mid-1950s through the early 1960s, CCC helped spearhead an effort to fluoridate New York City's drinking water [Lash 1956]. At times, CCC's attention spread beyond the strict confines of children's issues. In 1956-57, for example, the group explored the impact of the high cost of prescription drugs on middle- and low-income families [CCC 1958].

CCC's wide-ranging advocacy program reflected the varied interests and professional concerns of its members. So, too, did the tactics and strategies used by the CCC reflect its elite composition. The women and men who volunteered for CCC constituted the "social welfare elite of New York" [Romanofsky 1977: 52]. Many members had grown up with a family tradition of service in the community that instilled in them the notion that as educated, wealthy people, they had an obligation to be active leaders in their community.

Many of CCC's most important and influential members came from New York City's elite German Jewish society, and were reared with a family tradition of philanthropy. The father of Margaret Lewisohn, a charter member and early CCC board member, was the noted banker Isaac Seligman; her mother was the granddaughter of one of the founders of the great banking house of Kuhn, Loeb and Company. Born in New York in 1895, she married financier Samuel A. Lewisohn, a childhood friend, and was related through ties of family or close friendship to the highest strata of Jewish New York, including the Warburgs, Schiffs, Lehmans, and Sulzbergers. Fifty years old when she joined CCC in 1945, Lewisohn had spent most of her adult life engaged in philanthropic activity. After graduating in 1914 from the Institute of Musical Art in New York, Lewisohn did "post-graduate" work teaching music at the Hudson Guild Settlement in New York City. From her parents she inherited an interest in progressive education, which eventually led her to help found Bennington College in Vermont and to head the Public Education Association of New York [Cohen 1964].

Like Lewisohn, CCC cofounder and first president Adele Rosenwald Levy also claimed affiliation with the upper levels of New York Jewish society, although she was not a New Yorker by birth. And, like Lewisohn, Levy was guided by familial philanthropic traditions. She was born in Chicago in 1892 into a distinguished and wealthy family whose liberal social philosophy and secure economic fortunes propelled its members into a wide variety of reform activities. Levy's father Julius Rosenwald, one of the founders of Sears Roebuck and Company, was a member of the finance committee of the Hull House Association board of directors during the 1920s [Sklar 1990]. Indeed, Levy traced her "passionate concern for people" back to her father, whom she credited with teaching her "the obligations that come with wealth. He always said wealthy people are just custodians for money" [She can't mind . . . 1945].

Such traces of noblesse oblige notwithstanding, it would be wrong to brand Levy as a mid-twentieth century version of Lady Bountiful. Her commitment to reform was real, and spread to over 35 charitable, artistic, and community organizations. Although she never attended college, Levy worked hard to project an image of herself as a hardheaded "professional volunteer," one informed by knowledge and experience, not unreliable humanitarian impulses.

Conciliatory and modest—and a woman in what was very much a man's political world—Levy managed to wield a great deal of power in New York by working quietly and indirectly. Like many women of her generation and class, Levy shunned outright assertiveness, which was contrary to the values her class upheld, and to her own view of herself as a helper and facilitator, not a leader. One longtime CCC member recalled an incident during the early 1950s in which Levy was to testify for CCC at a budget hearing in behalf of a proposal to include an additional child welfare worker in that year's budget. Annoyed by the usual stalling tactics and aware of mounting hostility in the room, Levy, anxious to keep a dinner date she had made for the evening, killed the crowd with kindness. Making her way to the microphone, she presented her testimony in her meek, sweet way, and just said, "How could you be against children? These are the facts, I just don't understand how you could be against this" [Bernstein 1991].

There was, of course, more to Levy's powers of persuasion than charm. First and foremost, there was money. A loyal Democrat, Levy consistently threw her considerable financial resources behind those politicians who appeared receptive and friendly to CCC's concerns. She and other CCC members such as Ruth Field, wife of philanthropist Marshall Field, gave generously to Democratic Mayor Robert F. Wagner's various campaigns, always with the expectation that once elected, he would support CCC. One of Wagner's former deputy mayors recalled an instance during the senate race of 1956, which pitted Wagner against incumbent Jacob Javits. While writing a sizable check payable to Wagner's campaign, Levy let him know that the hole in the ceiling at the Children's Center had still not been fixed, and she hoped he would do something about it. He did, and the subject was never broached again [Lowell 1991].

This episode—and there were many like them—is significant because it points out the importance of informal, unofficial contacts and indirect modes of influence characteristic of postwar politics and postwar child advocacy. It also underscores the permeable boundary between government and voluntary organizations. Simply put, the elite composition of CCC's membership fitted the elite structure of postwar New York City government. For CCC, the "perennial question" of working inside or outside the political system was simply never an issue [Jenkins 1987]. Its strategy of quiet, behind-the-scenes negotiations was always preferred over outright confrontation, and was helped along by the presence of several politically savvy members. Eleanor Roosevelt was a key figure in this respect. A member of CCC's board of directors from 1945 until her death in 1962, Roosevelt linked the group to important city, state, and national politicians, and acted as a conduit of information for CCC.

In her capacity as CCC Executive Director, Trude Lash also faciliated CCC's effective, mutually beneficial partnership with city officials. From the start, Lash understood that child advocacy was ultimately a political endeavor, one that required the same skills, techniques, tactics, strategies, and resources that other interest groups used. As an administrator, Lash understood the importance of picking issues for impact and for flexible strategies. Commenting on Lash's style, former CCC staff member Alfred Kahn recalled that she operated on a "very personal level. That was the nature of her kind of advocacy" [Kahn 1991]. After CCC had researched and published a report, for example, Lash would pick up the telephone and harangue the mayor or a commissioner, because, as Kahn stated, "someone had to tell [them] how to do it" [Kahn 1991].

Reassessment and Decline: CCC, 1964–72

By the early 1960s, CCC's influence had spread beyond the confines of New York. In 1961, for example, several CCC members helped draft President Kennedy's major welfare accomplishment, the Public Welfare Amendments of 1962. But by 1964, as the group celebrated its twentieth anniversary, a renewed interest in rights and entitlements and a national emphasis on self-help and participatory democracy challenged CCC's conception of what advocacy entailed, and who should do it. The civil rights movement and the antipoverty programs had spawned an array of parent groups and neighborhood and self-advocacy groups in New York City, each of which asserted new strategies and forms and mobilized new constituencies [Kahn et al. 1972]. Something like a child advocacy *movement* began to emerge, and the new organizations that constituted it looked very different in content, strategy, and style.

One of the most influential and best-known child advocacy groups to emerge in the eastern United States in the 1960s was United Bronx Parents (UBP), a grass-roots, self-help organization of Puerto Rican parents who lived in the South Bronx. UBP was launched on a volunteer basis when its director—the president of the local PTA—became increasingly concerned about the rigidity of school administration and the school system's unresponsiveness to what she defined as the needs of Puerto Rican students. UBP's staff and constituency were primarily Puerto Rican and African American, and its board of directors included 15 community residents who were parents of children currently enrolled in the local school system [Kahn et al. 1972].

UBP's major activity centered on training parents to act as advocates for their own children in the local school system. A series of programs was developed to teach parents how to evaluate curricula, teacher performance, administrative efficiency, and school programs generally. In addition, parents were also informed about relevant legislation, the role of local school boards, principals' and administrators' obligations and responsibilities, student and parental rights, and entitlements. The program organized parents to intervene in the school system on both an individual and a team basis—in effect, to act as advocates for their own children, and to view child advocacy as part of a broader effort in community development, with wider political objectives [Kahn et al. 1972].

In contrast to CCC's elite insider status and its preference for behind-the-scenes negotiations, groups such as UBP deliberately worked outside the political system, relying on militant and sometimes disruptive tactics to achieve their advocacy objectives. Borrowing heavily from the style and rhetoric of welfare rights groups, these newer child advocacy organizations began to take on a distinctly political slant that brought the issue of community control to the forefront. The concept of co-planning, or the effort to involve poor parents as active participants in program planning, management, and implementation in matters affecting their childrens' lives, became a hallmark of the new child advocacy movement. The empowerment of formerly marginal groups became a goal of these newer groups, which sought to represent the collective interest of their members through citizen participation or "consumerism." Indeed, such groups were judged legitimate and credible by the extent to which their decision-making structures included "consumers" and promoted "citizen participation" [Jenkins 1987: 302–305].

In addition to such "indigenous advocates," many middle-class parents also organized as child advocates. The issue of adoption, particularly adoption of so-called special-needs children, galvanized many parents across the country. In many states minority children, children with handicaps, or older children languished in the custody of out-of-home care and adoption agencies, and prospective parents found it difficult to surmount the rules and regulations of such agencies. The creation of parent advocacy groups, such as the Open Door Society of Montreal in the late 1950s, and the Council on Adoptable Children (COAC), first started by Joyce and Peter Forsythe in Ann Arbor, Michigan, in the mid-1960s, empowered parents, as did the very advocacy processes that enabled them to expand their efforts in the struggle to adopt special-needs children. Using an array of advocacy strategies, including organizing and training other parents, the media, the threat of litigation, and legislative lobbying, parents were, in many cases, able to circumvent adoption agency inertia. In the mid-1960s, the Ann Arbor chapter of COAC took matters into its own hands and created Spaulding, an adoption agency solely responsible for placing special-needs children. Soon after, many states followed suit.*

The inability, or unwillingness, of adoption agencies to place special-needs children raised fundamental dilemmas for would-be parents of adoptable children and for other advocacy organizations. Of particular interest to these newer groups were the related questions of objectivity and sanction. Children need advocates because they cannot speak for themselves and defend their own interests. But who can know for certain what those interests are? How can there be any assurance that advocates are responsive to children's interests, and not simply pressing for their own vision of those interests, unconstrained by clients [Mnookin 1985]? The idea that power could come from communities concerned about their own young raised the fundamental question of child advocacy as it emerged by the late 1960s—who calls the shots [Dicker 1990]? Within this atmosphere, CCC's approach to welfare and its top-down, bureaucratically oriented solutions seemed especially vulnerable.

The extent to which child advocacy had changed, politically and strategically, was not lost on CCC. As early as 1964, members voiced concern about the group's continued relevance in the child advocacy movement. "We are aware," CCC's executive director Trude Lash wrote, "that the psychology of privilege hampers our ability to communicate with those we wish to reach" [CCC 1965]. One board member came close to implying that the group's longtime interest in promoting concepts like service integration and top-down, bureaucratically oriented solutions, such as a Children's Bureau for New York City, were

---

*Personal correspondence with Claire McGinnis, Legal Aid Society, Cleveland, Ohio, June 27, 1994.

outmoded, given the changed political and social atmosphere.
While the group had generally been successful in getting better
and more services for children, she observed,

> we were not always successful in reaching the more de-
> prived groups because we were working on services of
> which most disadvantaged groups could not take advan-
> tage . . . Apparently, "middle-class services" are not the
> answer. [CCC 1964]

In an effort to find the answer, CCC began a conscious attempt at reorganization in 1968. One member, noting the proliferation of new advocacy groups that used more dramatic means
to gain their ends, pointed out that City Hall simply had no
choice but to listen to them "more than to middle-class civic
groups" [CCC 1968a]. He might have added that City Hall's new
occupant, John Lindsay, tended to bypass established civic
groups like CCC in order to develop direct contact with the city's
poor and minorities [Gottehrer 1975].

As CCC members saw it, the task facing them would be one
of finding the "method and means by which we pass our expertise down to those who are now being listened to" [1968a]. CCC
Vice President Ruth Field realized, however, that the end result
of passing down information to "these little groups" (as board
member Helen Hall referred to them) would eventually be to
leave CCC without an operating mission [CCC 1968a].

The problem, then, was how to leave CCC's elite, professional character and composition intact, while remaining credible to the city's neighborhood and parent advocacy groups. Some
members suggested that CCC invite selected "indigenous" community representatives to become members, people who would
in every sense be "peers" of present CCC members, even though
they happened to live "in deprived neighborhoods," and who
might "relate CCC to the neighborhoods" [CCC 1968b]. What
members did not recognize was that those "little groups" did not

seem particularly interested in CCC's help and "expertise" or its offer to "pass down information." The only real attempt the group made to involve itself with community advocacy groups failed, according to a terse note in CCC's files, because "suitable neighborhood groups were unable to be found, partly because of the growing tendency on the part of many black groups to find their own solutions to the problems which they identified as black problems" [CCC n.d.].

In the end, CCC's reorganization effort failed. No attempt was made to incorporate a more diverse membership, or to recruit new, younger members. Indeed, CCC board members defended CCC's existing composition by insisting that representativeness was never the goal. CCC thus emerged from the 1968 reorganization effort with its character fixed and no substantial alteration in its advocacy strategies or goals. As the 1970s dawned, a sense of impatience and even defensiveness surrounded the group. CCC consultant Alfred Kahn, for example, spoke derisively of the changes that had occurred in child advocacy during the preceding decade. "Contrary to conventional wisdom," Kahn stated,

> consumers do not have the requisite knowledge or expertise to design services and to make sure that they are effective. They can be fooled . . . the monitoring of services is a very complicated matter which requires considerable professional skill and experience; consumers are very naive about why services work or do not work. [CCC 1970]

Despite the obvious condescension in Kahn's words, he was right on at least one point: by the early 1970s, child advocacy was becoming an increasingly professionalized and bureaucratized activity. Legal advocacy for children intensified, for example, spurred by the public interest law movement of the 1960s. Unlike traditional child advocates, including CCC, who achieved their greatest successes in local and state legislatures, "modern" legal advocates typically shunned such bodies in favor of the federal courts, where they were more likely to win broad, substantial victories for children [Mnookin 1985].

When the Nixon administration created a National Center for Child Advocacy within the Office of Child Development (OCD) in 1971, the locus of activity for child advocates shifted once again to Washington, further removing CCC from the vanguard of the movement. Charged with "identifying and promoting improvements in conditions which adversely affect the growth and development of children," OCD was more precisely a vehicle to promote and represent children's interests *in government*. As such, it offered a national structure and platform for the formal sanction and development of child advocacy programs, something that, until then, had been the concern of local communities and local organizations [Steiner 1976].

Such recent methodological and institutional changes within the child advocacy movement highlight an important issue with which current child advocacy organizations, including CCC, which continues to advocate in behalf of children, must grapple. As Bing and Richart [1987] note, the history of government intervention in the lives of children and their families continues to shape the debate concerning the goals of child advocacy. Some advocates, for example, ask whether state intervention isn't more destructive for children than the condition that formed the basis for it. Though all advocates believe that government can play a role in helping and protecting children, many are cautious about the extent to which government intervenes, and for what purposes [Bing & Richart 1987].

Conclusion

CCC's advocacy program always sought to expand the reach and power of the state in behalf of children. As such, it represented the final incarnation of a pattern of child advocacy that dated back to the nineteenth century. Still, as this article suggests, and as CCC's own history demonstrates, the content and meaning of child advocacy have shifted through the postwar decades, as have the types, strategies, goals, and ultimately, the impact, of child advocacy organizations themselves. By the early 1960s, such phrases as *community action* and *maximum feasible participation* revealed an increasingly paternalistic—or, more correctly, maternalistic—nuance in the concept of advocacy as practiced by CCC.

As Bing and Richart [1987] observe, the children's constituency is unique because it lacks the power to vote and to exercise normal constituency powers, to articulate self-interests to politicians, and to work towards specific goals. In this light, they question whether it is "possible to envision a child advocacy movement which is not fundamentally elitist" [Bing & Richart 1987: 6–7]. Perhaps, as Muncy [1991] notes, when one group in society advocates in behalf of another, the result will inevitably prove intrusive and to some degree authoritarian, regardless of intent. ◆

References

Bender, T. (1992, October 24). For better or worse, it happens in New York first. *New York Newsday*, pp. 33-36.

Bernstein, B. (1991, July 16). Interview by author.

Bing, S. R., & Richart, D. W. (1987). Fairness is a kid's game: A background paper for emerging state-based child advocacy organizations. Prepared for the Lilly Endowment, Inc., Indianapolis, IN.

Carr, C. (1946, August 4). Speech broadcast on WQXR. In papers of Dr. Viola W. Bernard, Hammer Health Sciences Library, Columbia University, files marked "Correspondence, 1945-1949."

CCC. (n.d.). *Milestones in the CCC's history of concern and achievement in child care issues.* CCC library files, New York.

CCC. (1970, November 7). Minutes of the meeting of the Task Force on Social Services. CCC library files, New York.

CCC. (1968a, May 20). Minutes of the meeting of the Ad Hoc Committee on CCC Goals and Priorities. CCC library files, New York.

CCC. (1968b, April 30). Minutes of the meeting of the Ad Hoc Committee on CCC Goals and Priorities. CCC library files, New York.

CCC. (1965). *Twentieth anniversary report, 1944-1964*. CCC library files, New York.

CCC. (1964, April 10). Minutes of the meeting of the Board of Directors. CCC library files, New York.

CCC. (1958). *Modern prescription drugs: A report on their impact on the family budget*. CCC library files, New York.

CCC. (1955). New York City's foster care program and the 1954 forecast on population trends. CCC library files, New York.

CCC. (1954). *The uprooted: Children in need of foster care*. CCC library files, New York.

CCC. (1953a). *Annual report, 1952-53*. CCC library files, New York.

CCC. (1953b). *Activities of the institutional and foster care section*, December 1946-June 1952. CCC library files, New York.

CCC. (1952). *Annual report, 1951-52*. CCC library files, New York.

CCC. (1946). *First annual report of the CCC*. CCC Library Files, New York.

Cohen, S. (1964). *Progressives and urban school reform: The Public Education Association of New York City, 1895-1954*. New York: Bureau of Publications, Teachers College, Columbia University.

de Schweinitz, K. (1943). *England's road to social security*. New York: A. S. Barnes and Company, Inc.

Dicker, S. (Ed.). (1990). *Stepping stones: Successful advocacy for children*. New York: Foundation for Child Development.

Geertz, C. (1983). *Local knowledge*. New York: Basic Books.

Gottehrer, B. (1975). *The mayor's man*. Garden City, NY: Doubleday & Company.

Hall, H. (1971). *Unfinished business in neighborhood and nation.* New York: The Macmillan Company.

Hays, S. (1987). The politics of environmental administration. In L. Galambos (Ed.), *The new American state: Bureaucracies and policies since World War II* (pp. 21-53). Baltimore: Johns Hopkins University Press.

Jenkins, J. C. (1987). Nonprofit organizations and policy advocacy. In Walter W. Powell (Ed.), *The nonprofit sector: A research handbook* (pp. 302-321). New Haven, CT: Yale University Press.

Kahn, A. (1991, September 15). Interview by author.

Kahn, A., Kamerman, S., & McGowan, B. (1972). *Child advocacy: Report of a national baseline study.* New York: Columbia University School of Social Work.

Lash, T. (1956, May 28). Memorandum to members of the CCC.

Lowell, S. (1991, July 16). Interview by author.

Matusow, A. (1984). *The unraveling of America: A history of liberalism in the 1960s.* New York: Harper and Row.

McDonald, M. J. (1993). The Citizens' Committee for Children and the evolution of child advocacy, 1945-72 (Published Ph.D. dissertation, New York University.)

Mnookin, R., Burt, R., Chambers, D., Wald, M. S., Sugarman, S., Zimring, F. E., & Solomon, R. L. (1985). *In the interest of children: Advocacy, law reform, and public policy.* New York: W. H. Freeman & Co.

Muncy, R. (1991). *Creating a female dominion in American reform: 1890-1935.* New York: Oxford University Press.

Payton, R. (1991, November). *Philanthropy in a liberal education.* Paper presented at Indiana University Center on Philanthropy Colloquium, Indianapolis, IN.

Romanofsky, P. (1977). Saving the lives of the city's foundlings: The Joint Committee and New York City child care methods, 1860-1907. *New York Historical Society Quarterly, 51*(1-2), 49-68.

Sayre, W., & Kaufman, H. (1950). *Governing New York City: Politics in the metropolis.* New York: The Russell Sage Foundation.

She can't mind her own business. (1945, December 3). *New York Post.*

Sklar, K.K. (1990). Who funded Hull House? In Kathleen D. McCarthy (Ed.), *Lady bountiful revisited: Women, philanthropy, and power* (pp. 105-110). New Brunswick, NJ: Rutgers University Press.

Sobie, M. (1987). *The creation of juvenile justice: A history of New York's children's laws.* Albany, NY: New York Bar Foundation.

Steiner, G. (1976). *The children's cause.* Washington, DC: Brookings Institution.

15

INFORMATION SOURCES ON CHILD WELFARE ARCHIVES: HOW TO IDENTIFY, LOCATE, AND USE THEM FOR RESEARCH

Murray Wortzel and Laura Delaney Brody

Archives provide a wealth of material for the historical researcher, as well as an obstacle course for the unwary. Questions about archive identification, location, and provisions for access are discussed. Published catalogs, directories, and guides to archives containing, among other items, manuscripts, documents, social agency records, oral history transcripts, and machine-readable data are examined. Suggestions on how to identify sources of interest are offered, along with a general approach to locating archives for research.

Murray Wortzel, M.S. in L.S., Cert. of Adv. Libnshp. (Ret.), was Associate Professor and Chief, Periodicals Division, Lehman College Library, City University of New York, New York, NY. Laura Delaney Brody, M.S. in L.S., is Social Work Librarian, Whitney M. Young, Jr. Memorial Library of Social Work, Columbia University, New York, NY.

Child welfare is "that part of human services and social welfare programs and ideologies oriented toward the protection, care, and healthy development of children" [Barker 1991: 35], and social welfare archives are "among the cumulative by-products of social welfare activities" [Klaassen & Steinwall 1987: 150]. Social welfare archives may include accreditation reports and responses, annual reports, budgets, biographical information, bylaws, charters, client case records, contracts, constitutions with amendments, consultants' reports, correspondence, manuals and handbooks, minutes, photographs, reports, and salary schedules, among other items [Barbeau & Lohmann 1992]. The researcher should consider which of these will be of importance in examining archival records.

A General Approach to Sources of Archival Material

Colleagues are often invaluable in suggesting archival sources to the prospective researcher, and reference and subject librarians can also be helpful at every stage of the research process. The following are resources to consider in finding archival materials: (1) general histories of social welfare; (2) documentary histories; (3) annotated bibliographies; (4) directories of archival and manuscript collections; (5) journal articles; (6) published inventories of oral history collections with reference to primary source materials; (7) The Social Welfare History Archives Center at the University of Minnesota; (8) social agencies and historical societies; and (9) abstracts, indexes, reference guides, and electronic services.

A Generic Approach to Finding and Using Archives

General Histories of Social Welfare

The General Index to David Schneider's *The History of Public Welfare in New York State* [1938] refers to "child welfare in New Netherland, care of dependent children, 15–19." On these pages is a reference to "orphan masters." A footnote there refers the reader to chapter note no. 25 and "New York City Orphan Masters 1902–7." The full reference on page 27 is "New York City Orphan Masters. *Minutes of the Orphanmasters of New Amsterdam: 1655–1663*. New York, 1902–7." In the New York City Municipal Reference and Research Center, this topic is not locatable under New York or New York City, but does appear under New Amsterdam [New York (NY) Orphanmasters 1902–1907].

Documentary Histories

In the area of children and youth, one documentary history is unusually complete for the period it covers. Compiled by Bremner [1970–1974], *Children and Youth in America: A Documentary History* is a multivolume set that includes citations from many archives covering the period from 1600 through 1973. It has a fine bibliography and is painstakingly indexed. Material from a number of the White House Conferences on Children is included.

Annotated Bibliographies

Annotated bibliographies not only provide the complete bibliographic information on a work, but also describe its coverage and scope. If available in a subject area of interest, annotations may lead the researcher to important material. For example, *Social Welfare in America: An Annotated Bibliography* [Trattner & Achenbaum 1983] includes monographs, journal articles, and dissertations from the mid-1940s through early in the 1980s, with some titles going back to the 1600s. Under the heading *Child Welfare*, the subject index yields a reference to a survey of child welfare literature spanning 75 years [Brown 1960].

Directories of Archival and Manuscript Collections

One ongoing compilation of monumental proportions is the *National Union Catalog of Manuscript Collections* (NUCMC), which began publication with its 1959–61 volume [Library of Congress 1962]. Collections are listed if they are "located in a public or quasi-public repository that regularly admits researchers." It does not list collections that are logically part of a functioning institution or organization such as municipal materials in a municipal agency, but it does include "archival records found outside the normal archival repository" [Library of Congress 1962: vi]. A name index (personal and corporate), a subject index, and a repository index appear at the end of the volume.

Looking in the subject index under the heading *Child Welfare—U.S.*, one finds a number of references to Jane Addams, one of which mentions papers 60–2187 and page 241. In the body of the catalog volume, on page 241, is the Library of Congress entry number MS 60–2187, which reveals that the Addams papers, measuring 59 feet in length, are located at the Friends Historical Library in Swarthmore College's Peace Collection. Available in the library are a catalog of the correspondence and a checklist.

The NUCMC runs through 1992. Some collections include transcripts of oral history recordings. A geographical guide to repositories listed is included, and the bulk of information listed is organized first by state and then by city. Over the years, the NUCMC has issued various indexes covering different time periods. Early volumes included an index, and later ones had separate indexes. Since 1975, separate indexes appear annually and are eventually gathered into five-year cumulations. These are broken down by name, place, subject, and historical period.

According to editor Philip M. Hamer, the United State National Historical Publications Commission's *A Guide to Archives and Manuscripts in the United States* [1961] was planned as a guide to material for research, rather than a catalog. Each entry begins with "a general statement of its field of special interest and some indication of the size of its holdings. This is followed by special mention of groups of papers considered to be of special interest" [United States National Historical Publications Commission 1961: xvii–xviii]. Reference is made to printed sources of information on the holdings when they are available. As in NUCMC, the arrangement of the body of the work is alphabetical, by state and then by city.

A subject index contains the heading *Child Welfare*, which lists, on page 129, the Pan American Sanitary Library, its address, and the name of its librarian. Under the subheading *Holdings* is "Archives of the Pan American Sanitary Bureau, 1902 to date." These holdings include coverage of public health and sanitation, as well as material on maternal and child health.

The index also lists names of individuals. Looking up Edith and Grace Abbott produces a reference to page 160, which refers the reader to the University of Chicago Archives, listing both Edith and Grace Abbott as social workers and educators, giving their dates of birth and death, and mentioning that there are 20 boxes of papers. Reference is also made to a catalog of manuscripts in the university libraries in which the Abbotts' papers are described.

The *Directory of Archives and Manuscript Repositories in the United States* updates an earlier edition with more complete and current coverage of each repository, including name, address, telephone number, hours, public copying facilities, acquisition policy, and description of the holdings [United States. National Historical Publications and Records Commission 1988]. Its format resembles the two directories already covered. There are a large text index, a repository index, and a subject index. The text is organized alphabetically by state and then by city within each state. The subject index includes the heading *Children* with the subheading *Social Welfare*. Under this, one finds the information MA109–830, which refers to the University of Massachusetts Library's Manuscript and Archival Collections Department. This facility holds 375 cubic feet of material dating from 1800 to the present, including archives of the major nineteenth and early twentieth century child welfare agencies of Boston.

The *National Inventory of Documentary Sources in the United States* (NIDS), a remarkable product on microfiche, has been in production since 1985 and provides finding aids to federal, state, academic library, and other repositories of archives and documents. It includes three parts: (1) Federal Records (including the National Archives, the Presidential Libraries, and the Smithsonian Institution); (2) Manuscript Division, Library of Congress; and (3) State Archives, State Libraries, State Historical Societies, Academic Libraries, and Other Repositories [Chadwyck-Healey n.d.*a*: 5].

A two-volume printed index to parts 1 and 2 became available in 1985. Since then, it has been updated twice, first in microfiche, and more recently in CD-ROM format. The NIDS provides finding aids on microfiche for the sources it covers, in the form of checklists or inventories (not full-text coverage) of the information listed. It is, therefore, now possible to identify microfiche finding aids for the Children's Bureau archives currently held by the National Archives.

The publisher, Chadwyck-Healey, has divided the Children's Bureau microfiche into six parts: Part 1, Child Welfare; Part 2, Child Legislation; Part 3, Children's Bureau History; Part 4, Maternal and Child Health; Part 5, Children's Bureau Merritt Files (research files of Ella A. Merritt, a bureau staff member concerned with child labor and the bureau's role in the New Deal); and Part 6, Children's Bureau Chiefs' File [Chadwyck-Healey n.d.*b*: 8].

These finding aids guide the researcher through the contents of each collection by itemizing individual holdings. The microfiche for this collection begins with an introduction to the Children's Bureau's history. The material included is designated as "Records of the Children's Bureau, Record Group 102" [National Inventory of Documentary Sources in the United States 1985: 1]. Further information includes, as Item 10, "Lewis Hine Photographs for the National Labor Committee Jan. 5, 1908–May 27, 1912" [National Inventory of Documentary Sources in the United States 1985: 2]. An index to the Central File, listed on page three, is on 3x5 cards; and the Central File itself, covering the period from 1912 to 1940, includes 450 feet of material. Page four lists the "Reference File of Ella A. Merritt Relating to Federal Control of Child Labor," which is arranged by subject and measures 15 running feet in length; State Plans for the Maternal and Child Health Program 1936–1945, in 90 running feet (in boxes 1–269); and State Plans for the Crippled Children's program 1936–1947, in 82 running feet (in boxes 1–202). State Plans for the Program of Child Welfare Services from 1936 to 1949 are also listed.

A Central File Classification System appears on 27 pages of the microfiche set as Appendix 1. Principal headings include general child welfare and other general activities affecting children; maternal and child health; recreation—leisure-time activities; child labor and industrial conditions affecting children; children in need of special care (delinquent, dependent, neglected, and handicapped); publicity and exhibits; education; legislation; Children's Bureau studies in the first decade of the agency and later; administration of the Sheppard-Towner Act; current statistics in child welfare and related studies; and maternal and child health services under the Social Security Act.

In addition to NIDS, Chadwyck-Healey also issued *The Records of the Children's Bureau, 1912–1969.* Available only on microfilm, the set includes 294 reels and contains the full text of 147 of the 410 printed pamphlets, reports, and studies inventoried [United States Children's Bureau 1988/1989]. A printed guide to the set lists all 410 titles [United States Children's Bureau 1993].

To locate foreign archives, Chadwyck-Healey produced the following microfiche sets: the *National Inventory of Documentary Sources in the United Kingdom and Ireland*, the *Public Record Office Foreign Office Registers and Indexes of Correspondence 1793–1919* (including 55 volumes concerning the United States), and *Les Inventories des Archives Nationales de Paris*. For research regarding archival material in the United Kingdom or France, these sets may be most useful to examine.

Women's History Sources [Hinding et al. 1979] is another excellent resource for identifying archival information. This two-volume guide includes archives and manuscript collections in the United States and is arranged geographically by state and then by city. More than 80 collections are listed as containing some material on child welfare. The most pertinent are the Northwest Child Welfare Club (Hartford), the Hebrew Orphan Asylum, the Child Welfare League of America, the Florence Crittenton Association of America, the Minneapolis Humane Society, and the Ladies Industrial School Association.

Journal Articles

Scholarly journal articles on historical aspects of social welfare may sometimes refer to archival sources. G. J. Parr's article, "Case Records as Sources for Social History" [1977], for example, refers to case records as "the product of the more systematic approach to philanthropy characteristic of the last third of the nineteenth century." The article actually reproduces a case record from Dr. Bernardo's Homes in Essex, England. Regarding these case records, which cover "orphaned, deserted and dependent children who emigrated to" Canada from England before World War I, Parr describes some of the documents as Canadian government inspection reports created as part of an investigation of "pauper and philanthrophically assisted children" [Parr 1977: 123–6]. These materials are now a part of the Toronto Emigration Office Records, volume 22, located at Butler Library, Columbia University, in New York City. Other materials concerning these children are in the Records of the Department of the Interior and the Department of Agriculture at the Public Archives of Canada and in the Ministry of Health Series at the Public Record Office in London. In a note, Parr informs us that the volumes covering 1905 and beyond, located in London, are sealed under a "hundred-year rule" [Parr 1977: 126]. She also adds that the most useful case records may be found at the headquarters of Dr. Bernardo's Homes at Tanner's Lane, Brakingside, Essex, in England.

Oral History Collections

Unpublished personal memoirs and oral histories are other useful varieties of archival sources [Klaassen & Steinwall 1987]. The authors also refer to a National Association of Social Workers oral history project, which provided transcripts of interviews with distinguished social workers to repositories at the University of Minnesota, Columbia University, the University of Washington, and the Library of Congress; and to important oral history holdings at the University of California at Berkeley's Bancroft Library. These sources often provide valuable information not otherwise documented.

Published archival volumes of oral history collections enable the researcher to evaluate repository holdings before visiting specific institutions. *Oral History Collections* by Alan M. Meckler and Ruth McMullin [1975] is an example of this type of reference source.

The Oral History Research Office at Columbia University is a rich resource for transcripts of many interesting interviews dating from 1948. Its Social Security Project includes interviews with Arthur J. Altmeyer, Eveline M. Burns, Wilbur J. Cohen, Martha M. Elliott, Marion B. Folsom, and many others. *The Oral History Collection of Columbia University* [Columbia University Oral History Research Office 1979], last published in printed form in 1979, has been updated as an online database available through the Research Libraries Information Network (RLIN).

Another important oral history resource at Columbia University is the *Oral History Project* videorecordings [CUSSW Alumni Association, Committee on School History 1990]. Also known as *The Pathfinder Series*, this project produced documentary videotaped interviews with distinguished faculty and alumni of the School of Social Work, including Sidney Berengarten, Mitchell Ginsberg, Florence Hollis, Carol Meyer, and Herman Stein.

In addition to the *Oral History Project*, the Alumni Association's Committee on School History also sponsors the

Oral History Day program at the School of Social Work, which is coordinated by Professor Emeritus Sidney Berengarten. The program has resulted in an ongoing series of monographs, the proceedings of Oral History Day, edited by Professor Berengarten. The proceedings from the first Oral History Day are particularly interesting for child welfare historians. In this volume, Professor Berengarten reports on a school-initiated project, the Bureau of Children's Guidance, which began in 1922. He describes the project as "the first community psychiatric facility for children which was entirely administered and staffed by a School of Social Work" [Berengarten 1986: 6].

The Social Welfare History Archives Center

At the University of Minnesota is a unique repository, the Social Welfare History Archives Center. The printed guide to the Center's holdings, *Descriptive Inventories of Collections in the Social Welfare Archives Center* [University of Minnesota, Social Welfare History Archives Center 1970], covers about a quarter of its collections from national and local voluntary social welfare organizations. Included in its holdings are materials from the Child Welfare League of America, and the personal papers of Helen Hall, Paul Kellogg (editor of *The Survey*), Eduard Lindeman, Leonard Mayo, and Benjamin Youngdahl. Records from *The Survey*, an influential social welfare journal, are also in the collection. This material is available on 81 reels of microfilm in a set called *The Survey Associates Records*.

Social Agencies and Historical Societies

Certain institutions and social agencies retain their archival materials and are, therefore, not listed in the NUCMC. Some of these groups, identified by Clarke A. Chambers in the *Encyclopedia of Social Work* [1977], include the Merrill-Palmer Institute Historical Library in Child Development and Family Life in Detroit, as well as the national headquarters of the YMCA and the YWCA.

This is also often the case with historical societies and state and municipal archives. Of course, the National Archives continues to serve as a repository for many federal institutions, as has been mentioned in connection with the Children's Bureau. Schools of social work, including Smith College, have also gathered materials concerning their respective histories and their distinguished faculty members.

Abstracts, Indexes, Reference Guides, and Electronic Services

Secondary sources of archival information include abstracts, indexes, reference guides, and electronic services. They now offer coverage of most of the generally available literature. Some are highly specialized, as, for example, *Social Work Abstracts*; others are less specific, as is the case with the *Social Sciences Index*.

In the category of reference guides, one notable source is the *Guide to Reference Books*, now available in a tenth edition, which covers reference material through 1985 [Sheehy 1986], and its supplement, which covers additional titles published through 1991 [Balay & Sheehy 1992]. An eleventh edition is being developed. With a universal approach to all fields of knowledge, this guide includes most significant reference works on a given subject. Included are numerous annotated citations to archival resources.

Another useful reference guide is the compilation, *Subject Collections* [Ash 1993]. This two-volume work covers special collections and subject emphases in college, university, public, and special libraries and museums in the United States and Canada. Included are descriptions of 11 different collections related to child welfare, such as the Records of Children's Aid and Family Service (1910–1984) at the University of Massachusetts at Amherst.

A new source that identifies electronic services for book and periodical literature is *Books & Periodicals Online* [1994]. Its current edition is copiously indexed. Approximately 228 specialized journals are listed in the subject index under the heading *Social*

Services and Welfare. This does not include a count of the journals listed under the headings *Psychology, Social Sciences,* and *Sociology,* though there are a few duplications.

The alphabetical index, which contains over 1,700 pages, represents the body of the source, and mentions journals by name, the name of their sponsoring organization, their publisher, and then the indexing/abstracting services in which journal articles appear. It also states whether the journal is indexed or abstracted, whether coverage is full or selective, and the date that coverage commenced.

For the journal *Child Welfare,* for example, its prior title, *Child Welfare League of America Bulletin,* is given. The indexing and abstracting services mentioned include *Academic Index,* with indexing of selected articles since January 1987; *Agricola,* with indexing since January 1, 1970; *Applied Social Science Index & Abstracts* (ASSIA), with selective indexing and abstracting since 1987; and *Criminal Justice Abstracts,* with indexing and abstracting of selected articles since January 1, 1968. There is also selective coverage by *Medline, Nursing and Allied Health, Current Contents Service, PAIS International, Psychfile* and *Psychinfo, Social Sciences Index* and *Social Scisearch* and, finally, *Social Work Abstracts* in print and on CD-ROM.

Other indexes include a Database with Producer/Vendor Listing; a Producer Listing, and a supplement with 379 pages devoted to database listings. With its detailed indexing, *Books & Periodicals Online* is one of the most useful sources for identifying published material in electronic format.

Conclusion

The location and identification of archival sources in child welfare are complicated by their dispersal and a lack of uniform information. A sampling is given of various access points, such as social welfare histories, documentary histories, annotated bibliographies, directories of archival and manuscript collections, journal articles, oral histories, specialized archives, individual social agencies and historical societies, abstracts, indexes, reference guides, and electronic services. Advice from colleagues and librarians is most useful, and enlightened speculation on sources is required. ◆

References

Ash, L. (1993). *Subject collections: A guide to special book collections and subject emphases as reported by university, college, public, and special libraries and museums in the United States and Canada* (7th ed., rev. and enl.). New Providence, NJ: R.R. Bowker.

Balay, R. (Ed.), & Sheehy, E.P. (Special ed. advisor). (1992). *Guide to reference books. Supplement to the tenth edition.* Chicago: American Library Association.

Barbeau, E.J., & Lohmann, R.A. (1992). The agency executive director as keeper of the past. *Administration in Social Work, 16*(2), 15–26.

Barker, R.L. (1991). *The social work dictionary* (2nd ed.). Silver Spring, MD: National Association of Social Workers.

Berengarten, S. (1986). The school's role in establishing a new field of practice: Psychiatric social work/mental health services. In S. Berengarten (Ed.), *The Columbia University School of Social Work: A history of social pioneering. Proceedings of the first Oral History Day for entering students, September 18, 1986* (p. 6). New York: Columbia University School of Social Work.

Books & Periodicals Online. (1994). New York: Library Alliance.

Bremner, R. H. (Comp. & Ed.). (1970–1974). *Children and youth in America: A documentary history.* Cambridge, MA: Harvard University Press.

Brown, J. (1960). Child welfare classics. *Social Service Review, 34,* 195–202.

Chadwyck-Healey. (n.d.*a*). *How to use the national inventory of documentary sources in the United States in your research* (publisher brochure). Alexandria, VA: Chadwyck-Healey.

Chadwyck-Healey. (n.d.*b*). *The National Archives. The records of the Children's Bureau* (publisher brochure). Alexandria, VA: Chadwyck-Healey.

Chambers, C. A. (1977). Archives of social welfare. In J.B Turner (Ed.), *Encyclopedia of social work* (17th ed.). (pp. 80–84). Washington, DC: National Association of Social Workers.

Columbia University Oral History Research Office. (1979). *The oral history collection of Columbia University.* E. B. Mason & L. M. Starr (Eds.). New York: Oral History Research Office.

CUSSW Alumni Association Committee on School History. (1990). *The oral history project* [videorecording]. New York: Columbia University School of Social Work.

Hinding, A., Bower, A.S., & Chamber, C.A. (Eds.). (1979). *Women's history sources: A guide to archives and manuscript collections in the United States.* New York: R.R. Bowker.

Klaassen, D. J., & Steinwall, S. D. (1987). Archives of social welfare. In A. Minahan (Ed.), *Encyclopedia of social work* (18th ed.) (pp. 150–156). Silver Spring, MD: National Association of Social Workers.

Library of Congress. (1962). *National union catalog of manuscript collections.* Ann Arbor, MI: J.W. Edwards.

Meckler, A.M., & McMullin, R. (Eds.). (1975). *Oral history collections.* New York: Bowker.

National inventory of documentary sources in the United States [microfiche]. (1985). Part 1—Federal Records. Records of the Children's Bureau. Teaneck, NJ: Chadwick-Healey.

New York (N.Y.). Orphanmasters. (1902–1907). *The minutes of the orphanmasters of New Amsterdam, 1655 to 1663.* New York: F. P. Harper.

Parr, G. J. (1977). Case records as sources for social history. *Archivaria, 4,* 122–136.

Research Libraries Information Network (RLIN). [Online]. Mountain View, CA: Research Libraries Group, Inc. (Producer) File: amc.

Schneider, D.M. (1938). *The history of public welfare in New York State, 1609–1866.* Chicago: University of Chicago Press.

Sheehy, E. P. (1986). *Guide to reference books* (10th ed.). Chicago: American Library Association.

Social sciences index. (1974/75). New York: H. W. Wilson Co.

Social work abstracts. (1994–). Washington, DC: National Association of Social Workers.

Trattner, W. I., & Achenbaum, W. A. (Eds.). (1983). *Social welfare in America: An annotated bibliography*. Westport, CT: Greenwood Press.

United States Children's Bureau. (1993). *The Children's Bureau, documentary sources from the National Archives*. Alexandria, VA: Chadwyck-Healey.

United States Children's Bureau. (1988/1989). *The records of the Children's Bureau, 1912– 1969* [microfilm]. Alexandria, VA: Chadwyck-Healey.

United States National Historical Publications and Records Commission. (1988). *Directory of archives and manuscript repositories in the United States* (2nd ed.). Phoenix, AZ: Oryx Press.

United States National Historical Publications Commission. (1961). *A guide to archives and manuscripts in the United States*. P.M. Hamer (Ed.). New Haven, CT: Yale University Press.

University of Minnesota. Social Welfare History Archives Center. (1970). *Descriptive inventories of collections in the Social Welfare History Archives Center*. Westport, CT: Greenwood Publishing Corp.